HERE COME THE HAWKS

Words and Music by
J. WAYNE SWAYZEE

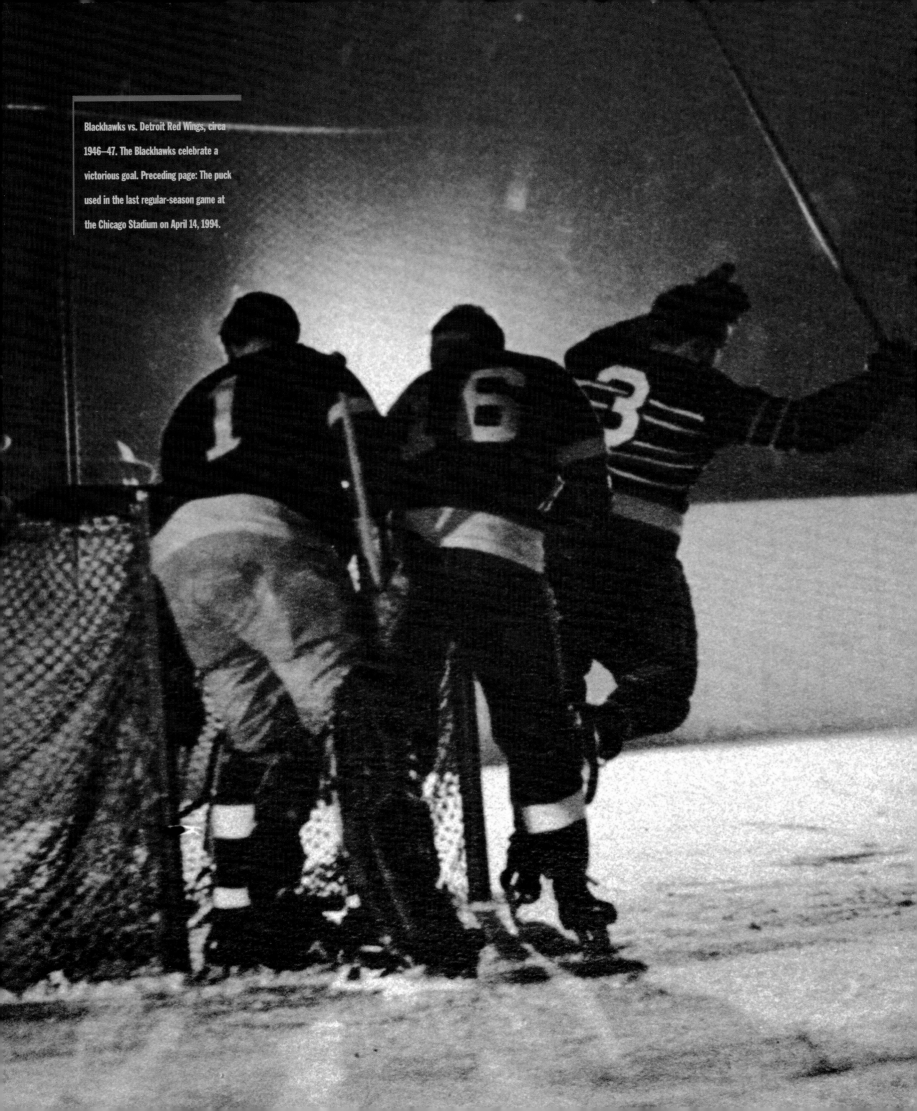

Blackhawks vs. Detroit Red Wings, circa 1946–47. The Blackhawks celebrate a victorious goal. Preceding page: The puck used in the last regular-season game at the Chicago Stadium on April 14, 1994.

If these players look surprised as well as jubilant, they had reason to be both. On April 12, 1938, the upstart Chicago Blackhawks defeated the Toronto Maple Leafs, 4-1, to win their second Stanley Cup. The Blackhawks, who finished a distant third in the American division during the regular season, were led by Bill Stewart, who had no previous experience as a coach, and eight American-born players.

Left wing Ethan Moreau (19), the Blackhawks' No. 1 choice in the 1994 amateur draft, storms the net protected by Dominik Hasek, all-star goalie for the Buffalo Sabres who served an apprenticeship in Chicago. Buffalo defenseman on the scene is Bob Boughner (6). On the right are winger Eric Daze (55) of the Blackhawks and defenseman Richard Smehlik (42) of the Sabres.

CHICAGO
SEVENTY-FIVE

BLACKHAWKS
YEARS

y BOB VERDI

OREWORD BY JIM BELUSHI

NTRODUCTION BY BILLY REAY

EHABI BOOKS

Tehabi Books developed, designed, and produced *Chicago Blackhawks: Seventy-Five Years*, and has conceived and published many award-winning books that are recognized for their strong literary and visual content. Tehabi works with national and international publishers, corporations, institutions, and nonprofit groups to identify, develop, and implement comprehensive publishing programs. The name *Tehabi* is derived from a Hopi Indian legend and symbolizes the importance of teamwork. Tehabi Books is located in San Diego, California.
www.tehabi.com

Chris Capen, *President*
Tom Lewis, *Vice President of Development*
Tim Connolly, *Director of Brand Publishing*
Andy Lewis, *Design Director*
Nancy Cash, *Editorial Director*
Vicky Vaughn, *Project Art Director*
Garrett Brown, *Project Editor*
Laurie Gibson, *Copy Editor*
Ray Grabowski, *Photo Editor*
Lisa Wolff, *Proofreader*
Ken DellaPenta, *Indexer*
William J. Martin, *Editorial Consultant*

Photography credits appear on page 180.

Library of Congress Cataloging-in-Publication Data

Verdi, Bob W., 1947–
    Chicago Blackhawks: seventy-five years / Bob Verdi; foreword by Jim Belushi;
  introduction by Billy Reay.
      p. cm.
    ISBN 1-887656-31-6 (hardcover)—ISBN 1-887656-32-4 (pbk.)—ISBN
  1-887656-30-8 (deluxe hardcover)—ISBN 1-887656-33-2 (limited collector's edition)
    1. Chicago Blackhawks (Hockey team)—History. 2. Chicago Blackhawks (Hockey team)—
  History—Pictorial works. I. Title.

GV848.C48 V47 2000
796.962'64'0977311—dc21   00-41780

The paper used in this publication meets the minimum requirements of the American National Standard for Information Sciences—Permanence of Paper for Printed Library Materials, ANSI Z39.48-1984.

Printed by Dai Nippon Printing Co., Ltd., in Hong Kong
10 9 8 7 6 5 4 3 2 1

Contents

"What'd you say? I'm sorry, what did you say?"

I've found myself repeating that question a lot over the past ten years. Sure, I've gotten a little older—and more mellow—but I chalk up at least part of my hearing loss to that 1991–92 championship season when the Chicago Blackhawks went to the Stanley Cup finals. The sound at the old Chicago Stadium during the playoffs that season was deafening. I knew I should have worn earplugs, but I guess I thought, "Hell, I've seen Grand Funk Railroad and Eric Clapton perform, and I was there when the Chicago Bears won the Superbowl." I thought nothing could be louder than that. Boy, was I wrong! The Chicago Stadium was loud, and it had the loudest crowds. Blackhawks fans there would scream the entire game—even through the national anthem.

When I go to Kings or Lakers games in L.A., their fans go to their cars before the end of the game, and are *nowhere* near as loud. Not Blackhawks fans! Especially in 1992, when the possibility of bringing home the Stanley Cup not only deafened the crowds, but also probably popped a lot of vocal cords.

I nearly popped a vocal cord myself during the first game of the Stanley Cup finals in Pittsburgh.

Before the game, I appeared on every sports channel screaming, "Pass the Cup! Pass the Cup!" I had boards made up that said, "Pass the Cup," and the TV cameras caught me waving them during the game. When the Blackhawks scored a string of goals in a single period, my buddy Rob Curtis and I never sat down. We stood and screamed at the Pittsburgh fans the whole time. The crowd was dead silent, but you could hear us in every corner of that stadium. The Pittsburgh fans were . . . very polite. I don't think they knew what to make of me. They just stared at me. Unfortunately, the Penguins came back and won the game and the series. I ran out of that town with my tail between my legs, and I've never been back.

FOREWORD BY JIM BELUSHI

PASSING THE CUP

Far left: Hockey Night in the Chicago Stadium often featured fans who cherished their tickets but rarely used their seats. Standing and cheering during "The Star-Spangled Banner" or action on the ice was the rule rather than the exception and if you wanted to bring your own flag or headdress, so much the better. Left: Jim Belushi posing on the ice at the beginning of the 1991–92 season.

That kind of enthusiasm can get a guy in trouble. But my passion for Blackhawks hockey actually had a much quieter start. I began watching the Blackhawks on TV as a kid with my brother, John. In high school, I went with Rob to my first live game, where it was hard not to feel the pull of the game's speed. Much later, I became friends with Peter Wirtz, who eventually asked me if I wanted to become the team's celebrity captain for the NHL's seventy-fifth anniversary season in 1991–92.

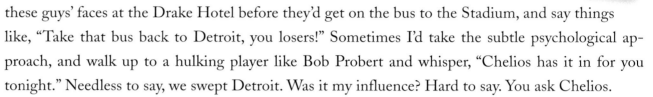

Right: The trading card of Jim Belushi as celebrity captain. Below: During a break in the action, four familiar names mark the National Hockey League's seventy-fifth anniversary season in 1991–92, replete with vintage Blackhawks jerseys. From the left, they are: defenseman Chris Chelios, a perennial all-star; Jim Belushi, famous actor and Blackhawks fan; Stan Mikita, the retired Hall of Famer who played his entire career in Chicago; and Steve Larmer, one of the finest two-way forwards in franchise history. Upper far right: Bobby and Brett Hull, the only father-son combination ever to win both the Hart and Lady Byng Trophies. Lower far right: Al Secord on the attack.

I played up my role well. Although you couldn't say I helped much with game strategy, I had my own brand of morale-building figured out. I would often harass the opposing team's players when they came to town. I'd get in these guys' faces at the Drake Hotel before they'd get on the bus to the Stadium, and say things like, "Take that bus back to Detroit, you losers!" Sometimes I'd take the subtle psychological approach, and walk up to a hulking player like Bob Probert and whisper, "Chelios has it in for you tonight." Needless to say, we swept Detroit. Was it my influence? Hard to say. You ask Chelios.

But as a member of the team, I also got a glimpse into the less public side of the Blackhawks' players and coaches. Mike Keenan was unbelievably intense as a coach, but he also had a vulnerable side that I was privileged to witness during the 1991–92 season. On the last night of the finals, after we lost, I saw Keenan holding his wife. Here was the coach, the toughest man on the team, and he was crying.

I've taken my son, Robert, to Blackhawks games for many years now. He likes going with me. I think he gets excited because I get excited about it. We've spent a lot of time in the tunnels and the locker rooms at the Chicago Stadium, talking to the players with their knees wrapped with ice. It's become a father-son thing.

After all the interviews and all the excitement in the locker room following the Detroit sweep, Chris Chelios, Robert, and I were walking out through one of the old tunnels. Chris stopped and handed Robert the stick he had used in the game. As Robert held the stick, Chris signed it and said, "This is for you." Robert is now a Blackhawks fan for life. It's men like Chris who make a difference and keep fans engaged with a team and the sport.

It's personal moments like this that keep me tied to the spirit of the Blackhawks—seeing that unforgettable look on my son's face; watching Keith Magnuson, Bobby Hull, and Stan Mikita on TV with my brother, John; getting run out of Pittsburgh with my buddy Rob; witnessing the sweeps, singing the national anthem, and so many others. We Blackhawks fans have a responsibility to pass on the spirit of hockey to our children, like Bobby Hull passing it on to Brett Hull, Pat Stapleton passing it on to Mike Stapleton, and Arthur Wirtz passing it on to Bill Wirtz and then on to Peter Wirtz (who, in turn, taught me everything about the game). It's not just about the stars of the game but also the adrenaline, the excitement, the speed, and most importantly, the relationships that come from being a Blackhawks fan.

Blackhawks hockey is all about the fans and the special excitement we share. Our eyes light up, we become animated in our storytelling, and we are *back* in front of the ice. And then the stories begin, "When my father and I were watching the Blackhawks . . . ," or "When my buddy and I went to the Stadium . . ." As for *my* favorite Blackhawks story . . .

When my son, Robert, was six, I took him to his first Blackhawks game at the Chicago Stadium. We were playing our great rival, the St. Louis Blues. You know how many fights happen with the Blues! Well, there was one big fight—one of those "lots of gloves on the ice, black and blue, and you know there are some stitches to be had" kinds of fights—and the crowd was screaming and cheering throughout the fight. After it was broken up and as the referee took Al Secord to the penalty box, Robert asked me, "Where's he going?"

I said, "He's going to the penalty box."

"Why?"

"Well, he broke the rules."

"What'd he do?"

"He started a fight on the ice."

"Oh."

After a pause, Robert asked, "Then why is the crowd cheering so loud?"

I said, "Ah, that's just Blackhawks hockey, son."

BLACKHAWKS PRIDE

Looking back at the seventy-five years of Blackhawks tradition, one can't help but appreciate the pride and the accomplishments garnered by the many players and coaches who have made their mark on hockey history. From their beginning in 1926 and later as one of the National Hockey League's Original Six, the Chicago Blackhawks have thrilled throngs of hockey fans with their energetic and spirited performances. Throughout their seventy-five-year history the Blackhawks have teamed together some of the greatest athletes in the sport of hockey. Their spirit not only epitomizes the pride of Chicago, it is the inspiration to many aspiring young athletes.

When I was a little kid growing up in Canada, I used to listen to the Blackhawks games on the radio. Charlie Gardiner was a goalkeeper at that time, and he was my idol. I'd always dreamed of wearing a National League jersey, and when it was the Blackhawks', so much the better. It really thrilled me to join the Blackhawks organization and then to be lucky enough to coach the team for the number of years I did. The boys who played for me were some of the greatest hockey players—Stan Mikita, Bobby Hull, Bill Hay, Eric Nesterenko, Chico Maki, Pat Stapleton, Bill White, Tony Esposito, Glenn Hall, Dennis Hull, Pit Martin, Jimmy Pappin— and they all were great guys. I always felt that they gave 100 percent of themselves to me and to the game. They were so proud of being Blackhawks. Wearing the Blackhawks crest really meant something to everybody who ever wore it. Each player gave everything he could, and was proud just to pull on that jersey. When I played for the Montreal Canadiens, I put on their jersey, and I was proud of it, and I gave it everything I had. But when I came here to Chicago and joined the Blackhawks, I didn't put on the uniform, I put on the cap, but I never felt more proud. Being with the Blackhawks was like being a part of one big, happy family.

Far left: The diminutive, Winnipeg-born Reay (standing) played for the Montreal Canadiens from 1945–53, twice winning Stanley Cups. After a brief tenure coaching the Maple Leafs, Reay took over the Blackhawks in 1963–64 from Rudy Pilous. Reay coached the Blackhawks to the finals three times and amassed 542 regular-season victories, 516 with the Blackhawks, the fourth-best record in the NHL. Left: One of the felt fedoras that dapper coach Billy Reay always wore behind the bench.

We really enjoyed ourselves. I don't think you could talk to anybody that played for me in that era who didn't enjoy playing here. And during the fourteen years I coached, I never had a player come to me and say he wanted to be traded.

Just wearing the Blackhawks uniform was special, and I always worked to help foster that pride in my players and encouraged them to be both proud and humble and respectful of each other because they were not only representing the Chicago Blackhawks, they were representing the fans of Chicago. They were representing their wives and their children. Never did any of the teams I coached ever let me down; they always demonstrated their incredible pride in their being Blackhawks, and the fans loved it. Even today people will stop me on the street to talk and tell me they're fans. They'll say, "Oh, I love Eric Nesterenko!" or "I love Lou Angotti!" They talk like they were family—and that's the way it was when I was coaching.

Here in Chicago, the fans are very lucky because the players are such outstanding guys, off the ice as well as on the ice. And, oh, how the fans love them! Of course each fan has particular likes and dislikes, and a player doesn't have to score fifty goals to gain their respect. It has always amused me how the players win over their fans and the way their fans appreciate them. Blackhawks fans are notorious for voicing their enthusiasm. The hairs on the back of your neck would stand up at the Chicago Stadium with the reaction of the crowd. They were so loud!

Below: Stan Mikita, always as colorfully attired as a rainbow off the ice, holds an autographed stick bearing his flowing signature, "Stan Mikita #21," standing next to the conservatively dressed but sartorially splendid Billy Reay. Reay was a "player's coach" who quietly got the best from those fortunate enough to play for him.

In the old building, the fans sat so close to the ice, their wild cheering would deafen us. But it was a thrill that I'll never forget, because the fans were always so enthusiastic. All the Chicago hockey fans want is a team that works hard and plays hard every night. Don't forget, when I was coaching here, they had never finished in first place in all the years they had been in the league. When we finished in first place for the first time, you'd have thought we had won the Stanley Cup—the fans were so proud! And the players were just as proud to bring it to them. It's a feeling that I really haven't got the words to express.

The strong Blackhawks tradition of pride was very important to me, too.

Regardless of what job I had in my life, I always wanted to be the best in whatever I did. I always stressed winning. Winning was everything, you know. I used to tell my team, "We're gonna play some games, and we're gonna play well, and we're gonna win; and we're gonna play some games, and we're gonna play well, and we're gonna lose." We had to balance that winning and losing. It was in finding that balance, my players afforded me respect, and they ac-cepted my authority. We had fun, and we won—we should have won the Stanley Cup, but we were out of luck. And that was about the size of it.

I once listened to an interview with Sparky Anderson when he was asked how he managed to have so much success. His answer, "I got the best ball players, I let them play, and we won." Hearing Sparky's reply, I thought to myself, "I was like that. I had good hockey players, I let them play, I cap-italized on what they did best, and we won." I felt that the players had a lot of fun, I had a lot of fun, and yet we had discipline. It was very rewarding for me.

In my house I have all kind of logos, so to speak, of the Blackhawks Indian head. I don't have any of the Montreal Canadiens, and yet I played for the Canadiens for eight years. The Blackhawks are my team now. Chicago is my city. I'm very proud of the Blackhawks, and I want them to do well. You never get hockey out of your system. Hockey is the best game in the world to play, and it's the best game in the world to watch. I was in it for thirty-eight years, and I love the game just as much today as I did when I was in it. I get a different kind of thrill watching it today than I did years ago. But when I see a guy today score a hat trick, I love it. I am forever a true-blue Blackhawks fan.

I can think of no better way to celebrate being a Blackhawks fan than this seventy-fifth-anniversary book. Reading about the history of the team and its many outstanding players reinforces the pride that I take in being a part of this remarkable franchise. Bob Verdi has done an exceptional job at bringing the characters and the spirit of the Blackhawks to life for the reader. This inspiring anniversary book is a great record of the triumphs and achieve-ments of the Chicago Blackhawks. I hope you enjoy reliving these memories— these moments in time—as much as I have.

Billy Reay

Left: Blackhawks Keith Magnuson (3) and Cliff Koroll (20) are the slices of bread sandwiching a hapless Detroit Red Wing who is airborne and about to land hard on the Stadium ice. The Blackhawks won the match, 2-0. Below: Alternate captains Stan Mikita and Bobby Hull share smiles with coach Billy Reay.

It is one of the most exclusive fraternities in the world of sports: the Original Six of the National Hockey League. Along with the Boston Bruins, the New York Rangers, the Detroit Red Wings, the Toronto Maple Leafs, and the Montreal Canadiens, the Chicago Blackhawks hold an honored place in sports history. There are now five times as many teams, but only the Original Six can claim to have been around for seventy-five years or more. That's a lot of history. When the Blackhawks played their first game in the NHL, Babe Ruth was still a year away from hitting sixty home runs for the New York Yankees. The stock market hadn't yet crashed. And a four-term presidency was unimaginable; Franklin Delano Roosevelt wasn't even the governor of New York then.

At that time, ice hockey was still unfamiliar to most in the Windy City. Baseball was America's pastime then, thanks in great part to Babe Ruth, who single-handedly revived confidence in a sport that had been scarred by the conspiracy to throw the 1919 World Series—plotted by Chicago's own White Sox. Boxing and horse racing were also popular sports with such giants as Jack Dempsey in the ring and Earl Sande on the racetrack. But ice hockey was, for the most part, a novelty and a curiosity. Americans skated for recreation but not yet with a stick and a puck.

Gradually, hockey had made its way down to the United States from Canada where the sport was—and still is—an essential part of the Canadian soul. (The first recorded game was played in 1875 in Montreal's Victoria Skating Rink between two teams of McGill University students.) On an amateur level, hockey was played by college students in New England, but it wasn't until the formation of the National Hockey League in 1917 that the "fastest game on earth" became a more recognized professional entity. Boston was the natural choice for a franchise in 1924. New York and Pittsburgh followed suit in 1925. Chicago seemed a viable place for a franchise, but the league had to find a man who was willing and ready.

TOUGH TEAM TOUGH TOWN

Far left: 1929–30 team photo taken on January 25, 1930, in Atlantic City, New Jersey, the temporary home of the Pittsburgh Pirates. Top row, left to right: Ty Arbour, Duke Dukowski, Stew Adams, Tommy Cook, goalie Charlie Gardiner, Rosie "Lolo" Couture, Frank Ingram, Taffy Abel, John Gottselig, and referee Bill Stewart. Bottom row: Helge Bostrom, Art Somers, Harold March, and Teddy Graham. Left: An early Blackhawks patch. The name was made one word in 1986–87 after William Wirtz noticed it was written that way on the original charter. This book uses the one-word spelling throughout for consistency.

Enter Major Frederic McLaughlin, a local coffee tycoon, polo player, Harvard grad, and quite a character. The Major was also a gambler. Betting on the growing popularity of the sport and the appeal of a New York–Chicago rivalry, McLaughlin gathered some well-heeled friends to post the $12,000 entry fee. For that amount, McLaughlin was allowed to pick a name for his team, and he chose the Blackhawks. The name was significant for him, since he had been a commander in the 333rd Machine Gun Battalion of the 85th Division of the U.S. Army during World War I. Members of his division called themselves the Black Hawks in honor of the Sauk Indian chief who sided with the British in the War of 1812 but was overcome in a territory dispute in 1832 by—who else?—troops from Illinois. To this day, the head of an Indian remains the centerpiece of the Blackhawks' distinctive uniform.

McLaughlin's means for building his team were no less distinctive. To round up players, McLaughlin bought the Portland Rosebuds of the Western Hockey League for $200,000, and formed the nucleus of his team with Charles "Rabbit" McVeigh, George Hay, Percy Traub, Dick Irvin, and goalie Hugh Lehman. McLaughlin bought Cecil "Babe" Dye, who would lead the team with twenty-five goals during that first sea-

son, from the Toronto St. Pats. Both Dye and Lehman were later enshrined in the Hockey Hall of Fame. With a team finally in place, McLaughlin secured a 4-1 victory on opening night—November 17, 1926—against the Toronto St. Pats before nine thousand spectators at the Chicago Coliseum, a converted Civil War–era prison. However, the Blackhawks won only nineteen of forty-four games that first season, lost twenty-two, and tied three for a third-place finish and a

brief playoff sortie (two losses to Boston and out) that opening season. Being the demanding fellow he was, McLaughlin figured he deserved more for his money, and he excused coach Pete Muldoon from further obligations. He wasn't the first coach that McLaughlin fired, and he was certainly not the last, but few personnel conflicts would yield as much fodder for Blackhawk lore. Before Muldoon cleaned out his desk, he reportedly left behind the "Curse of Muldoon," which, for a hoax, enjoyed a remarkably long life.

Though the Blackhawks weren't really cursed, they performed in their second season as though they had been witnesses to

the fictional exchange between McLaughlin and Muldoon. They won only seven games under two other coaches, Barney Stanley and Lehman. After Stanley was cashiered at midseason, ex-goalie Lehman took over and soon regretted that he had not retired. In his debut as coach, the Montreal Canadiens buried the Blackhawks 10-0. By this time, McLaughlin had hired a professional cheerleader—a deep-voiced jewelry auctioneer from Saskatchewan—to fire up the crowds. Fans who had been content to applaud politely, as if at the opera, now shouted and cheered their team on.

To prove their second season's travails were no accident, the team won only seven of forty-four games in 1928–29 under Herb Gardiner, the Blackhawks' fourth coach and a member of the Hall of Fame for his record as a defenseman. That 1928–29 squad, amazingly enough, failed to score a single goal during an eight-game stretch in February, and was shut out in twenty of its forty-four contests—both existing records. The Blackhawks tallied only thirty-three goals all season, also a record, and they had literally become road warriors. McLaughlin's lease on the Coliseum expired on January 20, 1929, and construction of the much-anticipated Chicago Stadium was delayed, so the Blackhawks played some home games in other cities.

McLaughlin experimented with a number of coaches during the Blackhawks' first decades (three in 1932–33) with varying results. The most successful was Dick Irvin, one of the players McLaughlin acquired from the Portland Rosebuds, who scored eighteen goals for the Blackhawks in their debut season. Irvin coached one full season—leading the team to the 1931 Stanley Cup finals only to be beaten by Montreal—and part of another before being shown the door. Later, as coach of the Toronto Maple Leafs, Irvin eliminated the Blackhawks from the playoffs in 1932, and proved a rousing success as a coach of the Montreal Canadiens, whom he led to three Stanley Cups.

If Irvin's discharge was a mistake to be rued later, one of McLaughlin's more unusual choices proved to be a miscalculation from the beginning. Godfrey Matheson coached a Winnipeg team to a midget championship, a feat that caught McLaughlin's eye, as did a dazzling letter of application that Matheson wrote. But his coaching skills never quite matched his literary talents. Matheson chose to use a dressmaker's dummy between the pipes during practice instead of expending the

Above: Miniature hockey stick autographed by the 1930–31 club, which nearly brought home Chicago's first Stanley Cup. Lower left: Wearing the executive dress of the day for traveling hockey players—suits, ties, topcoats, and hats—the 1930–31 Blackhawks are shown arriving at Montreal's Windsor Station on April 8, 1931, after the long train ride from Chicago during the three-out-of-five-game 1931 Stanley Cup finals.

energy of his fine goalie Charlie Gardiner. This decision may have reserved Gardiner's strength for games, but it depleted the offensive players' opportunities to better their skills against flesh-and-blood goalies. Matheson also had the Blackhawks' tiny Harold "Mush" March, all five foot, five inches, and 155 pounds of him, deftly stick-handling into opposing territory, thereby attracting the opposing team's defensemen, at which point March would leave the puck for Clarence "Taffy" Abel, who weighed in at 225 pounds. Abel would promptly pick up the puck and barge into the vacuum created by March's subterfuge, all the better to score. While this strategy sounded okay in theory, it never quite worked that way in practice. The dressmaker's dummy didn't last for long; neither did Matheson. His official coaching record: two games, two losses.

In the midst of these disappointments, the Major did find himself a fine organizational type in Bill Tobin, who worked his way up from being an executive handyman, and a quality coach in Tom Gorman, a former sportswriter who took over for Matheson. Gorman quickly proved his status as a card-carrying member of this feisty franchise from Chicago. Late in the 1933 season, the Blackhawks were leading against Boston 2-1 when legendary defenseman Eddie Shore scored a tying goal with two seconds remaining. The Bruins' Marty Barry scored in overtime, but the Blackhawks vehemently disputed the goal, and referee Bill Stewart skated over to their bench. Gorman promptly pulled Stewart's jersey over his head and started punching. Stewart punched back. Stewart then ejected Gorman, who agreed to leave with one caveat: his players had to follow him to the locker room. And they did. When none of the Blackhawks returned, the game was lost by a forfeit. Stewart dropped the puck with six Bruins on the ice, and Cooney Weiland scored in the empty net.

With that kind of fighting spirit, is there any doubt how Gorman led the Blackhawks to their first championship game in the following season? The 1934 Stanley Cup was actually somewhat of a surprise, since the team had finished in second place, only three games over .500. But Gorman was given a relatively free hand by McLaughlin, who had his own fires to put out. McLaughlin repeatedly sparred with NHL officials and resigned as the team's governor, delegating his duties to Tobin. McLaughlin also cried foul over fees for playing home games at the Stadium, and at the risk of violating his contract with the new building, he had the Blackhawks move back to the Coliseum until the crisis was resolved. McLaughlin also rejected repeated offers from James Norris, a Chicago resident who had taken control of the Detroit franchise, to buy the team.

Nobody ever accused the Blackhawks of being dull, even though they won only fourteen of their forty-eight games during the 1937–38 season and finished a distant third—thirty points behind first-place Boston. By no coincidence, this team's makeup reflected the influence of McLaughlin, who had decreed toward the end of the previous season that coach Clem Loughlin try to recruit a different breed of player.

Right: Despite his diminutive size (five foot, five inches, and 155 pounds), Harold "Mush" March was one of the most effective and popular forwards ever to play for the Blackhawks. March played right wing from 1928 through 1945, scoring 153 goals, none more important than the one he collected in sudden-death overtime to beat the Detroit Red Wings 1-0 and bring Chicago its first Stanley Cup in 1934.

CHICAGO STADIUM REVIEW

PRICE 15¢

HOCKEY

"Mush" March

Left: The Blackhawks made their debut with the 1926—27 season. Players, from left to right, were: goalie Hugh Lehman, defenseman Bob Trapp, defenseman Percy Traub, defenseman Duke Dukowski, defenseman Gord Fraser, forward Dick Irvin, forward George Hay, forward Mickey Mackay, forward Cecil "Babe" Dye, forward Cully Wilson, forward Eddie Rodden, and forward Charles "Rabbit" McVeigh. Above: 1930s shin pads featured heavy felt padding on the sides and top, grain leather lined on the inside with cane or bamboo sticks to protect the shins, and heavy felt-lined grain leather cushioned knee pads. The shin guards were so thin that they are hardly noticeable under the long stockings of the 1926—27 players.

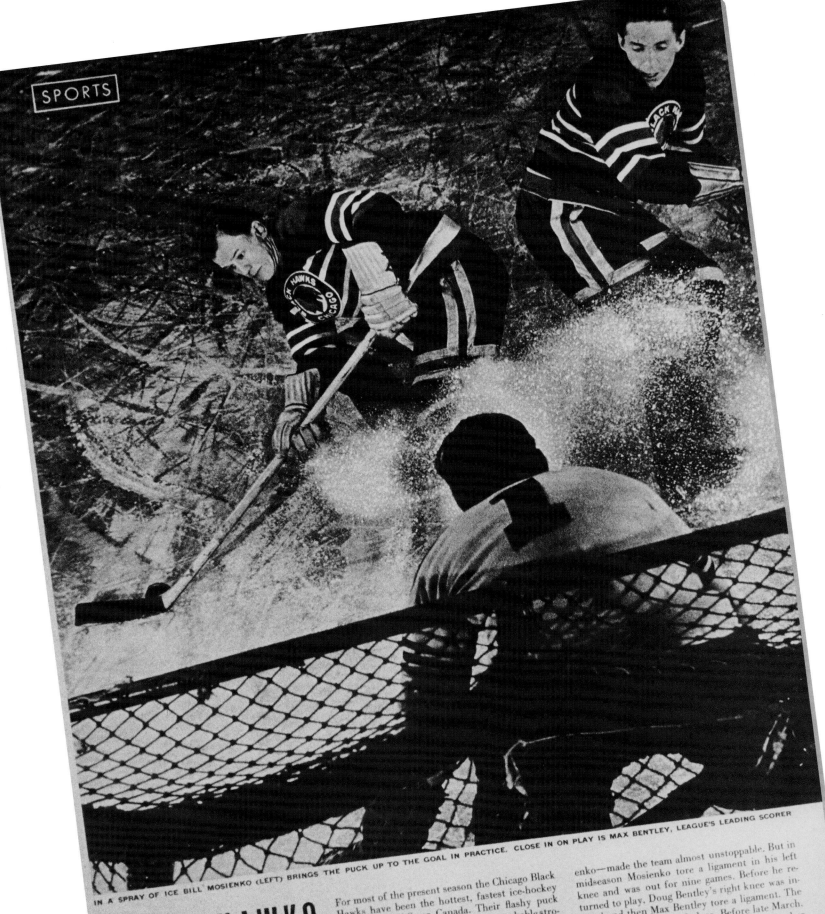

IN A SPRAY OF ICE BILL MOSIENKO (LEFT) BRINGS THE PUCK UP TO THE GOAL IN PRACTICE. CLOSE IN ON PLAY IS MAX BENTLEY, LEAGUE'S LEADING SCORER

BLACK HAWKS

Despite injuries, Chicago hockey team leads the league in scoring

For most of the present season the Chicago Black Hawks have been the hottest, fastest ice-hockey team in the U.S. or Canada. Their flashy puck handling, which is shown in these remarkable stroboscopic pictures by LIFE Photographer Frank Scherschel, put them at the top of the National Hockey League in January, when five of their players ranked among the league's seven top scorers. The speed and teamwork of their forward line—the Bentley brothers, Max and Doug, and Bill Mosi-

enko—made the team almost unstoppable. But in midseason Mosienko tore a ligament in his left knee and was out for nine games. Before he returned to play, Doug Bentley's right knee was injured and then Max Bentley tore a ligament. The team dropped to second place. Before late March, however, the famous line will be playing together again. Then the Chicago Black Hawks, who are certain to enter the Stanley Cup play-offs, expect to win the cup and with it the world championship.

CONTINUED ON NEXT PAGE

McLaughlin, never having been too keen on the Canadian dominance in hockey, wanted dearly to suit up Americans, and he instructed Tobin to juggle the roster accordingly. Art Ross, the Bruins' boss, dubbed McLaughlin's patriotic idea a farce and suggested that he be removed as the Blackhawks' owner. Ross was not alone in his dismay, but each of McLaughlin's critics received equal treatment: the rebuff, "Keep your nose out of our affairs."

McLaughlin got the last laugh, because his Blackhawks—with eight Yankees on the roster—came out of nowhere to win the Stanley Cup in 1938. Defying all odds, the Blackhawks, who had won only fourteen games during the entire season, won half as many during three playoff series over three weeks to seize their second championship. And who coached this miracle? None other than Massachusetts-born Bill Stewart, the same Bill Stewart who, as a referee, had sentenced the Blackhawks to that forfeit only five years earlier. And Stewart was still feisty. Before game one of the Stanley Cup finals against Toronto, Stewart exchanged punches with Conn Smythe, the president and general manager of the Maple Leafs.

Left: Forwards Bill Mosienko and Max Bentley, who starred for the Blackhawks during the 1940s and 1950s, spray ice in practice before playing the New York Rangers, as captured by a stroboscopic camera for a three-page spread in *Life* magazine. Right: Skates worn by fiery Bill Stewart, who coached the Blackhawks to their second Stanley Cup in 1938. Lower right: The legendary "Pony Line."

One might think that after choreographing such a miraculous feat, Stewart would have a job for life—or at least for another season. Stewart gladly accepted the Stanley Cup before a packed Chicago Stadium on opening night the next November, but he was let go midway into the 1938–39 season. Paul Thompson followed Stewart, and he lasted as player-coach and then as a coach until 1944, the year McLaughlin died. In many ways, McLaughlin *was* the Chicago Blackhawks and the force of his personality carried the team through good times and bad. The team continued to reflect his spirit and personality long after his death. In recognition of his contributions to his team and the sport, McLaughlin was inducted into the Hall of Fame as a builder in 1963.

Before McLaughlin died, he did witness one more trip to the Stanley Cup finals for his Blackhawks in 1944. But they lost four straight games to Montreal, the last of which by 5-4 after leading the Canadiens 4-1 entering the third period. That would be the Blackhawks' last trip to the finals until 1961. It wasn't because the Blackhawks didn't have some fine players. Bill Mosienko, a right wing, arrived in the 1941–42 season, and on February 8, 1942, in a game against the New York Rangers, scored two goals within twenty-one seconds—a feat he would later top. Soon he would join brothers Max and Doug Bentley as center and left wing on coach John Gottselig's feared "Pony Line."

The defense was anchored by John Mariucci, a 200-pound former University of Minnesota football player and one of the most feared "policemen" of his day. One of his many fights, vs. Black Jack Stewart of the Canadiens, lasted almost fifteen minutes—the equivalent of five rounds of boxing with no intermissions. Earl Seibert was another steady rear guard who could carry the puck. He was either a first- or second-team all star for ten consecutive seasons and a future Hall of Famer. But those were lean times. For two decades, from the 1940–41 season until 1960–61, the Blackhawks posted only one winning record (1945–46), and finished last nine times.

In 1946, Tobin's syndicate bought major-ity interest in the team for $350,000 from McLaughlin's heirs, but Tobin dared to trade the ever-popular Max Bentley to Toronto for five players a year later. For a while, fans came in droves. When Emile "The Cat" Francis debuted against Boston on February 23, 1947, there were 20,004 spectators crammed into the Stadium.

However, attendance gradually dwindled, and the Blackhawks were left on thin ice. After winning only seventeen of seventy games in 1951–52, the Blackhawks were sold to the prosperous owners of the Chicago Stadium, James Norris, his son James D. Norris, and Arthur M. Wirtz.

These entrepreneurs drew upon all the resources at their disposal to resuscitate the team's reputation. The elder Norris promptly dismissed rumors of the Blackhawks' imminent demise by stating that he could afford to lose $1 million a year for two centuries. Still, dollar bills couldn't skate. The new owners needed players, and NHL partners knew it. The Maple Leafs traded four bodies to Chicago for one, and the most valuable acquisition for the Blackhawks was goalie Al Rollins. Montreal sent Ed Litzenberger to the Windy City. Sid Abel, a star for Detroit but past his prime, came to Chicago to coach and to play. He managed to get the Blackhawks into the playoffs for the first time in seven years in 1952–53, and they actually took a 3-2 lead in games against the mighty Canadiens before losing the series.

The most significant change was the acquisition of the Red Wings' coach, Tommy Ivan, in July of 1954. Ivan had coached the Red Wings to six straight first-place finishes and three Stanley Cups. He had talent at his fingers, specifically the line of Gordie Howe, Ted Lindsay, and Sid Abel. Chicago, by contrast, was a blank canvas. The diminutive Ivan could not refuse the lure of becoming a general manager at a mere forty-three years of age. Ivan summed up his decision, "I wanted a new challenge other than coaching, and I got one in Chicago."

Ivan provided stability, patience, and knowledge—qualities the defeated Blackhawks desperately needed. The franchise had a wonderful building, a captive audience waiting to be entertained once again, and an ownership that hardly lacked for funds. What the Blackhawks needed now was a plan.

Ivan tried everything. He replaced Sid Abel with Frank Eddolls, whose 1954–55 team won only thirteen of seventy games. Ivan then turned the coaching job over to Irvin, who had made his mark in Montreal. Irvin's directive was to finish third. He finished last. Ivan even resorted to appointing himself coach the next season, but the Blackhawks landed in last place for the fourth straight season and the eighth of nine.

But Ivan didn't rely exclusively on trial and error to lay a surer foundation for his team. Aware that the Blackhawks had, for too many seasons, recruited players who had seen their best days in other uniforms, Ivan decided to seek out new talent that could be trained and polished for the NHL. Since the youth of North America couldn't be tapped all at once, Ivan dealt in quantity, if not in quality. For $150,000, he purchased the Buffalo minor league team, which included a promising defenseman, Pierre Pilote. Ivan also entered into a sponsorship of a junior club, the St. Catherines Tee Pees, which included another defenseman with considerable potential, Elmer "Moose" Vasko. In addition to these acquisitions, one transaction stood out. In July of 1957, Ivan sent Johnny Wilson, Forbes Kennedy, William Preston, and Hank Bassen to the Red Wings in exchange for Glenn Hall and Ted Lindsay. The latter still had some steam in him, scoring forty-four goals in three seasons for Chicago, but Detroit's management was upset at Lindsay's efforts in forming a players union. Ivan wasn't concerned about that. His eye was on Hall, who had tended goal for two full seasons for Detroit and might be the man to solidify the Blackhawks' most important position. Ivan was right.

The rest, as they say, is history. Remember those St. Catharines Tee Pees? They contributed not only Vasko to the Blackhawks but also Bobby Hull, Stan Mikita,

Above: 1930s gloves featured vented horse-hide palms and genuine leather cuffs, covered by protective inserts of cane. In 1933, the professional model of these gloves was expensive, $9.50, which would be well over $100 today. Below: The distinctive tie-neck wool sweater of the St. Catherines Tee Pees, the Blackhawks Junior A affiliate. Its colorful style is prophetic of the future many Tee Pees would have as Blackhawks.

Goalie Al Rollins, defending the Blackhawks' goal against the Toronto Maple Leafs, was an outstanding netminder during some lean times in the 1950s. (Masks were not worn until 1959.) In 1953–54, Rollins accomplished the near impossible feat of winning the Hart Memorial Trophy as most valuable player in the NHL—despite the fact that the Blackhawks won only twelve of seventy games and finished last. In this photo, Ron Stewart of the Toronto Maple Leafs stands over the action, while teammate Ted "Teeder" Kennedy, toppling another player, makes his best effort to control the puck.

and a coach, Rudy Pilous, to point them to the promised land. In 1961, the Blackhawks were No. 1 among the Original Six. Twenty-three long years after they had won their second Stanley Cup, they won their third on a snowy night in Detroit.

The Blackhawks were a force through the 1960s, and in the final season of the Original Six, 1966–67, they finished in first place: forty-one wins, seventeen losses, and twelve ties; ninety-four points, seventeen more points than the runner-up, Montreal. The next season, a vibrant NHL doubled its size in an expansion unmatched in professional sports. Philadelphia, Los Angeles, Minnesota, St. Louis, Pittsburgh, and Oakland formed a new western division, while the Original Six comprised the eastern division.

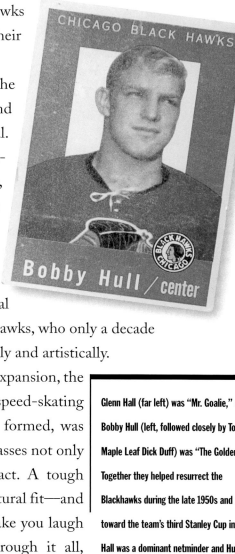

The NHL entered a brave new era. Such a venture was possible only because of the demand for hockey and the stability of the Original Six. This was a boon to the Blackhawks, who only a decade before were floundering, financially and artistically.

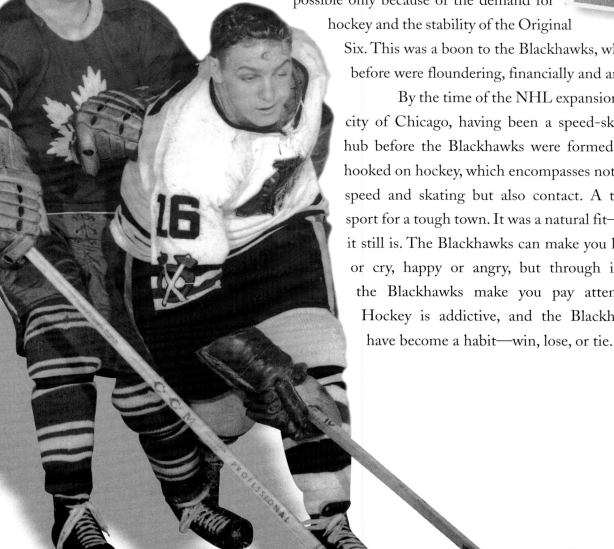

By the time of the NHL expansion, the city of Chicago, having been a speed-skating hub before the Blackhawks were formed, was hooked on hockey, which encompasses not only speed and skating but also contact. A tough sport for a tough town. It was a natural fit—and it still is. The Blackhawks can make you laugh or cry, happy or angry, but through it all, the Blackhawks make you pay attention. Hockey is addictive, and the Blackhawks have become a habit—win, lose, or tie.

Glenn Hall (far left) was "Mr. Goalie," and Bobby Hull (left, followed closely by Toronto Maple Leaf Dick Duff) was "The Golden Jet." Together they helped resurrect the Blackhawks during the late 1950s and move toward the team's third Stanley Cup in 1961. Hall was a dominant netminder and Hull an explosive left wing, though you'll note that he arrived in Chicago as a center and the first number he wore was No. 16, not his familiar No. 9. Above: A valuable trading card of a young Bobby Hull.

CURSE OF MULDOON

Like New York Yankee Babe Ruth's supposed "called shot" during game three of the 1932 World Series against the Cubs at Wrigley Field, there are many chapters in Chicago sports lore. And it doesn't seem to matter whether they're based on fact or fiction. One thing is for sure: after Pete Muldoon cleaned out his desk following his only season as coach of the Blackhawks in 1927, little could he have imagined . . .

Muldoon's curse on the Blackhawks can be attributed to the curse of daily deadlines on newspaper columnists.

James Coleman, a distinguished reporter for Canada's national newspaper, the *Toronto Globe and Mail*, possessed a clever, impish wit. Many years after Pete Muldoon had been fired as the coach of the Blackhawks, Coleman tapped his fertile imagination and concocted the following story in order to account for the Blackhawks' poor record:

The Hawks are victims of a hex Pete Muldoon put on them many years ago, after he was fired as coach. He had a stormy session with Major Frederic McLaughlin, the strange eccentric who owned the Hawks when they were admitted to the NHL in 1926. Muldoon coached the Hawks to a

third-place finish in their first year, but McLaughlin was not impressed. "This team was good enough to be first," he said.

Muldoon was amazed at McLaughlin's criticism, but not to the point of shutting up. "You're crazy," Muldoon said.

McLaughlin was outraged by such heresy. "You're fired!" he roared.

Muldoon flared back in a black Irish snit. "Fire me, Major, and you'll never finish first! I'll put a curse on this team that will hoodoo it till the end of time."

And so, kiddies, that's why the Hawks always fail to grab the flag in the NHL. They cannot beat the Curse of Muldoon.

Little did James Coleman realize the shelf-life that this fictional exchange would have. Whatever the story's origins, lore about the Curse of Muldoon grew stronger with fans and players with each passing season. The team did not finish first until 1967—forty years after Muldoon was shown the door.

OUR BLACK HAWKS ARE WORLD CHAMPS!

Dodgers Wallop Pirates, 13-6; ~~Tangles with Conlan~~ **Rally to Rout Red Wings, 5-1**

Chicago Daily Tribune

HALL'S WORK IN NETS

17,204 See Black Hawks Win Stanley Cup

CHICAGO ✦ AMERICAN

SECOND SECTION   CHICAGO, WEDNESDAY, APRIL 13, 1938   25

Hawks Flying High!

CHICAGO SUN-TIMES

MONDAY, MARCH 25, 1963

60

Hawks Nail 2d Place

TRIP BRUINS 4-3; VEZINA TO HALL

THEY HAVE A RIGHT TO SMILE

Hawks Eliminate Canadiens 2-0
HALL BRILLIANT, FACE TORONTO IN CUP FINALS

Sun-Times Special

BOSTON — Chicago's relaxed Black Hawks bagged three goals in a third-period flurry Sunday night to beat the Boston Bruins 4-3 and take second place in the final National Hockey League standings.

The result also won the

Montreal and Toronto lose. Gordie Howe scoring champ. Stories on Page 58.

Vezina Trophy for Hawk goaltender Glenn Hall and primed the Chicagoans for their Stanley Cup playoff opener at home Tuesday against the Detroit Red Wings.

The Hawks finished a single point behind first

Fear Not, Goals Will Come: Reay

BY DAN MOULTON

Coach Billy Reay figures that if his Black Hawks merely continue to play their game, the goals will have to start coming again.

Thus he plans nothing startling for tonight's Stadium match against the New York Rangers, in which the Hawks will be attempting to snap a scoreless streak at three games and climb back into the race for the National Hockey league championship.

"I might have six defensemen dressed for the game and keep one forward out of uniform, but that's about all," said Reay.

"Matt Ravlich [who has missed six games because of a groin injury] will be playing tonight, and I want to get both him and Doug Jarrett back into action, so we might go with the extra defensemen.

"But we don't need any-

BLACK HAWKS AREN'T CELEBRATING YET

By Julius Silverstein

The Black Hawks were taking nothing for granted after their 5-2 victory over the Detroit Red Wings in the second

Bobby Hull's injury obviously tempered the players' jubilation.

With left-winger Ron Murphy also sidelined, with an in-

Doug Bentley (7) whirls around to fire a backhand against the Maple Leafs goalie "Turk" Broda. When Bentley, a Saskatchewan wheat farmer, first arrived at the Chicago Stadium, he said, "This old barn could sure hold a lot of hay." Bentley and his brother, Max, developed the "flip" pass in the 1942–43 season. Doug said, "You see, we don't slide the puck on the ice when we pass. We flip the puck over our opponent's sticks."

When Frank Mahovlich, right, arrived in the NHL during the late 1950s, the Toronto Maple Leafs knew they had someone special. The Big M scored twenty goals in his first full season, then exploded for forty-eight goals during the 1960—61 campaign. That was the same season the Blackhawks won the Stanley Cup, but the Blackhawks still had an eye on Mahovlich. Here Mahovlich pins Tom Johnson of the Montreal Canadiens to the boards as he maneuvers for control of the puck.

THE MILLION-DOLLAR CHECK

In October 1962, just a year after the Blackhawks' third Stanley Cup win, James D. Norris—who was not content to rest on his laurels—decided to go after Frank Mahovlich, the Maple Leafs' twenty-four-year-old left wing who had garnered forty-eight goals during the previous season. Norris knew that Mahovlich was angling for a better contract, and thought he could relieve the Maple Leafs' management of the chore. So Norris broached the subject of buying Mahovlich with Harold Ballard, Stafford Smythe, and John Bassett at a party at Toronto's Royal York Hotel on the night before the annual NHL all-star game.

"I'll give you a million dollars for the right to negotiate with Mahovlich."

"You'll give us how much?" Ballard asked incredulously.

"You heard me," Norris persisted. "I'll pay you one million dollars."

"Every man has his price," Ballard said. After adjourning briefly to confer with general manager Tommy Ivan, Norris pulled ten crisp $100 bills from his wallet and returned to the party. He flashed Smythe his down payment, to which Smythe intoned, "You've got a deal."

Ballard promptly scribbled the essence of the deal on a cocktail napkin. Norris then instructed Ivan to place a call to Chicago, where then Blackhawks' publicity director, John Gottselig, could take down details and release the news to the papers.

"HAWKS BUY MAHOVLICH FOR $1 MILLION" screamed the headlines the next day. But fans in Toronto reacted so unfavorably to the story that the Maple Leafs' executives were forced to call an emergency meeting.

"I will not consider such a deal," Smythe insisted, even after receiving Norris's $1-million check from Ivan. "Frank Mahovlich is not for sale at any price. We decline. The money is going back to Chicago."

Later, many criticized Norris for staging a publicity stunt. No one can deny that Norris had an eye for talent. Mahovlich scored 533 goals during a brilliant NHL career with Toronto, Detroit, and Montreal, and was elected to the Hockey Hall of Fame in 1981. Perhaps the most telling piece of evidence of what really happened is the item that hung in a small frame on the wall of Ivan's Stadium office for many years: a check from James D. Norris to the Toronto Maple Leafs for $1 million, dated October 6, 1962.

Left: A $1-million check made out to the Toronto Maple Leafs by James D. Norris and the scribbled notes of a proposed blockbuster transaction whereby the Blackhawks would have purchased Frank Mahovlich before the 1962 season. The "deal" came about one evening at Toronto's Royal York Hotel, which is where it ended the morning after. "They welched on us," huffed Norris, who was not bashful about spending to build another Stanley Cup champion. Below: James D. Norris, left, and Tommy Ivan.

MOMENTS IN TIME: 1917–52

The National Hockey League was still in its early years when an eccentric coffee baron bought a franchise for his hometown of Chicago. Separated from Canada by the Great Lakes, the Windy City was pretty unfamiliar with the sport. But Major McLaughlin's Chicago Blackhawks changed all that. The team had a tough, gritty attitude that resonated well with the city's hard-boiled residents.

NOVEMBER 22, 1917
The National Hockey League is organized in Montreal.

NOVEMBER 17, 1926
The Blackhawks play their first game at the Chicago Coliseum and defeat the Toronto St. Pats 4-1 before a crowd of about eight thousand fans. Stones for the building had been transported from Europe to the South, where the structure served as a prison during the Civil War, and was later brought to Chicago and converted into the city's primary indoor arena for a variety of attractions.

MARCH 28, 1929
The Chicago Stadium opens to the public with a boxing match. The Stadium is the enterprise of Paddy Harmon, a sports promoter, and is built at a cost of $6 million.

SEPTEMBER 25, 1926
The NHL grants a franchise to the city of Chicago to be owned by Major Frederic McLaughlin, president of McLaughlin's Manor House Coffee. The Major, well-known in Chicago high-society circles, heads a group of local businessmen who pay $12,000 for a team to be known as the Blackhawks. The team will practice on an outdoor rink beside the south-side Chicago Beach Hotel. Left: Cecil Dye, one of the Blackhawks' first forwards.

DECEMBER 18, 1932
The Chicago Bears defeat Portsmouth 9-0 for the NFL's first title game played indoors at the Chicago Stadium.

MARCH 14, 1933
The Blackhawks forfeit only game in team history when the players refuse to return to the ice after their coach, Tom Gorman, is ejected by referee Bill Stewart. Boston is given a 1-0 victory.

MARCH 19, 1933
First afternoon game ever in NHL is played in Chicago. Detroit defeats Chicago 4-3.

JUNE 13, 1934
Blackhawks goaltender Charlie Gardiner dies of a brain tumor at age twenty-nine, just eight weeks after the team wins the Stanley Cup.

MARCH 8, 1937
Canadien Howie Morenz dies in a Montreal hospital thirty-nine days after suffering a broken leg in a collision with Blackhawk Earl Seibert. Cause of death: pneumonia, nervous exhaustion, and a "broken heart," according to line mate Auriel Joliet.

APRIL 3, 1938
Alfie Moore plays his one and only game as a Blackhawk against Toronto in a Stanley Cup game and helps the team beat the Maple Leafs 3-1.

DECEMBER 15, 1929
Before a crowd of 14,212 people, the Blackhawks make their debut in the new Chicago Stadium by beating the Pittsburgh Pirates 3-1 for their fifth consecutive victory. Vic Ripley scores two powerplay goals within thirty-five seconds of the second period, and Frank Ingram adds an insurance goal, also on a powerplay, later in the session.

APRIL 10, 1934
With almost nineteen thousand fans in attendance, the underdog Blackhawks win their first Stanley Cup by defeating the Detroit Red Wings 1-0 at the Chicago Stadium to win the best-of-five final series, three games to one. Harold "Mush" March scores at 10:05 of the second overtime period on the Blackhawks' fifty-fourth shot against Detroit goalie Wilfred Cude. Charles Gardiner (right), the Blackhawks' outstanding goalie, posts his second shutout in eight playoff games.

MARCH 18, 1940
The Chicago Blackhawks take the first chartered flight in NHL history to Toronto for the first round of the Stanley Cup finals.

MARCH 4, 1941
Sam LoPresti makes eighty saves on eighty-three shots against Boston; however, the Blackhawks lose to the Bruins 3-2.

MARCH 16, 1941
Blackhawks coach Paul Thompson pulls goaltender Sam LoPresti for an extra attacker in the season's final regular-season game. This is the first time the tactic is used in a Blackhawks game.

JANUARY 3, 1943
Blackhawks forward Reg Bentley scores a goal with assists from his brothers Max and Doug in a 3-3 tie at New York. It is the first goal in NHL history with all three points from the same family.

FEBRUARY 20, 1944
A "perfect game" is played at the Chicago Stadium between the Blackhawks and the Maple Leafs. The game ends in a scoreless tie (0-0), and there are no penalties called.

DECEMBER 17, 1944
Major Frederick McLaughlin, first owner of the Blackhawks, dies.

JANUARY 28, 1943
Max Bentley registers four goals and three assists for the Blackhawks in a 10-1 Stadium rout of the New York Rangers. His mark of five points in a single period (the third) ties a franchise record set by Les Cunningham in 1940. Left: Doug and Max pose suiting up for a *Sport* magazine feature.

APRIL 12, 1938
The unheralded Blackhawks, with a roster liberally sprinkled with American-born players, win their second Stanley Cup, beating the stunned Toronto Maple Leafs 4-1 before 17,205 fans in the Chicago Stadium. Cully Dahlstrom (right) scores in the first period to give the Blackhawks a 1-0 lead. Then, after Gordon Drillon tallies for Toronto, the Blackhawks get three straight goals from Carl Voss, Jack Shill, and Mush March.

The tone of the rough series is set in the first period, when there are three different fights. But the mood eases thereafter, although Leafs defenseman Red Horner refuses to shake hands with the Blackhawks afterward. Harvey "Busher" Jackson of the visitors is friendlier, waving to the crowd and holding his stick aloft before he tosses it into the stands as a souvenir.

MARCH 4, 1945
Forward Clint Smith joins Busher Jackson and Max Bentley with an NHL record: scoring four goals in a single period. The Blackhawks win 6-4 against the Montreal Canadiens at the Chicago Stadium.

FEBRUARY 23, 1947
A crowd of 20,004 is on hand on a snowy winter night at the Chicago Stadium. The Blackhawks lose to the Boston Bruins 9-4, but the attendance breaks the Stadium record of 19,749, set in January 1946. Before the game, Dit Clapper of the Bruins is honored for his induction into the Hockey Hall of Fame.

OCTOBER 13, 1947
Before a sold-out crowd at Maple Leaf Gardens, Blackhawks' left wing Doug Bentley scores the game-winning goal in the first NHL All-Star Game.

NOVEMBER 4, 1947
The Blackhawks trade Max Bentley to Toronto for Gus Bodnar, Gaye Stewart, Bob Goldham, Bud Poile, and Ernie Dickens.

NOVEMBER 3, 1948
The Blackhawks host their first NHL all-star game at the Stadium before a crowd of 16,681 fans. The NHL all-stars defeat the defending Stanley Cup champions, the Toronto Maple Leafs, 3-1. Breaking the customary code of all-star games, Detroit's Gordie Howe and Toronto's Gus Mortson engage in a spirited fistfight.

SEPTEMBER 25, 1951
The Blackhawks complete the largest cash deal in NHL history by purchasing six players from the Red Wings for $75,000. The players are forwards Jim Peters, Jim McFadden, Max McNab, and George Gee and defensemen Clare Martin and Clare Raglan. The largest cash transaction before that was in the 1930s when Toronto agreed to pay $35,000 to Ottawa for King Clancy.

JANUARY 17, 1952
Bill Mosienko scores his 200th career goal.

MARCH 23, 1952
Twenty-nine-year-old Bill Mosienko (left) collects an amazing three goals in twenty-one seconds at Madison Square Garden in a 7-6 Blackhawk victory over the New York Rangers. Left: An artist's rendition of Wee Willie with the three pucks that he had given to Coach Ebbie Goodfellow. The circular inset portrait captures Mosienko's third goal, a backhand lift shot to the opposite top shelf. The soft-spoken Winnipeg native scored 258 goals and 540 points in 711 NHL games over fourteen years, all as a Blackhawk. In twenty years of professional hockey, he played 1,030 games, accumulating a paltry 129 penalty minutes. It is no wonder he won the Lady Byng Trophy in 1945.

Wayne Gretzky had serious reservations about whether the 1991 NHL all-star game should be played. The annual all-star game was to be held at the Chicago Stadium on January 19, two days after the beginning of Operation Desert Storm. Gretzky was concerned about escalating global tensions, and he was not alone.

"I don't know if it's right," said Gretzky, who was then with the Los Angeles Kings. "Should we be over here in America having a good time while soldiers are over there, risking their lives in the Persian Gulf?"

The NHL eventually decided that the forty-second all-star game should proceed as planned, but there was much to indicate that this was no ordinary game. Between periods, players on both sides adjourned to their locker rooms to watch breaking news from the war on television. "No Flag Burners Here" was written on one banner that was hung from the second balcony, and "God Bless the U.S.A." was written on a bedsheet that hung from the first balcony. Of the 18,472 spectators who crammed into the Chicago Stadium on

West Madison Street, thousands carried American flags of various sizes. There were some Canadian flags, too. And sparklers. Most of all, there was noise from start to finish of the 11-5 victory of the Clarence Campbell Conference over the Prince of Wales Conference. After it was over, Gretzky was found in the locker room, shaking his head.

"I was standing next to Mark Messier during the national anthems," Gretzky began. "I said to him, 'This is unbelievable. I've heard it as loud in here before, but never as emotional.' The flags of both countries, the banners, the vibrations. You could tell that the fans, like us, were thinking of other things.

"There was such a mood in that rink, such patriotism," Gretzky marveled. "It was good for hockey, probably good for the country. I love this building. It's the best place to visit in the league. Whenever you come in here with a rookie on your team, you tell him to be ready, because there's nothing like Chicago Stadium. And today was unreal.

REMEMBER THE ROAR

REMEMBER THE ROAR

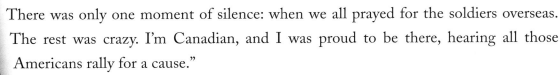

There was only one moment of silence: when we all prayed for the soldiers overseas. The rest was crazy. I'm Canadian, and I was proud to be there, hearing all those Americans rally for a cause."

The game was televised nationally on a Saturday afternoon by NBC. Several months later, William W. Wirtz, the president of the Blackhawks, had occasion to meet General Norman Schwarzkopf after the general returned from his victorious tour of duty. Schwarzkopf told Wirtz that he had seen and heard the noise while watching the telecast in the Persian Gulf, and found it so remarkable that he showed it to his 541,000 troops, who were uplifted by the knowledge that they had that kind of support back home.

"It was extra loud," Wirtz said. "But I didn't have the heart to tell General Schwarzkopf that it wasn't much different from what goes on every night we play at the Stadium."

Chicago Stadium is no more. 1800 West Madison Street has been reduced to a parking lot for the United Center across the street, where the Blackhawks now play. The United Center is about three times the size of the old stadium, and has all the amenities of a modern facility. But for anyone who has ever watched a hockey game at the old "Madhouse on Madison" . . . well, you had to hear it to believe it.

According to hockey historians in Chicago, the tradition of applauding during the national anthem began in 1985. The Blackhawks were engaged in the playoffs that spring, having beaten Detroit and Minnesota. Gretzky's Edmonton Oilers were the prevailing dynasty, and they proved themselves once again by whipping the Blackhawks 11-2 and 7-3 in the first two games of the best-of-seven Clarence Campbell Conference finals in Edmonton, Alberta. When the Blackhawks returned home, they needed some extra fuel, and they got it from their fans. Harvey Wittenberg, the public address announcer and a seemingly permanent fixture of the venue, went through his usual pre-ambles and the starting lineups: "Tonight's referee is . . . Please no smoking and no throwing objects on the ice. . . . And now, ladies and gentleman, will you please rise and join organist Bob Raatz. . . ." That's where the intelligible words stopped for the next few minutes. If you listened carefully, you could hear "The Star-Spangled Banner" being played in the background. For the most part, all you could hear was unabashed yelling and screaming from the seats way up in the second balcony to the seats against the glass.

In some sports arenas, it might be considered uncouth, or at least unusual, for spectators sitting in the most expensive seats to join those in the cheaper seats in any commotion, but such things were never a concern at the Stadium. The seats in the two balconies seemed to be right on top of the mezzanine seats, which were right on top of the loge, so it wasn't always clear where the din began or ended. What was evident was that sound collected. The Stadium, which was once described as having the acoustics of a soup can, held its noise well, and on occasion, the decibel level was the equivalent to a jet plane taking off. In any case, game three of the Stanley Cup semifinals on May 9, 1985, is generally pinpointed as the night when fans commenced the practice of voicing over "The Star-Spangled Banner." The Blackhawks won that night, 5-2, and again in

Above: Bill Wirtz president of the Blackhawks and a long-standing member of the Hockey Hall of Fame. He says, "I grew up in the Stadium. My mom went there just about every night to be with my dad, and she felt we should go along to be with him, too." In 1952, Bill joined the family company built by his legendary father, Arthur, and to this day he oversees the Wirtz empire. Bill loves all sports, but calls hockey "the greatest game in the world." Far right: Bill Mosienko, who played right wing for the Blackhawks from 1941 to 1955. His record—three goals in twenty-one seconds—has stood since 1952.

game four, 8-6, due in part to audience participation. The Blackhawks did not win the series, but they were up against one of the best teams ever. The Oilers lost only three of eighteen playoff games in 1985 as they romped to their second consecutive Stanley Cup in a run of four Cups in five years. Nevertheless, the Stadium was so exceptional as a conduit for the speed and energy of the game that one wondered whether the fans fed off the players or the players fed off the fans.

The Stadium was the perfect venue for hockey, but it was by no means just a frozen pond. The greatest professional basketball dynasty ever—the Chicago Bulls, six championships in eight years—won their first three there. Michael Jordan played his last NBA game in the Stadium on June 18, 1993. In a charity exhibition game later, shortly before the opening of the United Center, Jordan played once more at the Stadium, and concluded his cameo by kneeling on the ground, kissing the floor, and exclaiming, "I love the old building!"

Nobody loved the old building more than Patrick T. "Paddy" Harmon, a self-proclaimed "bullheaded Irishman" with vision and money. Harmon dearly wanted to have his own hockey team, and so in 1926, he ventured to an NHL meeting in Montreal where expansion was being discussed. Harmon brought with him a black satchel containing fifty one-thousand-dollar bills. He was prepared to leave that cash in exchange for a franchise, but he had come to the bargaining table too late. Major McLaughlin beat him to it for a mere twelve thousand dollars. Harmon left disappointed but undaunted.

"Everybody laughed at me," Harmon said of his dream to build a new stadium, but he showed everybody by laying out $2.5 million of his own money and borrowing the rest from friends to finance the construction. If he couldn't own the team, he would at least have it as the primary tenant in a building of his own construction. Harmon's dream became a reality on March 28, 1929, when the Stadium opened its doors for a boxing match between light heavyweight champion Tommy Loughran and middleweight champion Mickey Walker. That first event at the Stadium set a new record for gross indoor receipts: $187,000. Harmon beamed at his success.

Far left: The Blackhawks celebrate their four-game sweep in a best-of-seven playoff series against the Detroit Red Wings in 1992. By winning the division finals, the Blackhawks advanced to the conference finals, during which they also swept the Edmonton Oilers. In all, the Blackhawks won a franchise-record eleven consecutive postseason games that spring, vaulting them to the Stanley Cup finals.

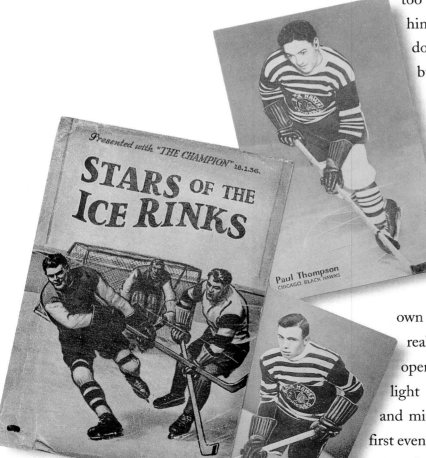

Presented with "THE CHAMPION" 18.1.36.
STARS OF THE ICE RINKS

Paul Thompson
CHICAGO BLACK HAWKS

Harold (Mush) March
CHICAGO BLACK HAWKS

to the second balcony as a sixty-two year-old tradition ends with the final regular season game against the Toronto Maple Leafs on April 14, 1994. Players stand for a rousing rendition of the Canadian and American national anthems. Note the flags and banners as devoted fans pledge to "remember the roar" and, according to one bedsheet, also "remember the view."

The Blackhawks played their first game at the Stadium on December 15, 1929. They beat the Pittsburgh Pirates 3-1 before 14,212 fans—6,000 more people than the largest home-game hockey crowd ever at the Coliseum. After a scoreless first period, the Blackhawks scored three times on powerplays by Vic Ripley at 8:15 and 8:50, both on assists by Marvin "Cyclone" Wentworth and Ernest Arbour. Later in the middle session, Frank Ingram tallied on a pass from Wentworth. In the third period, Tex White clicked on a Pittsburgh powerplay against goalie Chuck Gardiner. That game marked the fifth straight victory for the Blackhawks, who quickly learned that playing in the Stadium was to their distinct advantage because visiting teams were invariably awed, intimidated, or simply overwhelmed by their surroundings.

Far left: Earl Seibert's sweater from the 1935–36 season. For the first time, the Blackhawks abandon their barberpole sweaters for a new look, which lasted only one season. The Indian head has essentially stayed the same from 1926 to 2000. Lower left: Seibert at a practice rink wearing the traditional barberpole uniform.

Like the United Center that came after it, the Stadium was considered state-of-the-art architecturally when it was built. It boasted a 37,000-square-foot main floor, a 185-foot ice surface from end to end (that's actually fifteen feet shorter than the current regulation length), and over 16,600 seats—8,000 more than Madison Square Garden, which was the largest sporting venue at the time. One of the most impressive innovations was the Stadium's modern ventilation system, which delivered 600,000 cubic feet of fresh air to the building every minute.

"It is not hard to please the public," Harmon said. "All you have to do is remember that we are all born children, that we all die children, and that in between times, we are children."

Sadly, Harmon was only able to see the pleasure the Stadium brought the public for just over a year. He was killed when his new Packard sedan flipped over in suburban Chicago on July 22, 1930. He died with less than three dollars in his pocket and to his name. His last wish—to be "laid out" at the Stadium—was granted. Friends paid for his funeral, and the Stadium was draped in black and purple as hundreds of people paid their respects.

Below: Although Chicago Stadium was a special venue for hockey, the building also served as an all-purpose facility for a variety of other sports and entertainment. In particular, the Stadium was a mecca for boxing, as witnessed by the capacity throng that attended the annual Golden Gloves tournament in March of 1940.

The Stadium was, of course, a multi-purpose venue. It was a mecca for boxing. A veritable *Who's Who* of the sweet science fought there: Max Baer, Carmen Basilio, Primo Carnera, Ezzard Charles, Jack Dempsey, Gene Fullmer, Kid Gavilan, Rocky Graziano, Jake LaMotta, Sonny Liston, Joe Louis, Rocky Marciano, Archie Moore, Floyd Patterson, Sugar Ray Robinson, Barney Ross, Jack Sharkey, Ernie Terrell, Joe Walcott, and Tony Zale. Muhammad Ali won the Golden Gloves light heavyweight title there as Cassius Clay during the Golden Gloves 1960 tournament.

13TH ANNUAL GOLDEN GLOVES TOURNAMENT
CHICAGO STADIUM   MARCH 6. 1940

Chicago Stadium featured a sea of red seats, closely cropped near the action. But the vibes were so exhilarating that paying customers frequently found themselves standing to cheer, applaud, or sing. At the Stadium, it was always a chicken-egg riddle: that is, did the fans feed off the players, or did the players reap all that extra energy from the crowd?

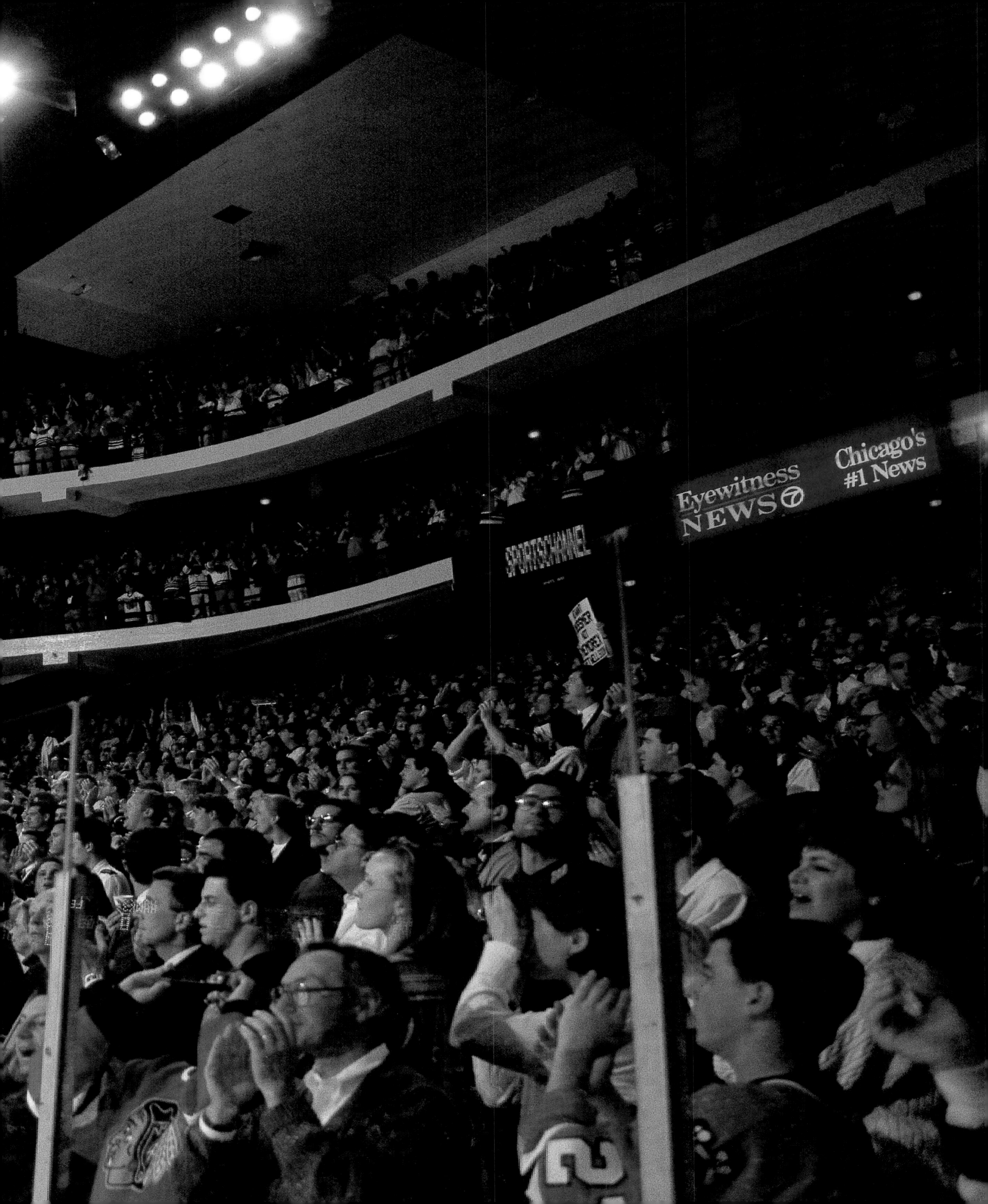
SPORTSCHANNEL
Eyewitness
NEWS 7
Chicago's
#1 News

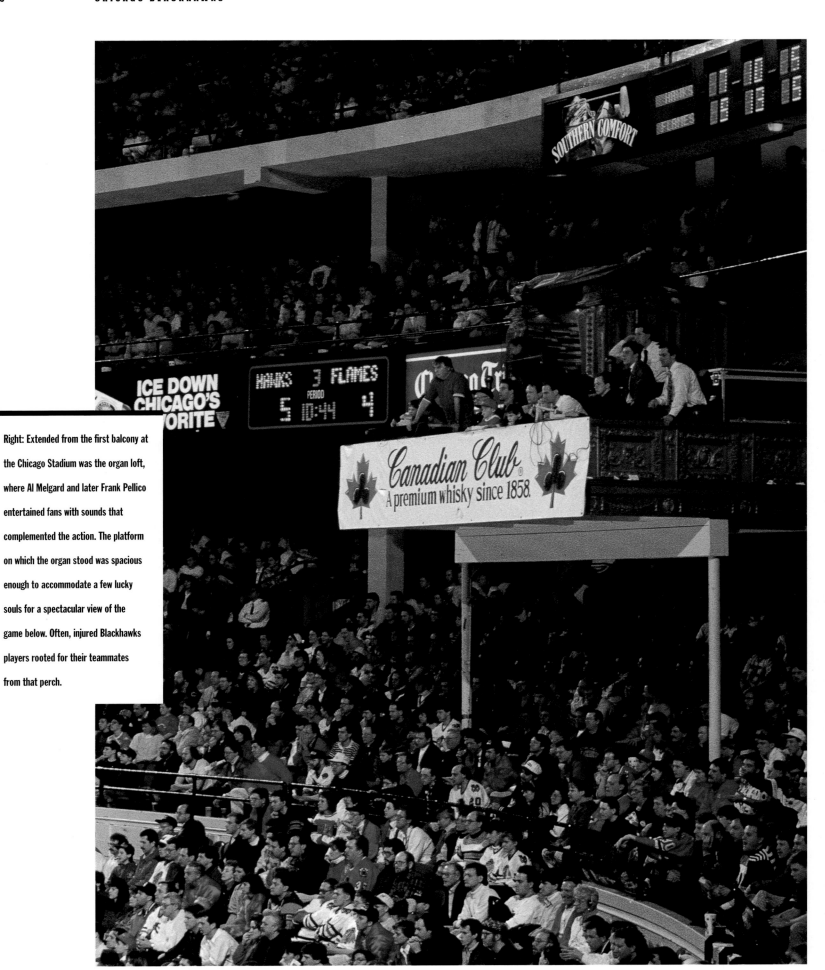

Right: Extended from the first balcony at the Chicago Stadium was the organ loft, where Al Melgard and later Frank Pellico entertained fans with sounds that complemented the action. The platform on which the organ stood was spacious enough to accommodate a few lucky souls for a spectacular view of the game below. Often, injured Blackhawks players rooted for their teammates from that perch.

The Stadium played host to many political conventions. Republicans and Democrats both came in 1932 when President Roosevelt first uttered the term "New Deal." Roosevelt returned in 1936 and 1940. Both parties held conventions at the Stadium in 1944. Four days after he attended a Stadium rally organized by Mayor Richard Daley, John F. Kennedy was elected president in 1960.

Countless singers and entertainers performed at the Stadium, from Frank Sinatra, Bing Crosby, and Bob Hope to Elvis, John Denver, the Rolling Stones, Kiss, and Chicago. It was also home to the "Greatest Show on Earth," the Harvest Moon Ball, Easter sunrise services, the Hollywood Ice Revue (starring Sonja Henie), the Bulls before Michael Jordan, the Bulls with Michael Jordan, the Chicago Opera, the roller derby, and the rodeo. The Stadium was used for bicycle races, college basketball games, professional wrestling matches, indoor soccer games, and track and field events. The Stadium was even used for Mayor Anton J. Cermak's funeral in 1933 and Virginia and Arthur Wirtz's fiftieth wedding anniversary in 1976. The idea for the latter was cooked up by the couple's children. Knowing her husband to be a baron of the bottom line, Virginia later remarked: "Wasn't that thoughtful of our kids? I do hope Arthur gave them a good deal on the rent."

Left: Hockey gloves developed longer cuffs to protect players' wrists from slashing sticks. Early gloves were not pre-formed to the hand as today's models are, and each player had to mold the horse-hair-stuffed fingers to his grip, often by dipping his hands in hot water before donning the gloves. The small insets at the knuckle were a modest attempt at flexibility and protection.

Lester Modesti, chief of the Frain ushers for almost half a century, says he saw thirty-five thousand people cram into the Stadium in 1937 when the janitors' union convened to elect a president. Two years later, sixty thousand people packed the Stadium for a dance put on by the Chicago Federation of Musicians to honor Mayor Ed Kelly. That's considerably more than the 11,198 people who witnessed the first professional football game held in the Stadium on December 18, 1932. Yes, the NFL indoors! The Chicago Bears beat the Portsmouth Spartans 9-0 for the league championship. Bronko Nagurski passed two yards to Red Grange for the only touchdown scored on a shortened, eighty-yard field. Wrigley Field, the Bears' usual home, was iced over, so the game had to be moved to the Stadium, where one kickoff almost sailed through a window onto Wood Street.

Flying objects are part of the ambience during hockey games, particularly if you are a member of the press corps. The NHL had five other buildings during the era of the Original Six, and all five had press boxes along one side of the rink, well above the flight patterns of wayward pucks. Not so at the Stadium. Newspaper reporters watched games from a box at the west end of the arena, behind the net, and suspended from the first balcony—and they were obliged to watch nearly every second of a game, lest they be stunned or bruised by a missile launched from the ice below. Many a puck was deflected toward the press box.

Left: The neoclassical limestone majesty of the Chicago Stadium, as seen from the north side of Madison Street, showing Gate 2, the Main Entrance at 1800 W. Madison. Greek Olympian figures adorned the facing beneath the roof on all sides of the building. Fire escapes were strategically placed at exits for the mezzanine and the first and second balconies. Above: This ticket stub was used on January 7, 1976, by 18,500 fans who watched the Soviet Wings beat the Blackhawks, 4-2, in a penalty-filled game (seventeen in all) with the Soviets outshooting Chicago, 30-18.

The back wall bore all the telltale signs of such deflections. The danger was not restricted to games, because those hard rubber disks had minds of their own during pre-game warm-up drills, too. For additional protection, the main press box had a small tin cover, not unlike the brim of a cap, to shield journalists from anything accidentally spilled by zealous spectators above them. The cover didn't always work, but it was a good place for fans sitting in the front row of the first balcony to rest their feet . . . or stomp them when they became overheated. As if the Stadium needed another noisemaker!

Being close to the action, however, did not always mean that members of the media could decipher a rather antiquated analog clock that hung above center ice. Again, other NHL arenas had digital timepieces with minutes and seconds precisely calibrated. If there was one minute and two seconds remaining in a period, you saw 1:02. Simple. But for many years, the clock at the Stadium had to be read by following the big hand around the dial. If that confused visiting teams, so be it. In the mid-1980s, the Stadium acquired a foghorn from Arthur M. Wirtz's boat that could lift spectators from their seats to celebrate Blackhawks' goals. It wasn't unusual for opposing players to jump out of their skates when that thing went off.

There were no elevators in the Stadium, so if you entered at street level and held a ticket for the second balcony, you probably reached your destination breathing heavily. Getting from point A to point B could be quite a haul, mounting various staircases through the mazes of the building.

"Don't tell me about stairs," said Stan Mikita. "Our dressing room was below ice level in the basement. To get to the ice before each period, we had to climb twenty-one steps in skates, which was always a trick. I counted them every time I went up them. . . . It's the third period. You're fatigued, you're getting the crap kicked out of you, and you think, 'God, do I have to go up those

stairs again?' Not that going down twenty-one steps was a lot of fun either at the end of each period."

Fair enough, but opposing teams had to perform the same ritual at the west end of the rink, and the proximity of Blackhawks fans hanging over the rail didn't always make for a pleasant arrival or departure. Visiting players spoke of being taunted and even pelted with objects until awnings were added to provide some protection from those sitting in that sea of fire-engine-red seats.

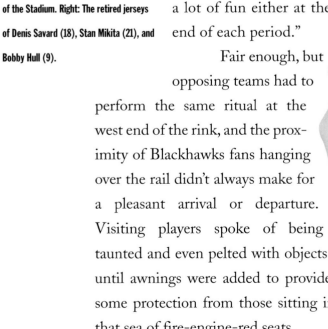

MUSIC FROM HEAVEN

TRIVIA QUESTION: Who played for the Blackhawks, Bulls, Harlem Globetrotters, and the De Paul Blue Demons? ANSWER: Al Melgard, who sat at the Barton pipe organ for decades at the Chicago Stadium, serenading spectators with a variety of songs, jingles, and just plain sounds. A railroad train down the track? No problem for Melgard. High above the east side of the Stadium, suspended from the first balcony on a moveable loft, the Barton organ was as much a part of the building's fabric as the glistening sheet of ice thirty feet below. It contained four thousand pipes and five thousand miles of wiring, and had required twenty-four railroad cars to transfer its components from Daniel Barton's factory in Oshkosh, Wisconsin, to the Stadium, where it was installed at a cost of $125,000 when the building opened in 1929. The organ could simulate, at full volume, twenty-five brass bands of a hundred instruments each. It could simultaneously recreate sixteen snare drums, eight bass drums, sixty violins, twenty-four flutes, sixteen trumpets, twelve saxophones, twelve clarinets, and seven French horns on six different keyboards and more than eight hundred different stops.

"One time I described it as being like the voice of God, like music from heaven," recalled Frank Pellico, who started playing the Barton organ at the Stadium in 1990 and now plays the organ at the United Center. "It had a massive, deep, heavy sound. The sound at the Stadium came from above your head and just fell down upon you."

Although not its original organist, Melgard was the maestro of the Stadium organ until he retired at the age of eighty-five in 1974, and he was more than merely accompaniment to the action. Al Melgard was part of the show, and he did it all with just nine fingers, having lost his left index finger in a carpentry accident.

Below: Al Melgard poses at the console of the $250,000 organ in the Chicago Stadium. When Paddy Harmon was building the Stadium, he asked the Bartola Musical Instrument Company to design and make an organ large enough for its sound to reverberate throughout the building. The first stadium organist was Ralph Waldo Emerson, named after the American literary giant. Emerson helped design the instrument, which featured six separate keyboards, shown below right.

Melgard reacted to whatever he witnessed. When Franklin D. Roosevelt was nominated in 1932, Melgard launched into a chorus of "Happy Days Are Here Again," and that song became indelibly associated with the four-term president. When two boxers returned to their corners for a one-minute break after pounding each other during a particularly brutal round, Melgard came up with "Give Me Five Minutes More." When spectators began fighting with each other one night, he pounded the organ so hard that some Stadium windows shattered, which stopped a potential riot.

Melgard was at his best when playing for hockey games. When the referee and two linesmen first skated onto the ice before a given game, he would welcome them with "Three Blind Mice." When a fan tossed a rabbit onto the ice, he played "Run Rabbit Run," or a coin, "Pennies from Heaven." Though he preferred to leave fans with a stirring version of his own composition, "My Vision," and of the Lord's Prayer at game's end, he wasn't averse to using those tunes (or "Put Your Arms Around Me, Honey, Hold Me Tight") as a means to restore peace during a particularly violent brawl between the Blackhawks and the evening's foes. When Melgard performed "The Star-Spangled Banner" before faceoff, the Stadium trembled.

As a rookie with the Blackhawks in 1972, Dan Maloney had heard all about the Stadium organ. One day, the team was practicing at the Stadium during training camp, and Melgard was up in his loft, tuning up his massive music machine after a long summer. Melgard took off for lunch, and Pat Stapleton, the veteran defenseman and a noted prankster, mentioned to Maloney that teammate Jim Pappin could play the organ as well as Melgard.

"Jimmy's taking piano lessons," Stapleton said of the right winger. "But he's already terrific at the organ."

Stapleton had arranged to have the Stadium electrician play a tape of Melgard's work over the sound system, and Pappin obliged, carrying the ruse forward. He climbed through the stands in his hockey gear to the organ, and presto, his hands began dancing across the keyboards. On cue, the tunes wafted through the building, and Pappin hammered it up with Liberace-like theatrics.

"There was poor Maloney coming back up to the ice from the dressing room," Pappin recalled. "He looked up and his jaw dropped. He couldn't believe it. Here I was, a mere hockey player, making all this great music on the largest organ in the country and most famous organ in the world."

When the Stadium closed in 1994, the organ was purchased by a fan, Bob Roppolo, who had it hauled in seven semitrailers to his nightclub in Lyons, Illinois. Roppolo then moved it again to Arizona, where the pipes were destroyed in a fire. Eventually, he sold the console to another private citizen, Phil Maloof, whose family owns the Fiesta Casino Hotel in Las Vegas. Maloof had the organ reassembled, refurbished, and restored in his Las Vegas home.

Above: The Blackhawks had a seventh "player" for those vibrant hockey games at the Stadium—Al Melgard, who could do everything with that huge Barton pipe organ but make it talk. Melgard's music was worthy of albums, yet some of his most brilliant moments occurred when he swiveled around in his seat and reacted intuitively to what he'd just seen on the ice with a song or, when two players collided, maybe the sound of a freight train.

Other improvements were made over time. The floors in the dressing rooms were carpeted. Mikita remembered that the wood floors were "warped, and slivers were everywhere. You even saw some nails sticking out. You were almost better off wearing your skates into the shower to protect your feet—if you could get into the shower. There were only six stalls for a team of twenty or so guys. We loved the place, though. And we did have a pool table."

When the Blackhawks retired Mikita's number on October 19, 1981, Mikita posed with family members and Robert Gammie, a construction worker who had overseen the birth of the Stadium. Gammie recalled, "We had two twelve-hour shifts, laying brick by brick around the clock. It was sturdy then, and it's sturdy now. It's a magnificent structure."

For more than thirty years, the rink above the boards was encircled by chicken wire to intercept pucks headed toward fans in nearby seats. Most of the time the wire sufficed, although it did not provide for optimum viewing. It wasn't the best situation for players, who would crash into jagged edges and come away with cuts. In 1960, Vic Stasiuk careened into the mesh and came away with a crimson reminder. He'd torn his face on the wire's jagged edges. The next year, panels of shatterproof glass fifty-six inches high were installed—yet another object for fans to bang on when they took issue with a referee's decision.

In January of 1995, the Blackhawks made their debut at a new ice palace, the United Center (below right), across West Madison Street from the Chicago Stadium. The United Center cost $175 million to build, contains 216 luxury boxes, and is almost three times the size of the former Stadium. But, for old-time's sake, the United Center still designates one of its many entryways as Gate 3½ (below left).

The Blackhawks played their final regular-season game at the Stadium on April 14, 1994. Among those present were all four of the Hall of Famers whose jerseys had been retired: Stan Mikita, Bobby Hull, Glenn Hall, and Tony Esposito. The Blackhawks lost to Toronto 6-4, but advanced to the Stanley Cup playoffs against the same Maple Leafs. In the first round of the Western Conference quarterfinals, the Maple Leafs prevailed four games to two. The last game ever at the Madhouse on Madison was played on April 28, when the Leafs won 1-0.

For the last time, players departed the Stadium through Gate 3½, a relatively inconspicuous black door on the west side of the building. Athletes and entertainers alike entered the building through Gate 3½ and left the same way, to reach their cars or limousines in the adjacent parking lot, which became a popular gathering place for fans seeking autographs or merely a close-up glance at their favorite stars. If you didn't have your own wheels and had to call a cab, you needed only to mention that you'd be waiting at Gate 3½. The cab drivers knew. As *Chicago Tribune* columnist Bernie Lincicome wrote, "It was only a door. It opened to dreams."

While the Blackhawks began to forge new memories and traditions at the United Center the following season, anyone who ever watched them play at the old Madhouse on Madison will remember the roar.

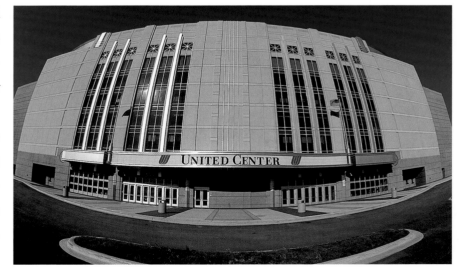

Chris Chelios was born in Chicago and born to play hockey. In his childhood, he could only dream of donning the jersey of his hometown Blackhawks and reporting to work through the players' entrance, the famous Gate 3½ on the west side of the Stadium. In 1990, Chelios and the Blackhawks had their wishes fulfilled when he was acquired from the Montreal Canadiens. Not surprisingly, Chelios was an all-star defenseman for the Blackhawks, too.

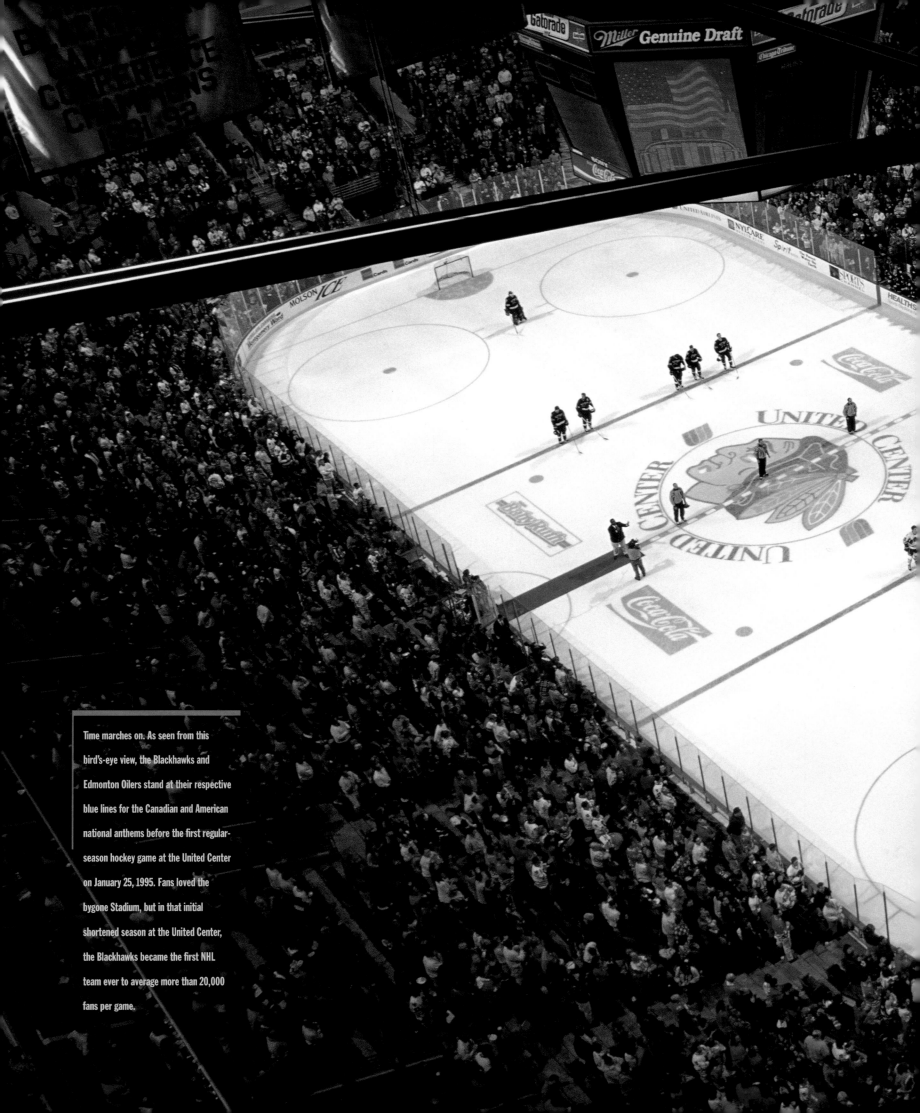

Time marches on. As seen from this bird's-eye view, the Blackhawks and Edmonton Oilers stand at their respective blue lines for the Canadian and American national anthems before the first regular-season hockey game at the United Center on January 25, 1995. Fans loved the bygone Stadium, but in that initial shortened season at the United Center, the Blackhawks became the first NHL team ever to average more than 20,000 fans per game.

BEHIND THE SCENES

The Chicago Stadium was the stage of many great games and many wonderful memories, too. Right: John Robertson has been with the Blackhawks almost from the beginning, and he's got stories spanning eight decades. Below: The Golden Jet, Bobby Hull, and his young family. Left to right: Bobby Jr., Mrs. Joanne Hull holding Michelle, Blake, Bart with his famous father, and Brett, who was six years old when he was photographed here. Just in case you don't feel old yet, in 2000, playing with the Dallas Stars, Brett surpassed his father's NHL total of 610 career goals.

There's a side of the game not seen by fans who filled the seats at the Stadium or tuned in to root for the Blackhawks on television. Only a few individuals, unseen themselves, have witnessed from behind the scenes the team's long run.

John Robertson didn't come with the new Chicago Stadium in 1929, but he arrived shortly thereafter, and has been with the Blackhawks ever since. You'll find him by the team's locker room on game nights, and if you don't have permission to enter, this local legend will stop you in a firm yet polite manner.

"I haven't had many problems through all these years," said Robertson. "Jack Adams, the general manager of the Red Wings, tried to get in between periods of a game a long time ago. He asked me if I knew who he was. I said, 'Yes, but you're not supposed to go in there, anyway.' I had to turn him around physically. He said, 'You won't be around much longer.' I saw Jim Norris the next day. He told me, 'Don't let it bother you.'"

In 1937, Robertson started dropping by after school to help out when his brother Ken was an assistant trainer for the team. Soon, John became a security guard on the Blackhawks' door. When Robertson's father took over his post, John moved over to the officials' room, where he stayed until 1977, when the senior Robertson returned the Blackhawks' door to his son.

"At the United Center, I have a TV monitor right across from me, so I can watch the game," Robertson said. "Or I can sneak behind the bench and see the real thing. At the Stadium, I would climb up the stairs to watch, and I'd often wind up with Bobby Hull's kids on my knees. Bobby scored a goal one night, and brought the puck down to Bobby Jr. I told Bobby he had to get one for Brett, too. Sure enough, he went out and scored during the next period, and brought another puck down for him."

Robertson claims that being around hockey players kept him young.

"I know times have changed," he said. "There's more money around now. Guys used to play more for the fun of it. But the hockey players are still the finest group of athletes you'll ever meet, whether it was 'Mush' March a long time ago or Phil Russell not so long ago. I'm not the only one who thinks that. Way back in the Stadium between periods, women used to come down to the locker room with drinks for the players. It was like a big social event then, like the opera, and these women would go to the concession stand nearby, buy drinks at the bar, and try to get them to the players. It never worked. And it didn't do me any good, because I never drank."

Harvey Wittenberg was another remarkable individual whose voice stood above the rest throughout all those noisy nights at the Stadium. Wittenberg started as the public address announcer in 1961, and hasn't changed his style one bit. "Don Cherry, the former coach turned broadcaster, criticized me for being monotone," said Wittenberg. "But that's just my style, and I've also received a lot of compliments on it. I give the fans

what they want, which is information. It's not that I don't root. Hockey and the Blackhawks have always been my passion. I am first and foremost a fan."

Wittenberg worked for the City News Bureau, alongside Mike Royko, when he began following hockey. Soon after, Wittenberg began a career as a radio station executive that lasted for more than four decades, but his first on-air exposure came as a Blackhawks' broadcaster. "That was 1959, the year they made the playoffs for the first time in a long time,"

Wittenberg said. "The Blackhawks didn't have a radio contract, and I kept bugging them about doing the playoffs. After getting permission, I had to get a sponsor and put everything together in a couple days. I wound up doing color beside Johnny Gottselig, who had become their publicity director after he retired as a player. He did the play-by-play. That was my first trip ever to the Montreal Forum."

For two years in the mid-1960s, he was the play-by-play man for the Blackhawks' road games on WLS-FM before an audience of friends and family "because FM radio wasn't big then." He also filled in on occasion for regulars with the Blackhawks' such as Lloyd Pettit and Pat Foley, and worked with another icon, Bob Elson, on closed-circuit theater telecasts of Blackhawks playoff games. But Wittenberg made his mark as the PA man.

"I used to work in the penalty box at the Stadium," he said. "But when you have a live microphone down there, and some angry players come in, yelling at each other after having a big fight . . . well, we had a problem once in a while and had to go someplace else. Most of the time, I was in the same press box with the newspaper guys, down at the west end of the Stadium, trying not to get hurt. Only once did I not duck in time, and a puck came flying up there and grazed my ear."

Remembering the roar of the old Stadium, Wittenberg observed, "Sometimes, when the time came to ask fans to stand for the national anthem, you could almost hear what I was saying."

Left: That voice you hear, and have heard for decades, at Blackhawk hockey games belongs to Harvey Wittenberg, the team's popular public-address announcer. Wittenberg's career has included several high-profile jobs as a radio executive and broadcaster, but his passion is the Blackhawks. Harvey's the man who tells you who scored that last goal, just in case you weren't sure.

The vast expanses of the United Center are evident by this ice-level panorama of a Blackhawks' game, photographed from a corner to the right of the visitors' net. The United Center ice surface is 200 feet by eighty-five feet, which is regulation size and larger than the one that existed at the Stadium. But, as you can see, the fastest game on earth is still that. And the players are bigger and quicker than ever, too.

MOMENTS IN TIME: 1952–72

Times were changing for the burgeoning NHL, and the Blackhawks proved that they could hold their own in the newly crowded field of competitors. A long-awaited Stanley Cup victory started off the 1960s, a decade defined by the superstars that graced the Chicago Stadium ice. Chief among them was legendary left wing Bobby Hull, who came to the team as a rookie. But the Blackhawks were more than the sum of their parts: They were a force to be reckoned with.

SEPTEMBER 11, 1952
Bill Tobin sells his controlling interest in the Blackhawks to the owners of the Chicago Stadium: James Norris, James D. Norris, and Arthur M. Wirtz.

JULY 8, 1954
Tommy Ivan is named general manager of the Blackhawks.

DECEMBER 18, 1954
Maurice "Rocket" Richard scores his 400th goal at the Chicago Stadium.

JANUARY 5, 1957
Employing cartoon character "Peter Puck" as an explanatory guide, the CBS network televises a Saturday afternoon game from the Chicago Stadium, the first national telecast of hockey in the United States. The New York Rangers defeat the Blackhawks 4-1.

OCTOBER 22, 1957
Rookie Bobby Hull scores his first NHL goal in his seventh game as the Blackhawks beat the Boston Bruins 2-1 at the Stadium. Eighteen-year-old Hull is the second-youngest player in league history, but he isn't a left wing in this landmark game against goalie Harry Lumley. He's playing center between Eric Nesterenko and Ron Murphy.

NOVEMBER 1, 1959
Jacques Plante wears a face mask for the first time in an NHL match. This is the same Plante who, as a rookie goalie, lifted the Montreal Canadiens to victory in a playoff series against the Blackhawks and eventually the 1953 Stanley Cup.

JANUARY 19, 1960
Blackhawks' captain Ed Litzenberger and his wife are involved in an auto accident. Litzenberger is seriously injured and his wife is killed.

MARCH 26, 1961
The Blackhawks defeat the Montreal Canadiens 2-1 in game three of the Stanley Cup semifinals when Murray Balfour scores after fifty-two minutes and twelve seconds of overtime at the Stadium. Balfour buries a backhand shot against goalie Jacques Plante on a powerplay, with Montreal's Dickie Moore serving a tripping penalty. Angered by the game's outcome, Canadiens' coach Hector "Toe" Blake takes a swing at referee Dalton McArthur.

OCTOBER 7, 1961
The All-Stars defeat the Blackhawks 3-1 in the second all-star game played in Chicago.

JANUARY 17, 1962
Goalie Glenn Hall plays his 500th consecutive game (including playoffs) as the Blackhawks challenged the Montreal Canadiens at the Stadium, where team co-owner James Norris presents "Mr. Goalie" with a new car. Hall's streak of 552 consecutive games ends the following season, at which point he had logged almost 32,000 minutes between the pipes.

MARCH 25, 1962
Bobby Hull scores his fiftieth goal of the season in the Blackhawks' 4-1 loss to the New York Rangers at Madison Square Garden. Hull ties Montreal's Maurice Richard and Bernie Geoffrion as the only players ever to reach the fifty-goal mark for a single season. Hull also ties the record of New York's Andy Bathgate with eighty-four points at season's end, and with more goals than Bathgate, secures the Art Ross Trophy.

APRIL 16, 1961
Ab McDonald and Reggie Fleming score second-period goals, then the Blackhawks add three more in the third period to win their third Stanley Cup with a resounding 5-1 rout of the Detroit Red Wings in the Detroit Olympia. The Blackhawks, who upset the defending champion Montreal Canadiens in their first series, outlast Detroit four games to two. Goalie Glenn Hall (whose jersey appears here) allows only twenty-seven goals in twelve playoff games and posts two shutouts, and is hoisted on the shoulders of his Chicago teammates following the contest.

NOVEMBER 7, 1962
Thirty-one-year-old Glenn Hall's streak of 502 consecutive regular-season games ends after he leaves the game with a pinched nerve. Denis DeJordy takes Hall's place as the Blackhawks win 3-1 at Montreal.

FEBRUARY 25, 1966
William W. Wirtz assumes the position of president of the Chicago Blackhawks.

MARCH 12, 1966
On assists by Lou Angotti and Bill Hay, Bobby Hull scores his fifty-first goal of the season before a standing-room-only Stadium crowd, becoming the most productive single-season goal scorer in NHL history. Hull tallies at 5:34 of the third period against goalie Cesare Maniago as the Blackhawks defeat the Rangers 4-2, breaking a three-game losing streak (all by shutouts). Hull winds up the 1965–66 season with fifty-four goals.

MAY 15, 1967
Chicago trades Phil Esposito, Ken Hodge, and Fred Stanfield to Boston for Gilles Marotte, Pit Martin, and Jack Norris in one of the biggest trades in franchise history.

JUNE 5, 1967
The Pittsburgh Penguins, Minnesota North Stars, Philadelphia Flyers, Los Angeles Kings, Oakland Seals, and St. Louis Blues officially receive their NHL franchises, marking the end of the Original Six era.

JANUARY 30, 1969
The Blackhawks win their biggest shutout ever, 12-0, at Philadelphia.

MARCH 30, 1969
Pat Stapleton matches Babe Pratt's twenty-five-year record of six assists by a defenseman in a single game. With Stapleton setting the pace, the Blackhawks win 9-5 against the Detroit Red Wings.

MARCH 12, 1967
The Blackhawks break the "Curse of Muldoon" by finishing first during the regular season for the first time in their history with a 5-0 rout of the Toronto Maple Leafs at the Stadium. Bobby Hull scores his forty-eighth goal of the season with nine games to go in the regular season, which the Blackhawks would complete with forty-one victories, seventeen losses, and twelve ties—seventeen points ahead of second-place Montreal in the standings. In addition to Hull's heroics, his outstanding teammate Stan Mikita completes a rare hat trick of honors: the Art Ross Trophy for scoring, the Hart Memorial Trophy for most valuable player, and the Lady Byng Memorial Trophy for sportsmanship and high-quality performance.

Sports Illustrated

JANUARY 25, 1965   35 CENTS

BREAKAWAY FOR THE RECORD

CHICAGO'S BOBBY HULL

JUNE 15, 1969
The Blackhawks claim rookie goaltender Tony Esposito from the Montreal Canadiens for $25,000.

FEBRUARY 21, 1970
Bobby Hull scores his 500th career goal against goalie Ed Giacomin in a 4-2 Blackhawks' victory over the New York Rangers at the Stadium. Some loyal fans insist it's actually Hull's 501st, since a goal by The Golden Jet against Detroit goalie Terry Sawchuk was mistakenly credited to Ab McDonald in 1962. McDonald tries to change the scoring after the game, but the official game report is already filed with the NHL headquarters.

APRIL 5, 1970
The Blackhawks complete an unprecedented worst-to-first turnaround by clobbering the Canadiens 10-2 at the Stadium. The Blackhawks score five of their ten goals on empty nets in the third period when the Canadiens pull their goalie in favor of a sixth attacker. The Blackhawks surrender eighty-four fewer goals in the standings, and amass ninety-nine points, a twenty-two-point improvement over the previous season.

JANUARY 19, 1971
Eleven Blackhawks on West All-Star squad beat the East 2-1 in Minnesota.

DECEMBER 12, 1971
Assisting teammate Chico Maki on a goal at 7:59 in the first period, Bobby Hull becomes the fifth player in NHL history to reach the 1,000-point mark. Hull leads his team to a 5-3 victory over the Minnesota North Stars.

MARCH 25, 1972
Bobby Hull blasts his 600th career goal past Bobby Orr and through goalie Gerry Cheevers in Boston Garden. The game ends in a 5-5 tie. A week later, in the Blackhawks' final regular-season game, Hull beats goalie Andy Brown of the Detroit Red Wings for his 604th and last regular-season goal for the Blackhawks. Hull's goal against Detroit is his fiftieth of the season, the fifth time he reaches that mark.

MAY 2, 1971
The Blackhawks advance to the Stanley Cup finals by defeating the visiting New York Rangers 4-2 in game seven of a grueling and dramatic semifinal series that features three overtime games. Pete Stemkowski wins two of the overtime games for the Rangers, and Bobby Hull (below) scores at 6:35 of the extra period to provide the Blackhawks with a 3-2 victory in game five. The series is hailed by many experts as one of the finest in the Stanley Cup annals.

MARCH 29, 1970
Rookie goalie Tony Esposito defeats the Toronto Maple Leafs 4-0 at the Stadium for his fifteenth shutout of the season, a modern record. Esposito winds up winning the Calder Trophy for best rookie and the Vezina Trophy for best goalkeeper. Esposito is seen here with Bobby Hull (left) and Gerry Pinder (right).

Nobody in the National Hockey League had ever witnessed the mood at the Stadium as they did on the night of April 5, 1970. Goal after goal after goal, the Blackhawks scored on an empty net. The palpable buzz in the sold-out, standing-room-only Stadium that had existed from the opening faceoff steadily grew with each pass, each rush, each shot by the hometown heroes. Everybody was standing and watching the Blackhawks pour it on. The question was not would the Blackhawks win, but rather by how much. By 10 P.M., the rout ended, and Blackhawks players rose from their bench and lifted coach Billy Reay on their shoulders. The most remarkable turnaround in NHL annals was official: Blackhawks 10, Montreal Canadiens 2. "WE'RE NUMBER ONE! WE'RE NUMBER ONE!"

FROM WORST TO FIRST

The Blackhawks have played many a glorious season throughout their history, but none was quite as stirring as the winter of 1969–70, the winter the Blackhawks made history by going from the bottom of the six-team Eastern Division to

WHATEVER IT TAKES

the top only a year later. All teams in all sports are subject to cyclical ups and downs—the thrill of victory and the agony of defeat. The Blackhawks are no different. But for all the resiliency this franchise has exhibited during three quarters of a century, nothing was quite like the 1969–70 season.

Expectations were not great, because after ten consecutive seasons in the playoffs, the Blackhawks had missed them in 1968–69. They had a winning record, 34-33-9, but they were in the Eastern Division comprised of the Original Six franchises. The Western Division belonged entirely to the six expansion teams admitted in 1967, and they simply did not have the depth of talent to compete with the establishment. Indeed, only one team in the West, the St. Louis Blues, had a better record than the Blackhawks in 1968–69.

But the Blackhawks did not delude themselves. They knew they had to make changes and play better, and they knew the principal area that needed improvement was between the pipes. During their

Canadian Magazine THE PROVINCE

THESE HAWKS AREN'T DOVES Page 19

trip to last place, they had surrendered 246 goals. Clearly, goalkeeping was part, if not all, of the problem. Tommy Ivan, the Blackhawks' wily general manager, sought to correct the situation immediately by plucking Tony Esposito from the defending Stanley Cup champion Canadiens. Esposito was left unguarded by Montreal, and Ivan grabbed him for the modest price of $25,000.

The plan was for Esposito to share netminding with incumbent veteran Denis DeJordy. Even if Esposito were up to the task, the Blackhawks still had other problems to contend with. Right wing Kenny Wharram, who had scored thirty goals the previous season, suffered a heart attack in September of 1969 and never played again. Bobby Hull, who had amassed fifty-eight goals the previous season, was under contract, but holding out to protest unfulfilled promises by management. He even broached the unthinkable—that he be traded to another team. On top of that, the players convened for training camp amidst a cloud of tension. During the off-season, Pit Martin, a respected veteran, criticized the Blackhawks' system. Hull and Stan Mikita were the stars, and according to Martin, all that mattered was whatever pleased them. For a long while, it was uncertain how Hull, Mikita, and Reay would react to Martin's frank criticisms.

Left: Tony Esposito posted a record fifteen shutouts during his rookie season in 1969–70, leading the Blackhawks from last to first place in the NHL standings. Above: Blackhawks' superstars Stan Mikita and Bobby Hull appear on the cover of *Canadian Magazine*. Right: Stan Mikita (21) fends off one of the strongest defensemen in the league, Tim Horton (7) of the Toronto Maple Leafs.

"I was glad to hear that Pit was so angry about the way we played last year," said Reay. "I was, too, and I intend to do something about it."

The Blackhawks themselves were not as responsive. Nobody blinked when they lost their first five games, and it wasn't until their sixth game—a 1-1 tie with New York—that the Blackhawks registered a point in the standings. Then, it clicked. Reay's decree sunk in: the players should pay more attention to defense.

Despite DeJordy's fine performance against the Rangers, Reay decided to follow a hunch, and pitted Esposito against his former employers on a Saturday night at the Montreal Forum. Esposito stoned the Canadiens 5-0. Disgruntled Blackhawks fans quickly ceased their "Goodbye, Billy" chant after the team won six games in a row, toward an unbeaten string of ten.

By that time, Hull was back on the ice after missing fifteen games. While not completely sold on the team's new defensive "none against" mode ("a goal prevented is as important as a goal scored"), The Golden Jet was mightily impressed by the zeal, energy, and work ethic of the games he saw on TV.

The team had not only changed its ways but also some of its members. The Blackhawks were unusually blessed with youth that season: Keith Magnuson, a fiery red-headed defenseman who came directly to the NHL from Denver University without stopping in the minor leagues; Cliff Koroll, a sturdy right wing who was Magnuson's teammate in college before spending one season at the Blackhawks' Dallas affiliate; Gerry Pinder, another rookie winger with excellent scoring skills; and last but not least, Esposito, who had played only twelve games with the mighty Canadiens during his apprenticeship.

"We wanted to get as much young blood in our lineup as possible," said Reay, as the Blackhawks turned a corner before his very eyes. "We expected it to take time. We knew it wouldn't be easy."

It wasn't, but it sure was fun. After thirty-five games, the Blackhawks were a .500 team: fifteen wins, fifteen losses, five ties. The objective was to make the playoffs, which meant finishing in the top four teams of six. Montreal, Boston, and New York were soaring. The Blackhawks, Reay figured, would have to beat out Toronto and Detroit. When Chicago's brilliant defenseman Pat Stapleton went down with a season-ending knee injury in early February, the mission seemed nearly impossible. The rookies were terrific, but so was the Eastern Division.

"It was as if we had to win every night just to keep pace," said Magnuson, who raised his play—and his fists—with each passing game. The Blackhawks summoned yet another rookie, defenseman Paul Shmyr, from their farm system. Then Ivan pulled another splendid trade with the Los Angeles Kings, exchanging DeJordy for goalie Gerry Desjardins and defenseman Gilles Marotte for defenseman Bill White, who was not flashy but consistently efficient. He fit the Blackhawks' scheme like a glove, and his steadying influence was the perfect match for the team's exuberant spirit.

Magnuson said the Blackhawks had to win almost every game, and they almost did. They lost only seven of their remaining forty-one games. On February 21, Hull became the third player in NHL history to reach 500 goals, and for good measure, he collected number 501 that night, too. When Esposito blanked the Maple Leafs 4-0 in the Stadium on March 29, it was his fifteenth shutout of the season. That was the modern record for goalies, and it still stands.

In spite of it all, the Blackhawks found themselves in a first-place tie with Boston with three games to go.

Billy Reay coached more games (1,012) and won more games (516) than any other man in Blackhawks history. His teams never had a losing season and missed the playoffs only once during his reign from 1963 until 1977. As Hall of Fame center Stan Mikita said, "Billy treated us like men. He was great to play for and, beyond that, a good friend."

The Blackhawks lost on April 1 at the Stadium to Detroit, but the Bruins lost in Montreal. On Saturday night, April 4, the Blackhawks went into Montreal and beat a desperate Canadiens' team 4-1, while the Bruins won in Toronto. There was still a tie at the top with one game to go. The Blackhawks had one significant advantage: they had five more wins than the Bruins (who had ten more ties), and that would be the difference if both Boston and Chicago won on closing night.

How desperate were the Canadiens? By the time they arrived at the Stadium, the mountain they had to climb had grown. The Rangers had tied Montreal for the fourth and final playoff spot with ninety-two points by beating Detroit in an afternoon game. The final was 9-5. So the Canadiens either had to defeat the Blackhawks or score at least five goals to avoid being eliminated from the playoffs for the first time since 1948! By scoring five goals, regardless of the game's outcome, the Canadiens would beat out the Rangers by virtue of the next tie-breaker.

What bedlam ensued! The proud Canadiens clicked early for a 1-0 lead, but Jim Pappin tied it for the Blackhawks at 15:49 of the first period. Then Martin tallied on a powerplay for a 2-1 Chicago lead. Hull made it 3-1 early in the second period with a blistering slapshot through Rogatien Vachon, the great veteran whose presence precipitated Esposito's departure to the Blackhawks. Jean Beliveau, the gallant Montreal captain, scored shortly after Hull, and it was 3-2. But then Martin, the man who had dared to challenge his teammates before the season, tallied twice within three minutes for a hat trick and a 5-2 Blackhawks' advantage.

Left: Well, Billy Reay almost always wore a hat while he was coaching the Blackhawks. But when they walloped the Montreal Canadiens 10-2 on the final night of the 1969–70 season to finish in first place, the players lifted their mentor on their shoulders, and off came his fedora.

Right: The bronze puck with accompanying tooth was a gift from teammate Bobby Hull after scoring his first NHL goal and winning his first NHL fight.

What followed was a scene not likely to be repeated in our lifetime. Montreal coach Claude Ruel abandoned any hope of winning the game, and instead sought to salvage a playoff berth by collecting goals. For the last eight minutes of the third period, whenever the Canadiens gained possession of the puck, Vachon left for the bench in favor of a sixth attacker. The visitors' net lay vacant, and the Blackhawks and the fans went thoroughly nuts. It didn't matter that Boston, starting an hour earlier at home, would whip Toronto, not when the Blackhawks saw that yawning net. Eric Nesterenko made it 6-2; then the Hull brothers, Bobby and Dennis, joined the feast, followed by rookies Koroll and Pinder. And then it was over.

"I've spent my whole life in hockey," gushed Reay, "but I have never had the thrills this team gave me. Every night was like the seventh game of the Stanley Cup finals, and they responded."

"I'm happy everybody took what I said the way I meant it," Martin added. "I meant it with respect. And we all came together, us veterans and all these kids. And nobody meant more than that guy over there."

He pointed to Tony Esposito, exhausted, seated at his locker, his body a kaleidoscope of multi-colored bruises. The Blackhawks had gone from worst to first, and it all started between the pipes.

KEITH MAGNUSON
1ST NHL GOAL
ASSIST BY B. HULL
1ST NHL TOOTH
EXTRACTED FROM HEISKALA
PHILADELPHIA AT CHICAGO
NOVEMBER 11, 1970

Stanley Cup I: The Economy Plan

The Blackhawks were, as they say in the thoroughbred industry, lightly raced in Stanley Cup experience when the 1933–34 season commenced. They had advanced to the finals only once in their brief history, and had missed the playoffs entirely in the previous season. Moreover, the Blackhawks' one flirtation with the Cup ended in heartbreak. They led the 1931 best-of-five final series, two games to one, and had a two-goal lead in game four before the Canadiens rallied from the brink of elimination to win 4-2 at home. Three nights later, the Canadiens won again 2-0, and it was over for the Blackhawks.

The 1933–34 squad had considerable talent, but it could have been mistaken for "The Gang That Couldn't Shoot Straight." At season's end, the Blackhawks finished second in the American Division, despite having scored a league-low eighty-eight goals in forty-eight games. But the Blackhawks made do with the economy plan, primarily because of their fabulous goalie, Charlie Gardiner, who had posted ten shutouts during the regular schedule.

For offense, the team relied on Paul Thompson, who led with twenty goals on left wing with center "Doc" Romnes and "Mush" March, the diminutive right wing. Johnny Gottselig tallied sixteen goals on left wing with Alex Trudel at center and Don McFadyen on the right side. The defense in front of Gardiner was anchored by Lionel Conacher, who would star for the Montreal Maroons both before and after that one season with the Blackhawks, to which he contributed ten goals and all-around skills—and toughness—that would land him in the Hall of Fame.

Right: Charlie Gardiner as he was shown on one of the first hockey trading cards. Gardiner was the iron man in the nets when the Blackhawks won their first Stanley Cup in 1934. Gardiner yielded only 101 goals during 48 regular season games for a brilliant 1.85 average. He also posted the first five playoff shutouts in Blackhawks history, including the 1-0 overtime clincher in 1934.

Gottselig's second goal of the game brought the Blackhawks a 3-2 victory over the Canadiens in the opener of the preliminary series at Montreal. March scored in game two, a 1-1 tie that sent the Blackhawks to the next round on the basis of total goals. The Blackhawks then whipped the Maroons in the next series clinched by Gardiner's 3-0 masterpiece.

Still, only the staunchest Chicago fans held out much hope for their heroes in the Cup final against the powerful Detroit Red Wings, who had finished first in the American Division, comfortably ahead of the Blackhawks. Another ominous aspect of the matchup: the climactic best-of-five final began with two games in Detroit, where the Blackhawks hadn't won a game in almost five years.

Perhaps it was then and there that the Blackhawks displayed their "whatever it takes" attitude. Conacher went end-to-end for a brilliant goal early, then Thompson tallied after twenty-one minutes and five seconds of overtime to provide the underdog visitors a gallant 2-1 conquest. The Red Wings must have been stunned, for they lost again at home, 4-1, two nights later.

Hockey publicity photos of the Golden Age depicted players such as Mush March, right, holding his stick for a teammate's wild, hair-raising leap at practice. Publicity shots always captured a snow-stormish spray of ice that the obliging pros could create with a well-executed hockey stop.

Earl Seibert decks a New York Americans player, causing the puck to fly forward to two on-rushing Blackhawks teammates.

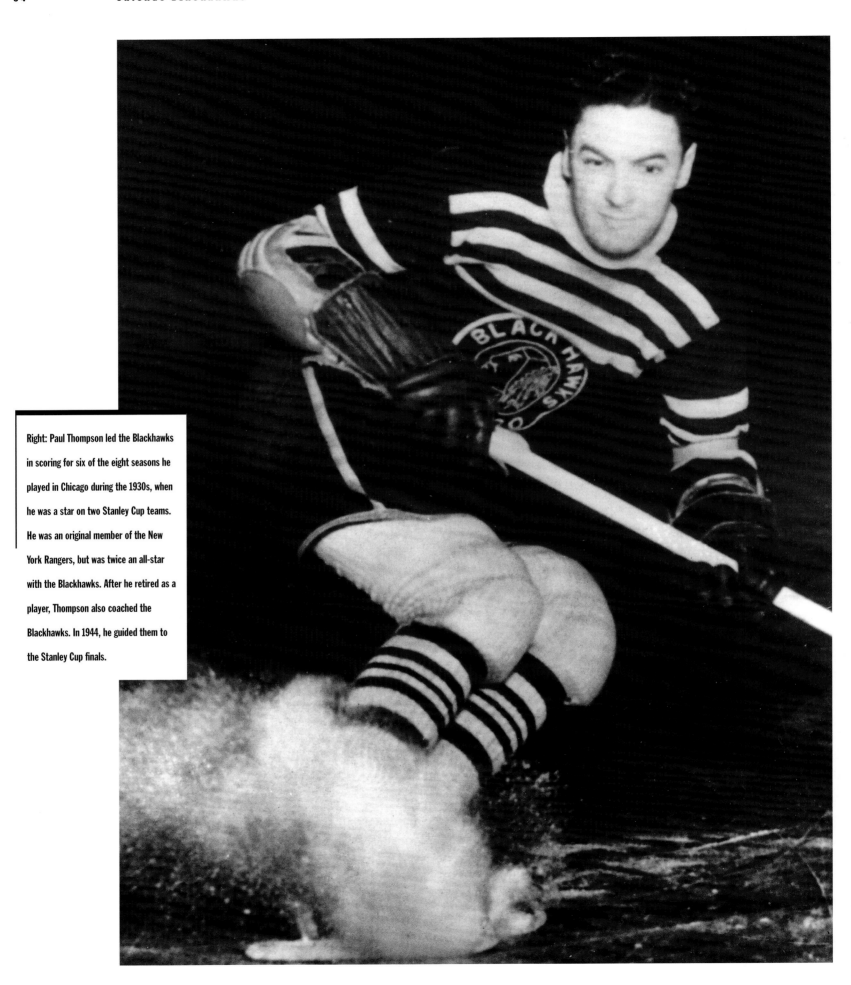

Right: Paul Thompson led the Blackhawks in scoring for six of the eight seasons he played in Chicago during the 1930s, when he was a star on two Stanley Cup teams. He was an original member of the New York Rangers, but was twice an all-star with the Blackhawks. After he retired as a player, Thompson also coached the Blackhawks. In 1944, he guided them to the Stanley Cup finals.

When the series moved to Chicago, the Stadium was packed with fans smelling a quick conclusion to a huge upset. The mood was enhanced when Thompson tallied twenty-seven seconds into the game, the third time in as many games that the Blackhawks scored in the first minute. Then in the second period, Detroit goalie Wilf Cude incurred a broken nose by accidentally coming in contact with Rosie Couture's stick. Alas, the Blackhawks fell 5-2. Cude was spectacular after pausing for repairs, and Gardiner was disconnected. A nervous type, Gardiner took this defeat particularly hard. So hard that he was sent to Milwaukee for a couple of days, to get away from the pressure. The Blackhawks didn't know whether he would return for game four. The Red Wings hoped he wouldn't.

But the high-strung Gardiner did come back, and he engaged Cude in a magnificent duel that ended at 30:05 of overtime when March brought eighteen thousand hockey fans to their feet by scoring the marathon's only goal on Chicago's fifty-third shot. March, who had scored only four goals in forty-eight regular-season games, scored twice in clutch playoff situations within three weeks. The Blackhawks won the game 1-0, the series 3-1, and their first Cup.

Defenseman Roger Jenkins picked a novel way to celebrate the title. He put Gardiner in a wheelbarrow, and took him through the Chicago Loop.

STANLEY CUP II: THE RED, WHITE, AND BLUE MIRACLE

If the Blackhawks' first championship was unlikely, their second in 1938 bordered on unbelievable. It's not often, after all, that you raise the bar by pulling a goalkeeper out of a tavern. Once again, since the Blackhawks had missed the playoffs in the previous season, expectations of a Cup were slim. Also, the Blackhawks wobbled through the regular schedule, winning just fourteen of forty-eight games for coach Bill Stewart, who had replaced Clem Loughlin after his three-year term ended.

The rest of the NHL was scoffing at the Blackhawks, whose roster had become Americanized at the directive of Major McLaughlin. That might not sound remarkable now, but in the 1930s, the first American on *any* roster was Clarence "Taffy" Abel, whose career was with the Blackhawks and Rangers. Abel was not with the Blackhawks, however, when McLaughlin injected four U.S.-born players into the roster mix toward the end of the 1936–37 season. McLaughlin didn't stop there, either. Threatening to rename his team the "Chicago Yankees," he added five more Americans in the 1937–38 season. Alex Levinsky, a defenseman from Syracuse, was so sure the playoffs would be a futile proposition that he sent his wife home when spring arrived, packed his clothes in his car in Chicago, and told her he'd be seeing her soon.

He was dead wrong, as were all the experts who had forecasted a quick exit for the Blackhawks. Few predictions changed

Below: When the Blackhawks won their second Stanley Cup in 1938, it caught a lot of experts by surprise, not to mention opposing teams. All the more reason for four of the most vital players on that squad to celebrate. They are, from the left: Jack Shill, Carl Voss, Cully Dahlstrom, and Mush March. That foursome contributed nine of the twenty-six goals scored by the Blackhawks during their dream postseason.

when they dropped their playoff opener to the Canadiens in Montreal. But Chicago's American-born goalie, Mike Karakas, and Gottselig, a force on the Blackhawks' first Cup team, keyed a 4-0 victory in game two. Then Thompson, another veteran from the 1934 champions, scored the winning goal in game three, and the Blackhawks advanced to meet the New York Americans. The Blackhawks set another trap by losing the opener. Then Karakas won game two by 1-0. The Blackhawks went into New York and won 3-2, eliminating the Americans.

That could have been the end of the line for the Blackhawks. Their opponent in the Stanley Cup final was Toronto, and the Maple Leafs were a prohibitive favorite. What is worse, Karakas had broken his toe in the last game against the Americans, so he was unavailable for the first game against Toronto. Management had sent Paul Goodman, the Blackhawks' twenty-eight-year-old spare goalie, home weeks before (perhaps for the same reason that Alex Levinsky sent his wife home). Stewart asked that the Blackhawks be allowed to borrow Dave Kerr from the Rangers as an emergency measure, but Conn Smythe, the Maple Leafs' boss, rejected the notion. Stewart became so furious that he threatened Smythe physically, but after a rather vigorous shoving match, Stewart backed off and accepted Smythe's suggestion to use Alfie Moore, a goalie who lived nearby. The next problem was finding the mystery man. He wasn't at home

Above: Clarence "Taffy" Abel was a robust 225-pound defenseman who played five seasons with the Blackhawks. He debuted in 1926 with the New York Rangers as the first American-born regular (Sault Ste. Marie, Michigan) in the NHL. Right: Alfie Moore had a much shorter career with the Blackhawks—one game, on an emergency basis, during the 1938 playoffs. But he won it, and was instrumental in leading the Blackhawks to a Stanley Cup. Far right: Howie Morenz's leather jacket from the 1933–34 season.

in Toronto, but his wife told the Blackhawks' search party of Gottselig and Thompson to try a corner tavern. Moore wasn't there, either, but he had been, and the bartender mentioned another watering hole a few blocks away. Sure enough, Moore was sitting there, well watered in mid-afternoon, only hours before the game. Gottselig and Thompson poured Moore into a taxi and brought him to the hotel, where Stewart took one look at his designated goalie for the night and exploded.

"Get him out of here!" yelled Stewart. But he cooled off and relented. Time was getting short, and besides, Moore had reason to sober up and play. He was property of the Maple Leafs, and he was miffed at Smythe for burying him in Toronto's minor league team in Pittsburgh all season. With a few cups of coffee, Moore was ready to seek revenge—well, almost ready. Toronto's first shot, by Gord Drillon, went in, and the score was 1-0. It started to look like it was going to be a long night for Moore and the Blackhawks. But that was the last puck that escaped Moore. Gottselig scored twice, Thompson once, and Chicago shocked Toronto, 3-1.

THE ONE THAT GOT AWAY

Defenseman Keith Magnuson says it all by burying his head in his hands in this painting by artist Rosa Lee. The Blackhawks led the best-of-seven 1971 Stanley Cup finals by two games to nothing, and led game seven on home ice by the score of 2-0. But still, the redoubtable Montreal Canadiens rallied to win the championship.

Ask any Blackhawk who was involved or any fan who was a witness, and the response will probably be the same: The game that hurt the most was game seven of the Stanley Cup finals on May 18, 1971, against the Montreal Canadiens at the Chicago Stadium. That was the one that got away. The best-of-seven series was as brilliant as it was heartbreaking. The teams each won three games on home ice. The Blackhawks jumped to a 2-0 lead with two victories in Chicago; the Canadiens returned the favor in Montreal. The Blackhawks won game five at home 2-0; the Canadiens, game six at the Forum.

Game seven unfolded on a Tuesday evening before a packed Chicago Stadium and a nationally televised, prime-time audience. The weather was warm, and the building's air conditioning system couldn't quite cool the Stadium, so the ice surface became shrouded in fog. The Blackhawks forged a 2-0 lead, just as they had in game six, and had numerous opportunities to expand their lead to 3-0, none better than Bobby Hull's drive that struck the crossbar. Canadien goalie Ken Dryden, the rookie-of-the-year netminder, also survived two excellent shots by Jim Pappin.

Montreal broke through goalie Tony Esposito when Jacques Lemaire beat him with a bullet drive from just past the center red line. Then Lemaire assisted on the Canadiens' tying goal by Henri Richard. Early in the third period, Richard broke down the left side, cut in on defenseman Keith Magnuson, and scored on Esposito from close in to make it 3-2 for the visitors. The Blackhawks stormed Dryden for much of the third period, but were unable to defeat him, and the Canadiens vanquished Chicago, four games to three.

"It's been almost thirty years since that game," said Cliff Koroll, a right wing on that Blackhawks' team, "and I still wake up at night, wishing it was a nightmare. That one really hurt."

Smythe was furious, and he had Moore ruled ineligible by NHL president Frank Calder for game two. So, two nights later, the Blackhawks summoned a rusty Goodman to Toronto. He had no NHL experience, and it showed as the Leafs romped, 5-1, in a rough contest. Red Horner, the Toronto defenseman, cross-checked Doc Romnes, and broke his nose in six places. March was already out with a groin injury, but the Blackhawks had gained a split of two games on foreign ice.

When they returned home for game three, there were 18,497 fans in the Stadium, a league record. The Blackhawks were ready and willing. Romnes, wearing a Purdue University football helmet, didn't play like a former Lady Byng Trophy winner. He went after Horner on numerous occasions, and he wasn't alone. Romnes also scored to snap a tie and lift the Blackhawks to an emotional 2-1 triumph behind Karakas, who was in the net wearing a customized boot to protect his toe.

In game four, Carl "Cully" Dahlstrom, the NHL Rookie of the Year, opened the scoring for Chicago. Carl Voss followed, and then Jack Shill, just trying to kill some time, lofted a 150-foot floater that fooled Turk Broda, Toronto's outstanding goalie. March tallied on a breakaway, and the Blackhawks whipped Toronto, 4-1, to clinch their victory. They staged a Stanley Cup party, and invited Moore down from Toronto. He received an engraved gold watch from Chicago manager Bill Tobin and three crisp $100 bills. Moore basked in the praise of Broda, who said, "He turned the whole series around in the first game. We threw everything at him but the house. Alfie Moore is the reason they won."

"We won it gangland style," added Thompson, "by roughing up Horner."

Alfie Moore and eight Americans: Sometimes truth is stranger than fiction.

STANLEY CUP III: THE LONG WAIT ENDS

After twenty-three seasons, many of them lean, the Blackhawks won their third Stanley Cup in 1961. Their *modus operandi* strongly resembled the plots of the two championships in the 1930s. They still hadn't finished first during a regular season; they were the underdogs.

But the 1960–61 squad had a number of pieces in place. General Manager Tommy Ivan had taken over a threadbare roster when he moved over from the mighty Detroit Red Wings in 1954, and his mission was to build from within. The farm system bore fruit. Bobby Hull, 21, scored thirty-nine goals. Stan Mikita, 20, chipped in nineteen. Glenn Hall, "Mr. Goalie," was in his prime. Pierre Pilote and Elmer "Moose" Vasko were exemplary defensemen. The team had some wonderful role players, and Reggie Fleming embodied a group toughness.

Earlier that season, the Blackhawks and Maple Leafs partook in a storied brawl at Toronto after Pilote whacked Toronto's Eddie Shack with his stick. Murray Balfour chased Carl Brewer of the Maple Leafs

Below: When the Blackhawks won the Stanley Cup in 1961, they were not only on top of the hockey world, but on top of soft drink bottles for a year after. The players on the Coca-Cola caps were: top row, Glenn Hall, Bobby Hull, and Stan Mikita; bottom row, Chico Maki and Ken Wharram.

Glenn Hall · goalie
CHICAGO BLACK HAWKS

around the rink, promising bodily harm, and it took a gaggle of police officers to quell the riot. Eight players were assessed game misconducts; twenty-one who left their respective benches were fined. The Blackhawks had personality.

Still, by finishing third, the Blackhawks drew the most difficult opening assignment against the Montreal Canadiens, who led the league and were homing in on a sixth consecutive Stanley Cup. Les Habitants won the first game at home, 6-3, but not before losing three players to injury—Jean Beliveau, Bill Hicke, and Donnie Marshall. Immediately the Blackhawks heard accusations of being a bit too chippy. Ed Litzenberger—acquired from Montreal in 1954—broke a tie in game two, and the Blackhawks prevailed, 4-3.

Game three in the Chicago Stadium was a classic. Balfour scored his second goal of a rough game at 52:12 in overtime for a 2-1 Blackhawks' victory. Dickie Moore was sitting out the marathon's twenty-sixth penalty for tripping Balfour, whose powerplay tally so enraged Montreal coach Toe Blake that he leaped onto the ice and took a swing at referee Dalton McArthur.

Right: Glenn Hall might have posed for this shot that appeared on his bubble gum card, but it wouldn't have been too difficult to catch him for an action photograph. Mr. Goalie played in a record 552 consecutive games (regular-season and playoff), a mark that this Hall of Famer just might hold for as long as hockey is played. Far right: The Stanley Cup in all its glory.

After the Canadiens pelted Hall with sixty shots in a 5-2 game-four win, they returned to the Montreal Forum with home ice advantage restored. But Hall was not to be beaten the rest of the series. He shut out the Canadiens twice—once in Montreal and again in Chicago—and the Blackhawks advanced, four games to two. Meanwhile, in the other semifinal series, Toronto was upset by Detroit, which had finished fourth during the regular season with a record below .500.

So the Blackhawks opened the finals at home and won game one, 3-2, on two goals by Bobby Hull. Terry Sawchuk, the Red Wings' great goalie, was injured and replaced by Hank Bassen, who played well in game two, which the Red Wings won at Detroit, 3-1. The teams traded home victories, 3-1 for Chicago, 2-1 for Detroit, and the series was tied, 2-2. In game five at Chicago, Mikita scored twice on Sawchuk, and the Blackhawks romped, 6-3. Then, Ab McDonald and Fleming clicked during the second period of game six at Detroit, and the Blackhawks added three more goals in the final period for a 5-1 victory that clinched the series, four games to two.

The Blackhawks hoisted Hall on their shoulders, but nobody else managed to become airborne that evening. There was a blizzard in Chicago, and the team was stranded in Detroit. Not to worry—owners Jim Norris and Arthur Wirtz staged an impromptu celebration at the Palace Theater where champagne glasses were raised to signal the end of a long drought. Coach Rudy Pilous hugged Hall, but the triumph perhaps was most satisfying to Ivan, who had left a secure situation in Detroit for a full-scale rebuilding job in Chicago. To beat the Red Wings with a goalie he acquired from them in his old backyard was special stuff. With victories such as this, the Blackhawks were poised to become one of the league's most entertaining teams for years to come.

It is difficult to fathom now, but at one time the Blackhawks were so troubled and so unloved that they almost moved to St. Louis. Imagine that: Chicago without the Blackhawks!

Some of the Blackhawks' troubles started with James Norris's purchase of the Detroit Red Wings in 1932 after Major McLaughlin prevented him from bringing a second NHL franchise to Chicago. Norris watched with glee as his Red Wings repeatedly buried McLaughlin's Blackhawks, but Norris's business partner, Arthur Wirtz, was not as amused, and he arranged to buy the Blackhawks franchise on September 11, 1952, with Norris's sons, James D. and Bruce.

Over the years, the interlocking relationship between the Norris and the Wirtz families proved helpful. For a while, the Blackhawks and Red Wings routinely exchanged players. Unfortunately, not many of the winning Red Wings' ways rubbed off on the Blackhawks, who had few players and few fans.

Matters were so desperate that the Blackhawks sought assistance beyond their friendly rivals in Detroit. The entire NHL cooperated in a "Help the Hawks" mission that brought Ed Litzenberger and Eric Nesterenko to Chicago. But the Blackhawks had to help themselves, and the new owners spared no cost in hiring Tommy Ivan from Detroit as the general manager in 1954. To his credit, Ivan immediately sought out particular

players—and even a Buffalo minor league club for $150,000—to fulfill his vision for the Blackhawks.

THROUGH THE THICK & THIN

When James D. Norris died in 1966, Arthur Wirtz's son William soon took over as the president of the franchise. During his long tenure, Wirtz was elected chairman of the NHL Board of Governors nine times, and is credited in part with ending a long, costly seven-year war with the rival World Hockey Association by taking in four WHA teams.

The many acts of kindness performed by William W. Wirtz, his brother Michael, and his sons, Rocky and Peter, are appreciated by those who know them best. To give just one example, there was a serious impasse between NHL management and the players association during the 1994–95 season. The two sides eventually settled, but it pushed back the start of the season to January. During the dispute, a number of NHL teams laid off employees to cut costs. Bill Wirtz did nothing of the kind. He paid every worker his or her due and decided that, even without games, 'twas the season to be merry. And so it seems that not all notable actions appear in the win-loss standings.

Far left: Jeremy Roenick (27) eagerly makes his way over the boards to the action. Left, left to right: Michael Wirtz, Arthur M. Wirtz, and William W. Wirtz. Below, left to right: Peter R. Wirtz, William W. Wirtz, Michael Wirtz, and W. Rockwell Wirtz.

BLACKHAWKS TROPHY CASE

ART ROSS TROPHY (highest point total)

1943	Doug Bentley
1946	Max Bentley
1947	Max Bentley
1949	Roy Conacher
1960	Bobby Hull
1962	Bobby Hull
1964	Stan Mikita
1965	Stan Mikita
1966	Bobby Hull
1967	Stan Mikita
1968	Stan Mikita

BILL MASTERTON TROPHY (perseverance, sportsmanship, and dedication to hockey)

1970	Pit Martin

LESTER PATRICK TROPHY (outstanding service to hockey in the U.S.)

1967	James Norris
1969	Robert M. Hull
1972	James D. Norris
1975	Thomas N. Ivan
1976	Stanley Mikita
1978	William W. Wirtz
1985	Arthur M. Wirtz

FRANK J. SELKE TROPHY (best defensive forward)

1986	Troy Murray
1991	Dirk Graham

JAMES NORRIS MEMORIAL TROPHY (outstanding defenseman)

1963	Pierre Pilote
1964	Pierre Pilote
1965	Pierre Pilote
1982	Doug Wilson
1993	Chris Chelios
1996	Chris Chelios

VEZINA TROPHY (outstanding goaltender)

1932	Charles Gardiner
1934	Charles Gardiner
1935	Lorne Chabot
1963	Glenn Hall
1967	Glenn Hall
	Denis DeJordy
1970	Anthony Esposito
1972	Anthony Esposito
	Gary Smith
1974	Anthony Esposito*
1991	Ed Belfour
1993	Ed Belfour

*Shared with Philadelphia's Bernie Parent.

WILLIAM M. JENNINGS TROPHY

(goaltender with fewest goals against average)

1991	Ed Belfour
1993	Ed Belfour
	Jimmy Waite
1995	Ed Belfour

JACK ADAMS AWARD (NHL coach judged to have contributed the most to his team's success)

1983	Orval Tessier

LADY BYNG MEMORIAL TROPHY

(sportsmanship and gentlemanly conduct)

1936	Elwin Romnes
1943	Max Bentley
1944	Clint Smith
1945	Bill Mosienko
1964	Ken Wharram
1965	Bobby Hull
1967	Stan Mikita
1968	Stan Mikita

HART MEMORIAL TROPHY

(most valuable player)

1946	Max Bentley
1954	Al Rollins
1965	Bobby Hull
1966	Bobby Hull
1967	Stan Mikita
1968	Stan Mikita

CLARENCE S. CAMPBELL BOWL

(Western Conference playoff champion)

1971*	Chicago Blackhawks
1972*	Chicago Blackhawks
1973*	Chicago Blackhawks
1992	Chicago Blackhawks

*Finishing first in the Campbell Division during regular-season play.

PRESIDENTS' TROPHY (team finishing first overall during regular-season play)

1991	Chicago Blackhawks

CALDER MEMORIAL TROPHY

(outstanding rookie)

1936	Mike Karakas
1938	Carl Dahlstrom
1955	Ed Litzenberger
1960	William Hay
1970	Anthony Esposito
1983	Steve Larmer
1991	Ed Belfour

MOMENTS IN TIME: 1972–92

During two decades marked by the aging and retiring of legends, the Blackhawks found solace in reaching milestones and demolishing records. Blackhawks greats Bobby Hull, Stan Mikita, and Tony Esposito all ended their Blackhawks careers, as did famed defenseman Bobby Orr, who played just twenty-six games with Chicago before retiring. Throughout the 1980s, the Blackhawks celebrated their past triumphs by retiring their first four jerseys, all the while hoping for a bright future.

APRIL 2, 1972
Bobby Hull scores his last goal as a Blackhawk (No. 604) against Detroit and goaltender Andy Brown.

JANUARY 29, 1974
The third all-star game held at the Chicago Stadium pits the West Division against the East Division. The West all-stars prevail, 6-4.

APRIL 6, 1975
The Blackhawks win their 1,200th game with a 5-0 victory over Minnesota. It's also the 500th NHL victory for coach Billy Reay.

OCTOBER 6, 1976
Bobby Orr, signed during the off-season as a free agent from Boston, makes his Blackhawks' debut in St. Louis. The legendary defenseman, however, is beset by knee problems, and is only able to play twenty-six games for Chicago before he retires.

FEBRUARY 27, 1977
Stan Mikita scores his 500th career goal against the Vancouver Canucks' goalie Cesare Maniago at the Stadium. Ecstatic fans stage a celebration, and the game is delayed for several minutes.

MARCH 13, 1979
The Blackhawks and the Atlanta Flames complete an eight-player trade. The Blackhawks acquire Tom Lysiak, Harold Phillipoff, Pat Ribble, Greg Fox, and Miles Zaharko in exchange for Ivan Boldirev, Phil Russell, and Darcy Rota.

FEBRUARY 3, 1982
Burly right wing Grant Mulvey scores five goals (once right after a faceoff, twice on his own rebounds, and twice on assists by Terry Ruskowski and Denis Savard) in a 9-5 rout of the St. Louis Blues at the Stadium. Mulvey's outburst establishes a franchise record for the most goals in one game, and his four goals in the first period tie a league record that still stands.

APRIL 4, 1982
Doug Wilson scores his thirty-ninth goal—a record for a Blackhawks defenseman.

MAY 10, 1982
The Blackhawks' farm team, the Moncton (New Brunswick) Hawks, captures the AHL Calder Cup. Coach Orval Tessier is chosen as the top AHL coach for 1981–82.

JUNE 8, 1982
At the annual NHL awards ceremony in Montreal, Doug Wilson wins the James Norris Memorial Trophy for best defenseman of the league. Wilson, the No. 1 draft choice in 1977, is the first Blackhawk rear guard so honored since Pierre Pilote, who won the Norris three consecutive times in the 1960s. Wilson scores thirty-nine goals—a high-water mark for an NHL defenseman, second only to Bobby Orr's record of forty-six in 1974–75, and he adds a total of forty-six assists for the season.

OCTOBER 19, 1980
The Blackhawks retire their first jersey, Stan Mikita's No. 21, in a historic pre-game ceremony at the Stadium. Mikita retired after the 1979–80 season, his twenty-first with the Blackhawks. Mikita remains the team's all-time leader in assists (926) and points (1,467), and his 541 goals rank second only to Bobby Hull's 604.

MARCH 22, 1982
Denis Savard, in his second season, registers his 108th point at Toronto's Maple Leaf Gardens, breaking Bobby Hull's previous record of 107 points (fifty-eight goals and forty-nine assists during the 1968–69 season). Savard finishes the season with 119 points on thirty-two goals and eighty-seven assists.

MARCH 20, 1983
Al Secord, the Blackhawks' powerful left wing, scores his fiftieth goal at the Stadium against the Toronto Maple Leafs, becoming the second player in franchise history to reach that plateau. Secord winds up with fifty-four goals for the season.

JULY 21, 1983
Arthur M. Wirtz, owner and chairman of the board of the Chicago Blackhawks, dies.

OCTOBER 30, 1983
Blackhawks' forward Tom Lysiak receives a twenty-game suspension, the second-longest suspension in NHL history, for upending linesman Ron Foyt, who had repeatedly thrown the Blackhawks' center out of faceoffs.

DECEMBER 18, 1983
The Blackhawks retire their second jersey, Bobby Hull's No. 9, before a roaring Stadium crowd chanting, "Bob-by, Bob-by!" Hull reiterates what he has said many times, that leaving the Blackhawks after fifteen years for the rival World Hockey Association's Winnipeg Jets "was the biggest mistake of my life."

JANUARY 7, 1987
Al Secord sets a franchise record by scoring four goals within eight minutes and twenty-four seconds of the second period at the Stadium. He tallied at 0:31, 3:36, 3:46, and 8:55 of the session, leading the Blackhawks to a 6-4 triumph.

JUNE 18, 1988
Blackhawks sign free agent goalies Bob Mason and Ed Belfour.

OCTOBER 15, 1983
The Chicago Blackhawks and Toronto Maple Leafs set the NHL record for the fastest five goals by two teams. Toronto's Gaston Gingras scores at 16:49 of the second period, Chicago's Denis Savard at 17:12, Chicago's Steve Larmer at 17:27, Savard again at 17:42, and Toronto's John Anderson at 18:13 for a 1:24 record. The first four goals also set a record for the fastest four goals by two teams. Toronto beats the Blackhawks 10-8.

NOVEMBER 20, 1988
Two more jerseys, Glenn Hall's No. 1 and Tony Esposito's No. 35, are retired during a pre-game ceremony, bringing the number of retired jerseys to four. Mr. Goalie and Tony-O are cheered vigorously as their banners are raised to the rafters of the Stadium.

MARCH 4, 1990
Defenseman Bob Murray plays his 1,000th NHL game, all in a Blackhawks uniform.

MAY 25, 1990
The Blackhawks' farm team, the Indianapolis Ice, captures the IHL Turner Cup. Coach Darryl Sutter is chosen as the IHL Coach of the Year.

JANUARY 19, 1991
The Blackhawks host their fourth NHL All-Star Game before a flag-waving, sold-out crowd. The Clarence Campbell Conference routs the Prince of Wales Conference 11-5, but the game is remarkable for the patriotic display by fans only days after war in the Persian Gulf broke out and for the return of former Blackhawk Denis Savard to the Stadium.

FEBRUARY 23, 1991
Michel Goulet of the Blackhawks scores his 1,000th point in a 3-3 tie at Minnesota. Goulet becomes only the thirtieth player in NHL history to reach the milestone, and he does so in style, with the third goal of a hat trick.

MARCH 10, 1991
Head coach Mike Keenan achieves his 300th NHL win as the Blackhawks defeat the New York Rangers, 5-2, at the Stadium.

MARCH 31, 1991
The Blackhawks close their regular schedule with a 5-1 victory over Detroit at the Stadium, and the two points bring the Blackhawks their first-ever Presidents' Trophy for best NHL record during the regular season. The Blackhawks amass 106 points, one shy of a franchise record, and tie team records with forty-nine wins, twenty-one on the road.

FEBRUARY 16, 1992
Michel Goulet scores his 500th career goal against Calgary at the Chicago Stadium. He becomes the seventeenth player in NHL history to reach the milestone.

MARCH 14, 1991
Goalie Ed Belfour beats the Los Angeles Kings 6-3 in Los Angeles for his thirty-ninth victory of the season, surpassing Tony Esposito's previous franchise high of thirty-eight in 1969–70. Belfour finishes the season with a league high of forty-three wins in seventy-four games, a team record. Belfour wins the Calder Trophy for best rookie and the Vezina Trophy for best goalie.

What makes the Chicago Blackhawks special? The Blackhawks' jersey is one of the most admired in professional sports, but it alone cannot account for the team's distinctiveness. The bygone Stadium and the brilliant new United Center have fostered the excitement of Blackhawks hockey, but context alone cannot determine the nature and significance of the game. The fans, from the newly hooked to the die-hard, are a constant source of strength, inspiration, and amusement, but while they may influence the outcome of a game, they don't make the game happen. No, what makes this franchise so special is the players.

Team members have come from different backgrounds, have spoken various tongues, and are of all shapes, sizes, and styles. Through the years, they've come from afar—from Canada's great white north, from Sweden and Russia and Czechoslovakia, from colleges around the United States—and from the suburbs and streets of Chicago. But once they don that uniform, they become brothers, bonded to each other

and their admirers, a family in a loose yet real sense. Just ask any careful observer of sports which athletes are unique, which athletes readily sign autographs, which athletes treat their fans as blood relatives, and which athletes give back to their community without hesitation, and he or she will tell you that hockey players invariably outrank their peers.

For three-quarters of a century, the Chicago Blackhawks have been blessed with a number of exceptional players whose contributions to the cause have exceeded sixty minutes of hard labor on game nights. Every fan wishes to identify with his or her favorite players, but when that feeling is mutual . . . well, perhaps that explains why Blackhawks hockey is so much about passion and soul.

The question is often asked, Why do so many players not from Chicago play in Chicago and then stay in Chicago? It's not because of the weather, so it must be because of the warmth. Here are many of the rare athletes who helped build the proud history and culture of the Chicago Blackhawks.

A GALAXY OF STARS

Far left: Blackhawks scoring leader Tony Amonte (10) jubilantly embraces playmaker Alex Zhamnov (13) in hockey's trademark celebratory post-goal scoring hug. Zhamnov and Amonte are constant scoring threats because of their bullet-like speed, agility, puck creativity, and deadly shots. Left: A young Bobby Hull stands ramrod straight with his stick erect in his right hand and his blade tip on the ice—a popular pose of the era.

CHARLIE GARDINER

The Blackhawks have had their share of excellent goalkeepers, and their first one came early, by way of Scotland. Charlie Gardiner took over during the second year of the franchise, 1927–28, and was revered for his effort through thick and thin. Gardiner became a goalie because he was a mediocre skater, yet he developed a reputation as the "Roving Scotsman" because he frequently ventured from his net to handle the puck or to improve his angle on an oncoming shooter.

Gardiner toiled during some lean seasons, but he was also the driving force of the Blackhawks' first Stanley Cup season. He posted a minuscule 1.63 goals against average that year, and was brilliant during the playoffs. Gardiner won his second Vezina Trophy that season, despite bouts with various illnesses. Teammates ascribed Gardiner's erratic health to his worrisome nature, but sadly, it proved to be much more than that. A few months after celebrating his Stanley Cup, Gardiner collapsed and died of a brain tumor.

In 316 regular-season games (forty-two of which were shutouts), Gardiner allowed only 664 goals for a goals against average of 2.02. In his twenty-one playoff games (five of which were shutouts), he allowed only thirty-five goals for a remarkable goals against average of 1.37! For this outstanding record, Gardiner was inducted into the Hockey Hall of Fame in 1945.

Right: Charlie Gardiner in white all-star sweater for the NHL's first all-star game in Toronto on February 14, 1934. Gardiner displays the typical goalie protection of the mid-1930s. His stick is heavily taped on the blade and the thick part of the lower shaft, and his forward-like gloves are merely mirror opposites. The Trapper and the Blocker had not yet been invented. Goalies' hands and palms took a pounding from deflecting shots back then.

HAROLD MARCH

When Harold "Mush" March started with the Blackhawks in the late 1920s, little was expected from this little guy, a five-foot, five-inch, 155-pound right wing. But March could skate. (March's nickname followed him to Chicago from Regina, Saskatchewan, Canada, where he was called "Mush Mouth" after a local cartoon character known for his small size.) He joined center Elwyn "Doc" Romnes and Paul Thompson to form one of the NHL's best lines during the 1933–34 season, when the Blackhawks won their first Stanley Cup. March scored a key

goal in the first series against the Montreal Canadiens, but that was just an appetizer.

In game four of the best-of-five finals against Detroit, a standing-room-only Stadium throng witnessed a classic. The contest was scoreless through regulation and the first overtime period. Midway into the second overtime, defenseman Ebbie Goodfellow was penalized, and the Blackhawks embarked on a powerplay. Romnes won a faceoff in Detroit territory and whipped the puck back to March, who fired "with everything I had" from forty feet away on goalie Wilf Cude. He got a piece of it, but the puck slithered behind him at 30:05 of overtime. The Blackhawks won 1-0 and took the Cup.

According to NHL minor official Jack Fitzsimmons, "Harold March was a two-way performer: his offensive skills were always productive, and at the same time, he was a defensive hockey player. He had many, many skills. You can't compare the game from the 1930s and 1940s to the game today; it was different. But he was a credit to the sport and, in fact, a credit to the sport world, whether it was hockey, football, or baseball. . . . The bottom line is [that] he is a class act. He was then, and he still is." Mush March played seventeen seasons with the Blackhawks, and scored 153 goals, but none was as important as the one that clinched the Stanley Cup.

EARL SEIBERT

Seibert began his NHL career with the New York Rangers in 1931, but he joined the Blackhawks in 1936 and made the first or second all-star teams for nine consecutive seasons in Chicago. He rushed the puck aggressively and was no less forceful with the physical aspect of the game.

Regrettably, Seibert was involved in a tragic encounter with the great Howie Morenz, who was on his second tour of duty with the Montreal Canadiens after making brief stops in Chicago and New York. On January 28, 1937, in a game at the Montreal Forum, Seibert body-checked Morenz, who went into the boards skates first. Morenz suffered a broken leg, and at age thirty-six, it was doubtful that he'd ever play again. Morenz died two months later.

Seibert went on to be a vital cog in the Blackhawks' 1938 Stanley Cup surge. He finished his career with Detroit, and was inducted into the Hall of Fame in 1963.

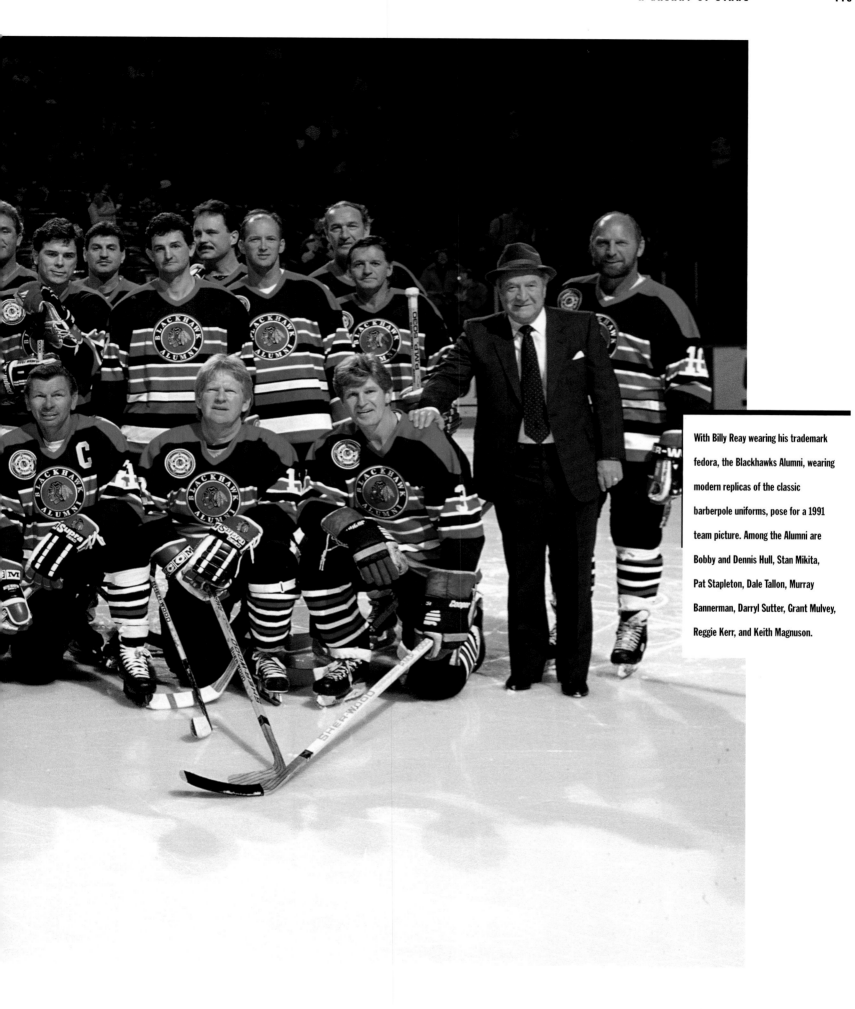

With Billy Reay wearing his trademark fedora, the Blackhawks Alumni, wearing modern replicas of the classic barberpole uniforms, pose for a 1991 team picture. Among the Alumni are Bobby and Dennis Hull, Stan Mikita, Pat Stapleton, Dale Tallon, Murray Bannerman, Darryl Sutter, Grant Mulvey, Reggie Kerr, and Keith Magnuson.

The Brothers Bentley

A five-foot, eight-inch, 140-pound dynamo, Doug Bentley, joined the Blackhawks as a left wing in 1939–40, and led the team in goals. Before long, he was scoring at such a clip that he led the NHL with thirty-three in 1942–43 and thirty-eight in 1943–44.

Max, the younger and slightly larger brother, joined the Blackhawks as a center a year after Doug, who served as the team's scout. "If you think I'm good," he informed the management, "you should see my brother back home." Coach Johnny Gottselig put the brothers together with Bill Mosienko for a spell, and they became known as "The Pony Line," although James Farrell, the team's colorful publicist, originally floated the idea of calling it "The Gazelle Line."

Max amassed seven points in one game (four goals and three assists), and led the Blackhawks twice in scoring. Max was traded to Toronto in 1947, and a blockbuster transaction it was. The Blackhawks were down, and they needed bodies. Doug retired in 1952 after collecting 217 goals in Chicago, but was coaxed into returning two seasons later to play with Max in New York. In their first game with the Rangers, the Bentley brothers bagged eight points.

Time has proven Doug Bentley one of the best Blackhawks players of all time. He won the Art Ross Trophy in 1942–43 for scoring. He made the all-star team twice, first in 1943–44 and later in 1948–49. During the 1949–50 season, Bentley was the first Blackhawks player to score 200 career goals. Max's status as one of the great Blackhawks players has fared no worse than his brother's. In his seven-year career with the Blackhawks, he claimed the Art Ross Trophy twice and both the Lady Byng Trophy and the Hart Trophy once. Doug was inducted into the Hall of Fame in 1964, and Max was inducted in 1966.

Bill Mosienko

Bill Mosienko scored two goals within twenty-one seconds in a match against the New York Rangers. That was in 1942, and quite a feat. But a decade later, Mosienko topped it by scoring three goals within twenty-one seconds, also against the Rangers.

Above: A fashionable hockey public-relations photo shows the Bentley brothers "throwing snow" at their goalie in practice. Lower right: Bill Mosienko in a primitive leather helmet, pictured separately on the following page. Players seldom wore these modest head protectors unless ordered to do so by team doctors because of an injury. Far right: Al Rollins demonstrates the advance in goalie equipment from Charlie Gardiner's day. Rollins wears a catching glove to trap the oncoming puck, while his blocker holds his goalie stick.

How remarkable is that? The previous record for the three quickest goals was held by Detroit's Carl Liscombe, who completed a hat trick in a paltry sixty-four seconds in 1938. And since Mosienko's amazing accomplishment on March 23, 1952, in New York, the closest any player has come was forty-four seconds by Montreal's Jean Beliveau in 1955.

What we shouldn't forget about Mosienko is that he achieved much more than his rapid-fire hat trick. Though he played for some modestly talented teams, Mosienko tallied 258 goals and 282 assists, marking a career total of 540 points during his fourteen-year career with the Blackhawks. For that, he was inducted into the Hall of Fame in 1965. Mosienko still ranks ninth on the team's all-time point list.

AL ROLLINS

Al Rollins might be the best goalie ever to get so little respect. Part of the reason was that he played during a time when the Blackhawks were down and almost out. In 1953–54, for instance, the team won only twelve of seventy games. Rollins won them all, and posted a 3.23 goals against average with five shutouts.

Despite the Blackhawks' last-place standing, Rollins won the Hart Trophy for the most valuable player in the entire league. However, praise found its limits, Hart Trophy or no. Rollins wasn't voted to either all-star team. Toronto's Harry Lumley was the first all-star goalkeeper, and Detroit's Terry Sawchuk was the second all-star that season.

Strangely enough, this didn't phase Rollins. As a player for the Maple Leafs in 1951, he was awarded the Vezina Trophy, but didn't qualify for either all-star team. That braced him for years of unfriendly fire in Chicago. Rollins was an island of stability. During his Hart Trophy season, the Blackhawks were so desperate that they played a home game at Indianapolis just before Christmas. They fared so poorly, financially and athletically, that rumors abounded of their imminent demise. But neither the Blackhawks nor Rollins folded.

LEADERSHIP

In addition to Tom Gorman, Bill Stewart, and Rudy Pilous, who led the Blackhawks to Stanley Cup triumphs, the franchise has been blessed with a number of revered coaches who have directed the team through some heady times.

No man held the job longer than Billy Reay, who took over in 1963, coached into the 1976–77 season, and won 516 games. Not once during Reay's thirteen full seasons behind the bench did the Blackhawks post a losing record, and only once did they miss the playoffs. Reay was in charge when the Blackhawks broke the "Curse of Muldoon" by finishing first for the first time ever in the regular 1966–67 season. Then, he made a practice of being on top—his teams won five other division titles. Three times he coached the Blackhawks to the Stanley Cup finals. Reay was a shrewd leader who benefited from his experience as a center with the Montreal Canadiens for eight seasons. Reay rarely put his foot down when the team was struggling. On the contrary, he believed that the time to declare himself was when the team was playing well. Reay's stern closed-door lecture during a fifteen-game unbeaten streak when he feared his athletes were in danger of believing the flattering press is a case in point. Reay was particularly brilliant in coaching the worst-to-first team (laden with rookies) in 1969–70 and in guiding the Blackhawks to the Stanley Cup finals the season after Bobby Hull left for the World Hockey Association in 1972–73 and most experts figured the team would take a serious tumble.

In 1977 the Blackhawks went outside the organization to hire Bob Pulford, who had crafted a great record with the Los Angeles Kings. He immediately coached the Blackhawks to consecutive division titles, then relinquished his bench duty to devote himself to the general manager's role. As a front office executive, Pulford preached the same strong-but-silent discipline that made him a Hall of Famer with the Maple Leafs. Along with assistant general manager Jack Davison, he oversaw the resurgence of the Blackhawks in the 1980s, during which the team jelled with No. 1 draft choices such as Denis Savard and Doug Wilson and with diamonds in the rough like Steve Larmer, who was selected in the sixth round and 120th overall in 1980 but became one of the best players ever to don the Indian-head jersey.

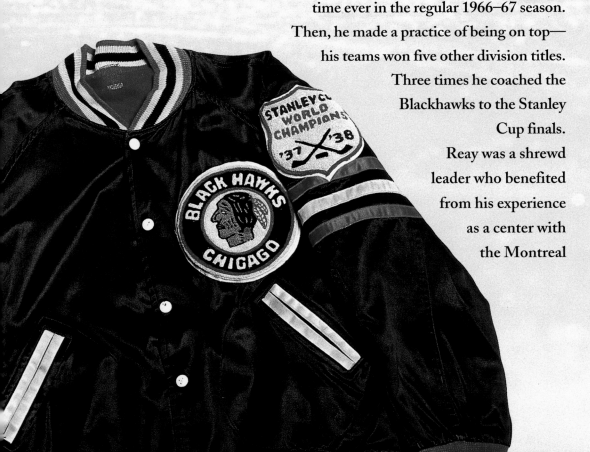

To spot and develop talent like Larmer's requires devotion to duty, and Pulford always did his home-work. Pulford earned the reputation as a "player's coach," having played in 1,079 NHL games and on five all-star teams.

If there was a common thread in the Blackhawks' leadership during the second half of the twentieth century, it was Tommy Ivan, who resurrected the franchise after being hired as the general manager in 1954 and coached the team briefly in the late 1950s. Although Ivan was careful around members of the press, he could not escape the trained eye of Stan Fischler, whose many books include *Hockey's 100*. Fischler listed Ivan as one of the ten best coaches and ten best general managers ever.

Few administrators in any sport faced the daunting task Ivan took on in Chicago after coaching the Red Wings to three Stanley Cups. The Blackhawks were down and out and without a plan. Ivan rolled up his sleeves and put the Blackhawks back on the map. He took a fair amount of criticism for pulling the trigger on a 1967 trade that sent Phil Esposito, Ken Hodge, and Fred Stanfield to Boston, where they all starred.

But Pit Martin, whom Chicago got in exchange, was a fine player, and Gilles Marotte, a defenseman also acquired from the Bruins, was used by Ivan in a subsequent transaction with Los Angeles that brought Bill White—a superlative defenseman—to the Blackhawks.

Some would say Tommy Ivan brought the Blackhawks back to life. After all, it was he who had hired Rudy Pilous to mold the Blackhawks into a winning team. Pilous had to think twice about taking the big jump to Chicago, because he feared it might be a plunge instead.

"It was a graveyard," said Pilous.

But when Pilous agreed to succeed Ivan midway during the 1957–58 season, the time seemed ripe. Several of the stars Pilous coached at St. Catharines—Bobby Hull, Stan Mikita, Chico Maki, Ab McDonald, Pierre Pilote, Wayne Hillman, Elmer Vasko—would wind up in Chicago. So why not the coach himself? Pilous led the Blackhawks to a series of third-place finishes and one of them, 1961, culminated in a Stanley Cup. He did not, however, repeat that accomplishment, nor did Pilous ever shatter the "Curse of Muldoon." He was replaced by Reay in 1963, and shortly there-after, the two men ran into each other at a Montreal racetrack during the summer.

"Any advice for me?" inquired Reay.

"Yeah," said Pilous, who had a quick wit. "Make sure you finish first."

Upper left: Bob Pulford joined the Blackhawks as general manager and coach in 1977 after a brilliant playing career and a successful term as coach of the Los Angeles Kings. He is still the Blackhawks' senior vice president. Above: Jack Davison, vice president and forty-year veteran of the Blackhawks front office, was a master of judging junior players and aided in drafting Denis Savard, Steve Larmer, Jeremy Roenick, and Doug Wilson. Below: Rudy Pilous, the witty and colorful coach, led the Blackhawks to their third Stanley Cup in 1961.

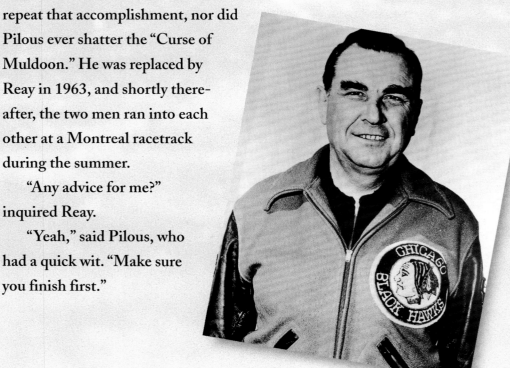

PIERRE PILOTE

Here's a trivia question for you: When Bobby Orr established a record for defensemen with sixty-four points in 1968–69, whose record did he break? Pierre Pilote's is the answer. The Blackhawks defenseman amassed fourteen goals and forty-five assists during the 1964–65 season, and those fifty-nine points seemed like a lot at the time.

When Pilote joined the Blackhawks in 1955, he had much experience as a center from his youth, which explains his deftness with the puck. But he easily adapted to the blue line, and was willing to mix it up whenever necessary. Pilote recalls once fighting both the Richard brothers, Maurice and Henri. "I started with the Pocket, and then came the Rocket," said Pilote, who won three consecutive Norris trophies in the mid-1960s.

Right: Pierre Pilote uses his stick to neutralize a Detroit attacker while keeping his eye focused on the puck. Below: Other than Gordie Howe, no player had better elbows than Eric Nesterenko (right), a relentless forechecker and backchecker who marched to the tune of his own drummer, often preferring to discuss literature than hockey. Far right: Glenn Hall leaps high in the air to snatch a flying puck.

Pilote succeeded Ed Litzenberger as team captain, played as a first-team all-star five years in a row, and chipped in eighty goals during his career, which merited his induction into the Hall of Fame in 1975.

ERIC NESTERENKO

"Swoop," "Elbows," "Flin Flon Flash." Eric Nesterenko had a number of nicknames and a number of interests beyond hockey. Well-read and cerebral, Nesterenko was one of the most interesting individuals ever to don a Blackhawks jersey, and he was a stabilizing presence for sixteen seasons and 1,013 games—the third-highest total in team history.

No job was too big or too small for Nesterenko. A fluid skater with terrific anticipation, he was a superlative penalty killer with a variety of partners: Bill Hay, who also centered the Million Dollar Line of Bobby Hull and Murray Balfour; Chico Maki, who shared regular shifts with Bobby Hull and Phil Esposito; and Lou Angotti, a tireless skater who did time at center between Hull and Nesterenko. In addition to his defensive talents, Eric scored 207 goals for the Blackhawks, twenty-two of them shorthanded. Nesterenko went on to become a ski instructor and a movie actor, starring in *Young Blood* with Rob Lowe. You name it, Nesterenko could do it.

Glenn Hall

You could always rely on Glenn Hall to show up in goal for the Blackhawks, and you could rely on the fact that Hall hated every minute of it.

"You've got to be a little sick to be a goalie," said Hall. "There were nights when I almost wished I didn't have to go out on the ice."

But he did for 552 consecutive regular-season and playoff games until November 7, 1962, when Hall had to leave the ice because of a back injury. In the current era of the two-goalie system, that record seems as safe as Hall's place in NHL history.

Before joining the Blackhawks, Hall won the Calder Memorial Trophy for best rookie with the Detroit Red Wings, for whom he played two full seasons. As a Blackhawk, he later won one Vezina Trophy for himself, and shared a second one with Denis DeJordy. Hall was instrumental in leading the Blackhawks to their first Stanley Cup win in twenty-three years in 1961, but no matter how well he performed, he always warned the Blackhawks at season's end that he was going home to paint his barn in Alberta and might never come back.

"It was pure torture for me," said Hall, who would routinely throw up before games because of his nerves. Shy and sensitive, Hall was drafted by the expansion St. Louis Blues at age thirty-five. He shared another Vezina Trophy there with Jacques Plante, and helped lead the Blues to the Stanley Cup finals, too.

Hall, who played goalie without a mask but with plenty of heart and lots of injuries, retired after the 1970–71 season with a spiffy 2.51 goals against career average and a 2.79 goals against average in 115 playoff games. He was voted to the first all-star team on seven occasions, and is the second-winningest goalie in Blackhawks history after Tony Esposito. Hall was elected to the Hockey Hall of Fame in 1975, and had his number retired by the Blackhawks in 1988. Now a goaltending consultant with the Calgary Flames, Hall is an active supporter of the Blackhawk Alumni Association. And he finally painted his barn.

Bobby Hull

"The Golden Jet" joined the Blackhawks in 1957 as an eighteen-year-old hulk of a youngster, and it wasn't long before opposing goalies throughout the NHL were ducking for cover. Hull's fabled slap shot was clocked at up to 120 mph, and there were many nights when he had to shed two or three checkers before he unleashed those cannon blasts.

Hull was a charismatic figure who dearly loved the game. He scored three goals in a Stanley Cup game in 1963 despite a broken nose. Years later, Hull incurred a broken jaw. A lesser athlete would have sat out indefinitely, but Hull missed only one game and then played for six weeks with his mouth wired shut. His only source of nourishment was what he called a "brownish ugh" from a blender. Remarkably, he still collected ten goals during that span! After Hull resumed eating solid food, he went on a binge with nineteen goals in fourteen games.

Hull was a fun-loving, vivacious soul. In his early days with the Blackhawks, he shared some railroad flares during the team's train ride from Boston to Montreal with unsuspecting mates. Hull was also famous for holding up team buses while he signed each and every autograph. The fans loved him, and he loved them. Hull's rink-length rushes brought fans to their feet throughout the NHL. He was a consummate entertainer and a force to be reckoned with. The Golden Jet broke the fifty-goal barrier five times with the Blackhawks, and he led the league in goals for a record seven seasons during his fifteen-year NHL career. Hull won the Art Ross Trophy for scoring three times, the Hart Trophy for most valuable player twice, and the Lady Byng Memorial Trophy for sportsmanship once.

Hull is the all-time leader in goals with the Blackhawks (604 regular season, 62 playoffs), and he ranks second in total points (1,153) and second in games played (1,036). When Hull left the NHL for the Winnipeg Jets in 1972, he virtually established the rival league. He scored 303 goals in the WHA, including 77 in 1974–75 with the Jets. A perennial all-star, Hull is considered the greatest left wing in hockey history. He was inducted into the Hall of Fame in 1983 as the NHL's fifth all-time goal scorer. There was only one Golden Jet.

Below: Bobby Hull launches his powerful slap shot, his entire muscular body behind it. Right: Stan Mikita, who is credited with the invention of the curved blade, doctors his stick in preparation for that night's game. (After playing with a cracked stick in practice, Mikita found that his shots dipped in ways that challenged league goaltenders.) Far right: Mikita, seen here wearing the fish-bowl helmet that he never stopped using, was a Blackhawks powerhouse and was voted an all-star every year from 1962 to 1970.

STAN MIKITA

Mikita was born in Czechoslovakia, but he immigrated to Canada at age eight to live with his aunt and uncle. He learned hockey and how to fend for himself, and evolved into a world-class player. List the best and brightest playmakers in NHL history, and Mikita is invariably cited among the select few.

What's amazing about Mikita's superb career is that he reinvented himself. When he arrived in the NHL, he was a chippy, ornery, smallish type who dished out and took punishment. In four of his first six seasons, Mikita logged more than 100 penalty minutes per season. But after he became a husband and, later, a father, he realized that he couldn't put bread on the table or points on the scoreboard from the penalty box. During the 1967–68 season, Mikita "reformed" and collected just twelve minutes, becoming the only player in NHL annals to win three major awards—the Art Ross Trophy for scoring, the Hart Memorial Trophy for most valuable player, and the Lady Byng Memorial Trophy for sportsmanship—in one season. And Mikita was so good that he repeated that accomplishment twice.

Mikita and Hull comprised a sensational one-two punch. Foes naturally presumed that shutting them down strongly enhanced their chances of beating the Blackhawks, but that was easier said than done. Moreover, Mikita was forever delving into areas beyond the game. He helped popularize the curved stick blade that rendered pucks more difficult for goalies to handle, and when headgear came into vogue, he designed a helmet that became a fixture for many players.

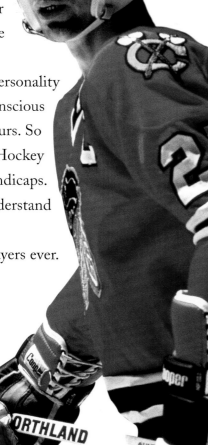

Mikita was more than just an athlete. His quick wit and personality made him a Chicagoan for all seasons, and Mikita was forever conscious about giving back to the community. As a child bucking the language barrier, he heard the slurs. So it was natural that he was a prime mover in the creation of the American Hearing Impaired Hockey Association for young hockey players who were eager to participate in sports despite their handicaps.

"I could identify with them," Mikita recalled, "because when I was a kid, I didn't understand what people were saying around me, either."

There's no misunderstanding now about Mikita being one of the greatest hockey players ever. He was a six-time first all-star who played in more playoff games (155) and produced more playoff points (150) than any other Blackhawk. He was inducted into the Hall of Fame in 1983, three years after his number was the first to be retired by the franchise for which he played a record 1,394 games.

Dennis Hull

For a man who encountered a great deal of pressure as the brother of a legend, Dennis Hull did just fine, thank you very much. Don't forget, Dennis not only followed Bobby to Chicago, but also played on the same Blackhawks' team for several years. While Bobby was in a league of his own, Dennis earned a reputation as a blue-chip scorer, too.

When Dennis arrived as a rookie in 1964, he lacked confidence. But coach Billy Reay took him aside and made Dennis a pet project. The results were outstanding. Dennis amassed 298 goals for the Blackhawks, the fifth highest total in franchise history and the sixth spot in total points (640). Moreover, after Bobby left for the World Hockey Association, it was the "MPH Line" of Pit Martin centering for right wing Jim Pappin and left wing Hull that keyed the team's drive to the Stanley Cup finals—and at just the time when experts had forecast that the Blackhawks would tumble without The Golden Jet. Dennis was known for his sharp and often self-deprecating sense of humor, and after he retired, he became one of the most popular after-dinner speakers throughout North America. When Dennis scored thirty goals and Bobby fifty-eight in 1968–69, the pair established a record that stood until the 1999–2000 season: eighty-eight goals in one season by brothers.

Far left: Dennis Hull charges forward, eyes exhibiting total concentration, his strong pride determined to reach the Rangers' goal. Bottom right: Tony Esposito uses his entire body—goalie pads, gloves, stick, and molded face mask—to defend his goal at all costs.

Tony Esposito

As a youngster, Tony Esposito closely observed his magnificent predecessor in the Blackhawks goal, Glenn Hall. Esposito developed a similar mindset as Mr. Goalie: Stopping pucks makes for a nice living, but sometimes it seems like a series of a near-death experiences.

"You always knew when it was game day, because Tony was miserable," quipped Stan Mikita. "You didn't say anything to him, and he didn't say anything to you. But he was *our* miserable, and he did a hell of a job."

On game days, Esposito was in a zone of his own as he built his concentration toward the task that evening. Few athletes prepared themselves as thoroughly as Esposito, who possessed an unconventional style and uncommon devotion to duty. Tony-O did his job, often in spite of injury, migraines, or illness. He was a warrior in every sense. To think general manager Tommy Ivan stole him from the Montreal Canadiens' crowded roster for only $25,000 in 1969—one of the all-time bargains in sports history!

In Esposito's rookie season, he single-handedly lifted the Blackhawks from worst to first with thirty-eight victories and fifteen shutouts. No modern goalie has posted more shutouts. Esposito's career total of seventy-four shutouts outranks all others on the list of illustrious Blackhawks netminders. He had two with the Canadiens, and his total of seventy-six is seventh on the all-time NHL list.

Although Esposito went on to work in the front office for the Pittsburgh Penguins and Tampa Bay Lightning, he will always be remembered as a member of the Blackhawks, who retired his jersey in 1988.

TONY ESPOSITO
BLACK HAWKS GOALIE

KEITH MAGNUSON

After the Blackhawks finished last in 1969, coach Billy Reay was looking for an injection of young blood. Reay wasn't completely sold on the possibility of a rookie defenseman coming right out of college to fill such a role, but Keith Magnuson was simply too determined, from day one of training camp, so he never spent a day in the minor leagues. Instead, the redheaded rear guard from Denver University contributed dearly to a renewed spirit of the Blackhawks, who vaulted to first place in his rookie season.

He once explained, "I came to the Blackhawks the year after they finished last in 1969. We had a lot of us rookies . . . [but] we wound up winning the division. So I had to be fortunate to be coming up at just that time."

Maggie was a ferocious competitor on the ice, unafraid of dropping his gloves and fighting anybody. Off the ice, he was a decent, well-mannered soul who was an integral part of the team's chemistry throughout his career. Maggie was destined to wear the captain's C as a player. He later became an assistant coach for the Blackhawks and, after that, a head coach. Thirty years after he broke in, Magnuson remains part of the family as president of the Blackhawk Alumni Association.

Above: Keith Magnuson's gloves with palms discreetly removed for a more natural "feel" to his stick—or all the better to grab an opponent by the jersey. Far right: Captain Magnuson, bloody but unbowed, shoulder pad exposed, wishing an opponent a good night with fire in his eyes. Lower left: Doug Wilson blasting his deadly accurate slap shot from the point.

DOUG WILSON

The Blackhawks have been blessed with a number of exceptional defensemen in their history, but none was as adept offensively as Doug Wilson, their first selection in the 1977 NHL draft and an important figure in the team's success during the 1980s. Wilson was a heady player and an effortless skater with a booming shot.

Wilson is one of only three Blackhawks defensemen ever to win the James Norris Memorial Trophy (1982), and it's unlikely that Wilson's production will be matched anytime soon. His 225 goals rank tenth on the all-time Chicago honor roll, and he collected an amazing 554 assists, behind only Stan Mikita and Denis Savard and just ahead of Bobby Hull.

Despite several injuries that at times forced him to wear a helmet, Wilson played almost his entire career without one. He played his thousandth game in 1992 with the San Jose Sharks, whom he later joined as a front-office executive.

Sitting on the players' bench, Blackhawks forward Doug Gilmour gazes intently at the center score board to watch a replay on the jumbotron during a stoppage in play.

STEVE LARMER

Talk about a diamond in the rough! In the 1980 NHL amateur draft, the Blackhawks selected Steve Larmer in the sixth round, 120th overall. Somebody in the organization did some extra homework, because Larmer developed into one of the most durable and reliable two-way forwards in franchise history. Larmer was a left-handed shooter who could play right wing and contribute both offensively and defensively.

Larmer bagged forty-three goals and forty-seven assists in his 1982–83 rookie season when he won the Calder Memorial Trophy, and he only got better. He was neither flashy nor particularly fleet, but he had an intuitive sense of the movement of the puck that can't be taught. Also, Larmer refused to bow to illness or injury. He played 884 consecutive games for the Blackhawks, a franchise record, not missing a single start from his opening game in 1982 to his final game in 1993. When his string stopped, Larmer's was the third longest in NHL history, and the two players ahead of him—Doug Jarvis and Garry Unger—were retired. During the 1990–91 season, Larmer scored forty-four goals and led the Blackhawks in scoring with 101 points. He matched the latter accomplishment during the 1988–89 and 1989–90 seasons, and scored forty or more goals in a single season five times. Larmer scored the third most goals in Blackhawks history (406)—behind only Bobby Hull and Stan Mikita—and then left for the New York Rangers, with whom he won the Stanley Cup in 1994.

DENIS SAVARD

As a youngster growing up around Montreal, Denis Savard could do it all, except grow. Perhaps his smallish size was a reason why the hometown Canadiens passed over Savard when making the No. 1 overall selection in the 1980 NHL amateur draft. The Blackhawks, picking third, didn't think twice, and were they ever blessed. Savard became one of the most electrifying players ever to skate in Chicago.

When he left home that first time, Denis promised in a tearful goodbye to his parents that he would make the team as a rookie. He knew no English and was somewhat awed by the big city, but he chose his friends well. Defenseman Keith Brown, a solid citizen, took Savard under his wing. Savard scored twenty-eight goals and added forty-seven assists in his first season. He never looked back.

By year two, Savard shattered Bobby Hull's single-season point total for the Blackhawks with 119. Denis went on to become one of the most feared and creative forwards in the league. He was a terrific skater and brilliant passer, and he was full of energy. Clearly, Denis enjoyed playing for the fans as much as the fans enjoyed watching him, and it's a fact that Savard's arrival helped precipitate a revival in the franchise during the 1980s. As the decade opened, the Blackhawks were still struggling to find a crowd-pleaser to replace the departed Bobby Hull and the retired Stan Mikita.

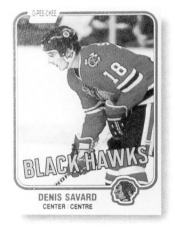

DENIS SAVARD
CENTER / CENTRE

Indeed, for Savard's opening game against Buffalo on October 9, 1980, there were 6,000 empty seats in the Stadium. But not for long. One look at this diminutive Flying Frenchman, and Blackhawks fans had a new hero. Savard scored many a picturesque goal after executing his spin-o-rama move, a 360-degree revolution, puck in tow, which left the opposing defender reeling and groping the air. Many found similarities between the outgoing Mikita and the incoming Savard. Assistant coach Cliff Koroll once put it this way: "There are undeniable similarities between Stan and Denis. One is between the ears and other is between the arm pits. Denis is a smart hockey player, just as Stan was. He also knows where the other end of the rink is. He has a lot of heart, just like Stan. Denis always puts the team's performance ahead of any individual accomplishments."

Savard, a personable sort, became a popular figure in the community. After he was traded to Montreal, where he won a Stanley Cup, and then moved on to Tampa Bay, Savard returned to finish his career with the Blackhawks and received a royal welcome. Savard's 377 goals rank fourth all-time with the Blackhawks. He is second only to Mikita with 719 assists and third behind Hull and Mikita in points with 1,096.

As an assistant coach with the Blackhawks, Savard had his jersey retired in 1998. His next stop will be the Hall of Fame.

Left: Denis Savard fiercely pursues the puck. Far left: Steve Larmer fearlessly defends the puck against the Red Wings. Though he seldom had his skates sharpened, Larmer could stop on a dime and leave change. Above: Denis Savard's O-Pee-Chee rookie trading card.

JEREMY ROENICK

Everything you wanted to know about Jeremy Roenick was evident early in his Blackhawks career. During a playoff game at St. Louis in 1989, Roenick lost a few teeth on one shift and then incurred a cut above his nose on another. But he still managed to score a goal on true grit, which was his calling card with the Blackhawks. They picked him first (and eighth overall) in the 1988 NHL amateur draft, and this feisty center from Thayer Academy proved to be a wise investment.

He was not particularly big, but he was utterly fearless, and he became a crowd favorite in his first full season, when he scored twenty-six goals. He then went on to forty-one goals, and in 1991–92, he became the third Blackhawk to break the fifty-goal barrier with fifty-three. The next season, Roenick hit fifty again, joining Hull as the only Blackhawks to have back-to-back fifty-goal seasons. He is the only player in franchise annals with three consecutive hundred-point seasons. Few players in the league got as much from a 175-pound frame as J. R. did.

Above: Jeremy Roenick defies gravity in a skillfully executed hairpin turn. Right: Hard-hitting defenseman Chris Chelios executes a deft maneuver. Far right: The supremely competitive center Stan Mikita uses his sweater to wipe the salty sweat he shed during one of his many on-ice battles.

CHRIS CHELIOS

Born in Chicago, Chris Chelios established himself as one of the league's premier defenseman with the Montreal Canadiens, whom he captained to a Stanley Cup championship in 1986. In 1990, Chelios was traded to his hometown Blackhawks in exchange for Denis Savard.

Chelios's intense style was quickly felt by the Blackhawks, who won the Presidents' Trophy in 1991 and then advanced to the Stanley Cup finals in 1992 on the wings of a franchise-record eleven-game winning streak in the playoffs. Chelios's six playoff goals during the 1991–92 season established a new franchise record for the most goals in a playoff year by a defenseman, outdoing the old record of five goals established by Earl Seibert during the Blackhawks' 1937–38 season.

In 1993, Chelios earned the James Norris Memorial Trophy as best defenseman in the league—just the third rear guard in Blackhawks history to achieve that honor. During the 1995–96 season, Chelios led the Blackhawks in scoring with fourteen goals and fifty-eight assists, becoming the first defenseman in team history to accomplish that feat. Chelios won another Norris Trophy in 1996, by which time he had been appointed captain in Chicago.

THE HAT TRICK

BY WILLIAM J. MARTIN

Far right: An elated Bill Mosienko
displays the three pucks he fired past
Ranger goalie Lorne Anderson in twenty-
one seconds on March 23, 1952, at
Madison Square Garden. Mosienko grew
up dirt poor in Winnipeg and spent every
hour he could skating furiously on black-
ice ponds in sub-Arctic temperatures.
His hard work paid off. Mosienko won
two NHL speed contests against
speedsters from other Original Six clubs,
and a poll of hockey journalists named
him the fastest skater in the NHL.

On the final night of the 1951–52 season, the sixth-place Blackhawks were playing the fifth-place Rangers at Madison Square Garden in a game with nothing at stake—both teams had missed the playoffs. As the third period started, the New York Rangers held a 6-2 lead. Rookie Ranger goalie Lorne Anderson had played impressively for two periods, frustrating the Blackhawks' line of Gus Bodnar centering left wing George Gee and right wing Billy Mosienko.

Mosienko recounted the feat that followed on a sweltering July afternoon in 1989 at his bowling alley, Billy Mosienko Lanes, in North Winnipeg. His ice-blue eyes sparkled as he grabbed a pool cue to demonstrate his 1952 record-shattering hat trick.

"In the first two periods," he began, "the kid in the Ranger goal beat me four times when I faked to the inside and went outside."

Crouching low, knees bent, eyes blazing, Mosienko took his position at the pool table and eyed the cue ball. "At 6:09 of the third period, Gus Bodnar won a center-ice face-off and slipped the puck to me. I skated full tilt down right wing and cut to the inside of the Rangers' Hy Buller inside the blue line. Heading toward the net, I took a forehand wrist shot on the ice," he said, whipping the pool cue with perfect follow-through.

"I beat Anderson to his right corner from about seventeen feet out.

"At 6:20 Gus Bodnar won the center-ice face-off again and took the puck straight toward the Ranger blue line before passing to me on right wing. I cut to my left, again getting past Hy Buller, kept cutting toward the middle of the Ranger zone, and took a wrist shot from twelve to fifteen feet out, beating Anderson in the same spot as my first goal."

Forwards played two- to three-minute shifts in the 1950s, not the forty-five-second bursts of today's game. Coach Ebbie Goodfellow toyed with taking Mosienko's line off after the second goal, but changed his mind.

Mosienko's wide blue eyes danced and twinkled as he transported himself in time to that night at the Garden. "At 6:30 Bodnar won his third straight faceoff in a row, and this time he passed to Georgie Gee on left wing. Georgie faked a shot but passed to me, and I cut hard to my left, moving in close to the net. I skated across the net before lifting a backhand shot from eight feet out into the opposite top shelf," he said excitedly.

"Ebbie left us out there. On the fourth faceoff, Bodnar again got the puck to me, and I swerved hard to my left, pulling the goalie with me, giving me a wide open net. I missed by inches. When I skated to the bench, Coach Goodfellow asked, 'What's the matter, Mosie, are you slowing down?' I'll never forget that."

Neither will the record book.

EVOLUTION OF PROTECTION

Top right: The 1974 popular fiberglass model that protected more of the netminder's face. It was designed by Ernie Higgins, a Needham, Massachusetts, plumber who made his first mask in 1965 for his son, a Boston University goalie, and went on to make hundreds more including one for Boston Bruin Gerry Cheevers. Lower left: The 1930s leather noseguard mask worn by Clint Benedict for one game after Howie Morenz broke the Ottawa goalie's nose. After losing 2-1 to the Blackhawks, Benedict quit using the mask. Lower right: A fiberglass mask designed by Detroit trainer Lefty Wilson for Terry Sawchuk and Roger Crozier in the mid-1960s. Far right: Blackhawk Murray Bannerman's mask, a model still molded to the face. With Eddie Belfour, upper left, and Jeff Hackett, lower left, their cages demonstrate the evolution of the mask away from the face for better vision and more protection with the head safely ensconced in a full helmet and the throat covered with a strong flap.

1974

CIRCA 1970

CIRCA 1930

ED BELFOUR

MURRAY BANNERMAN

JEFF HACKETT

Lloyd Pettit and Pat Foley. When you mention names that ring a bell in Blackhawks history, two of the most popular will be the charismatic broadcasters whose voices have warmed many winter nights on television and radio.

With the Blackhawks fast becoming one of the league's most exciting teams again in the mid-1960s, the demand was there for a full schedule of road games on WGN, Channel 9, Chicago's leading independent TV channel. Luckily, the Blackhawks tapped as their announcer Lloyd Pettit, who had a wealth of experience in sports and news. His booming voice and enthusiasm were perfect for hockey, and it was Pettit who brought home the exploits of such magnetic athletes as Bobby Hull and Stan Mikita: "A shot . . . and *a goal!*" That became Pettit's signature, although he was quite versatile. Nobody could call a hockey fight quite like Pettit.

When Pettit was transmitting those vivid images of Blackhawks' hockey on television and radio during the 1960s and 1970s, one of his most avid fans was Pat Foley, who grew up in the suburbs of Chicago. Foley attended Michigan State University, where he practiced his craft calling baseball and hockey games. After college, Foley worked for the Grand Rapids Owls of the International Hockey League. Then, a dream came true. Foley was offered and accepted a position as the voice of the Blackhawks. He completed his twentieth year during the 1999–2000 season. Whether the Blackhawks are up or down, Foley is generally regarded as the finest play-by-play broadcaster in Chicago sports. He has a distinctive voice, a quick wit, and a terrific passion for the game.

What a treat for Chicago Blackhawks fans. All those great players for all these years . . . plus Lloyd Pettit and Pat Foley, too.

BROADCASTERS

Below: Broadcasters Pat Foley (left) and Lloyd Pettit (right) pose for a photograph. Far left: Detroit Red Wing goalie Roger Crozier (1) prepares to fend off a shot by legendary Blackhawk Bobby Hull (9) during a game in the 1965–66 season. That is, if Billy Harris (14) doesn't stop him first.

MOMENTS IN TIME: 1992–2000

In a thrilling resurgence of strength, the Chicago Blackhawks muscled their way to the 1992 Stanley Cup finals. Though defeated by Pittsburgh, that stellar group of players set the tone for the decade to come. Hot young superstars like Chris Chelios and Tony Amonte brought fans as well as victories to the Chicago team, while relocation to the United Center, a plush new arena, brought the Blackhawks and their fans into the comforts and amenities of the twenty-first century. By their seventy-fifth anniversary, the Chicago Blackhawks had paved the way for dominance.

MARCH 7, 1992
In his hometown of Boston, Jeremy Roenick scores his fiftieth goal in a single season, and it's the game winner in a 2-1 decision over the Bruins. After Bobby Hull and Al Secord, Roenick is the third Blackhawk to reach the fifty-goal milestone.

APRIL 26, 1992
In a 6-4 win against the St. Louis Blues, the Blackhawks become the third team in NHL history, after the Montreal Canadiens and the Boston Bruins, to score 1,000 career playoff goals.

NOVEMBER 27, 1992
Chris Chelios scores his 100th career goal as the Blackhawks win 8-1 against the Edmonton Oilers.

MAY 22, 1992
The rampaging Blackhawks advance to the Stanley Cup finals by recording their eleventh straight playoff victory, a 5-1 romp in Edmonton. The Blackhawks lose two of their first three playoff games in the division semifinals before winning the next three to eliminate St. Louis. The Blackhawks then sweep Detroit and Edmonton.

JANUARY 16, 1993
Right wing Steve Larmer scores his 400th career goal. Larmer reaches his milestone in a 5-3 Chicago victory against the Toronto Maple Leafs.

APRIL 13, 1993
Goaltender Ed Belfour achieves his fortieth win of the season in a 3-2 victory over the Minnesota North Stars. Belfour joins Terry Sawchuk, Jacques Plante, Bernie Parent, and Ken Dryden as the fifth goaltender in NHL history with two forty-win seasons.

APRIL 15, 1993
Steve Larmer plays in his 884th consecutive and final regular-season game with the Blackhawks.

OCTOBER 6, 1993
The Florida Panthers play their first NHL game, meeting the Blackhawks at the Chicago Stadium. The game ends in a 4-4 tie.

APRIL 24, 1994
Joining Bobby Orr, Dick Redmond, Denis Potvin, Doug Halward, Paul Reinhart (twice), Al Iafrate, and Eric Desjardins, Blackhawk Gary Suter becomes the eighth defenseman in Stanley Cup playoffs history to a post a hat trick. The Blackhawks defeat the Toronto Maple Leafs 4-3 in overtime in game four of the Western Conference quarterfinals.

APRIL 28, 1994
The Toronto Maple Leafs beat the Blackhawks 1-0 in game six of their playoff series, thus eliminating the home team in the last hockey game ever played at the Chicago Stadium.

APRIL 14, 1994
The Blackhawks play their final regular-season game at the Stadium. In an emotional pre-game ceremony, the four banners representing the four retired jerseys are lowered from the ceiling and presented to the four legends in attendance: Stan Mikita, Glenn Hall, Bobby Hull, and Tony Esposito.

JANUARY 25, 1995
After the NHL season is delayed by a labor dispute, the Blackhawks finally debut in the new United Center, where Joe Murphy scores the first goal at 11:33 of the second period, assisted by Jeremy Roenick, in a 5-1 decision over the Edmonton Oilers before a crowd of 20,536 fans. The Blackhawks will average 20,833 fans per home game during the abbreviated season in their spacious new facility. The Blackhawks are the first team in NHL history to average 20,000 or more per date.

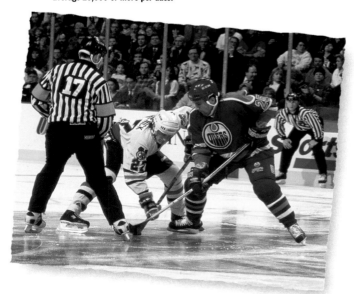

MAY 3, 1995
The Blackhawks finish the forty-eight-game regular season, allowing 115 goals for a 2.37 goals against average, to capture the William M. Jennings Trophy for the third time in five years.

MAY 19, 1995
The Blackhawks defeat the Toronto Maple Leafs 5-2 in game five of the Western Conference quarterfinals. It is the Blackhawks' first playoff series win against Toronto since 1938.

FEBRUARY 4, 1996
Brent Sutter scores his 350th career goal as the Blackhawks win 4-1 against the Anaheim Ducks.

AUGUST 16, 1996
The Blackhawks trade Jeremy Roenick to the Phoenix Coyotes for Alex Zhamnov, Craig Mills, and a 1997 first-round draft pick.

SEPTEMBER 14, 1996
In the third and final game of the inaugural World Cup of Hockey series, forward Tony Amonte scores the game-winning goal at 17:25 against Canada.

NOVEMBER 5, 1996
The Blackhawks' Executive Vice President Arthur Michael Wirtz, Jr. dies at the age of sixty-two.

FEBRUARY 22, 1996
Blackhawks winger Tony Amonte records the first hat trick in the United Center against the St. Louis Blues in the fifty-third game played at the arena.

NOVEMBER 30, 1996
Ed Belfour (below) earns his 200th career win in the Blackhawks' 5-3 victory against the Los Angeles Kings at the United Center. Tony Amonte leads the scoring with a hat trick.

FEBRUARY 15, 1997

For an afternoon game against Wayne Gretzky and the New York Rangers, a record Chicago hockey crowd of 22,819 turns out, and the Blackhawks respond with a 2-0 conquest.

APRIL 11, 1997

Alexei Zhamnov scores his fifth career hat trick in a 7-3 victory against the Calgary Flames at the United Center. Chicago qualifies for the playoffs for the twenty-eighth consecutive season, the longest active streak in professional sports.

JULY 30, 1997

Bob Murray is named general manager of the Blackhawks when Bob Pulford announces his retirement after twenty years with the team.

APRIL 18, 1998

The NHL's regular season ends and the Blackhawks fail to qualify for the Stanley Cup playoffs for the first time since 1969, ending a twenty-eight-year streak.

JULY 3, 1998

The Blackhawks sign free-agent center Doug Gilmour to a three-year, $18 million deal, the largest contract in Blackhawks history.

JUNE 24, 1999

The Blackhawks' Vice President Thomas N. Ivan dies at the age of eighty-eight.

SEPTEMBER 25, 2000

The Blackhawks' seventy-fifth anniversary.

MARCH 19, 1998

Before a game against the Montreal Canadiens, Denis Savard becomes the fifth Blackhawk to have his jersey retired. The entire ceremony is televised in English and French in Savard's hometown of Montreal, where he won a Stanley Cup as a member of the Canadiens in 1993. The popular No. 18 returned to Chicago to finish his active career, then joined the Blackhawks as an assistant coach in 1998.

LEFT WINGS

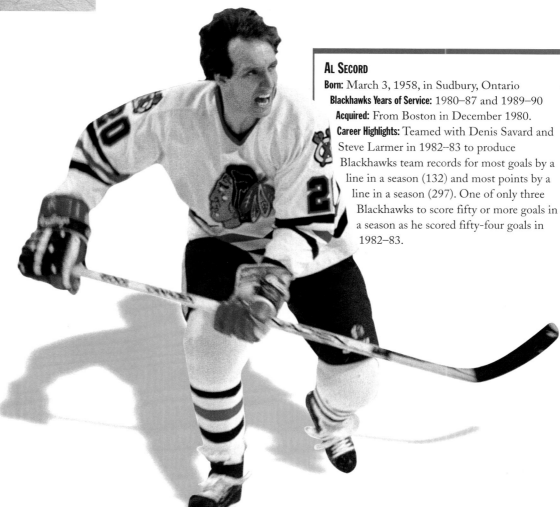

ROBERT MARVIN "BOBBY" HULL

Born: January 3, 1939, in Pointe Anne, Ontario
Blackhawks Years of Service: 1957–72
Acquired: From the St. Catherines Tee Pees (Jrs.) in 1957.
Career Highlights: Became the first player in the NHL to score more than fifty goals in a season. Is first on Blackhawks all-time goals scored list with 604 and second on Blackhawks all-time points scored list with 1,153 (in 1,036 games). Ranks seventh on NHL all-time goals scored list with 610.
Hockey Hall of Fame: Inducted in 1983.

DENNIS HULL

Born: November 19, 1944, in Pointe Anne, Ontario
Blackhawks Years of Service: 1964–77
Acquired: From the St. Catherines Tee Pees (Jrs.) in 1964.
Career Highlights: Ranks fifth on the Blackhawks all-time goals scored list with 298. Ranks tenth on the Blackhawks all-time assists list with 342. Ranks sixth on the Blackhawks all-time points list with 640. While his brother, Bobby, was known as "The Golden Jet," Dennis was known as "The Silver Jet."

AL SECORD

Born: March 3, 1958, in Sudbury, Ontario
Blackhawks Years of Service: 1980–87 and 1989–90
Acquired: From Boston in December 1980.
Career Highlights: Teamed with Denis Savard and Steve Larmer in 1982–83 to produce Blackhawks team records for most goals by a line in a season (132) and most points by a line in a season (297). One of only three Blackhawks to score fifty or more goals in a season as he scored fifty-four goals in 1982–83.

CENTERS

JEREMY ROENICK

Born: January 17, 1970, in Boston, Massachusetts
Blackhawks Years of Service: 1988–96
Acquired: First-round pick (eighth overall) by the Blackhawks in the 1988 entry draft.
Career Highlights: Was named by *The Sporting News* as NHL Rookie of the Year following the 1989–90 season. His fifty-three goals in the 1991–92 season broke a Blackhawks record (forty-seven) for most goals by a center; they also made him the third player in Blackhawks history to score more than fifty goals in a season.

DENIS SAVARD

Born: February 4, 1961, in Pointe Gatineau, Quebec
Blackhawks Years of Service: 1980–90 and 1995–1997
Acquired: First-round pick (third overall) by the Blackhawks in 1980 entry draft; reacquired from the Tampa Bay Lightning on April 6, 1995.
Career Highlights: Became only the second Blackhawk ever to score more than 100 points in a single season in 1981–82, and went on to accomplish the feat four more times. Holds the Blackhawks record for most points in a season (131 in 1987–88), most assists in a season (eighty-seven in 1981–82 and 1987–88), and most 100-point seasons (five).

STAN MIKITA

Born: May 20, 1940, in Sokolce, Czechoslavakia
Blackhawks Years of Service: 1958–80
Acquired: From the St. Catherines Tee Pees (Jrs.) in 1958.
Career Highlights: Ranks first in Blackhawks all-time games played with 1,394 in twenty-one seasons and first in Blackhawks all-time points scored with 1,467. Led all players in scoring in the 1961 playoffs as the Blackhawks took their third Stanley Cup. Became the first Blackhawk to have his number retired: October 19, 1980.
Hockey Hall of Fame: Inducted in 1983.

DEFENSEMEN

BILL WHITE

Born: August 26, 1939, in Toronto, Ontario

Blackhawks Years of Service: 1969–76

Acquired: From the Los Angeles Kings with Bryan Campbell and Gerry Desjardins on February 20, 1970.

Career Highlights: Made the second all-star team three seasons in a row, 1971–72, 1972–73, and 1973–74. Often described as the League's best defenseman during his career. Coached the Blackhawks during the 1976–77 season.

PIERRE PILOTE

Born: December 21, 1931, in Kenogami, Quebec

Blackhawks Years of Service: 1955–56 and 1956–68

Acquired: Broke into the NHL with Chicago in 1956 after serving his pro apprenticeship at Buffalo in the AHL.

Career Highlights: Never missed a game during his first five full seasons with the Blackhawks, but was finally forced out in 1962 with a shoulder separation. Voted to the NHL all-star teams eight consecutive seasons: second team, 1960–62, and first team, 1963–67.

Hockey Hall of Fame: Inducted in 1975.

CHRIS CHELIOS

Born: January 25, 1962, in Chicago, Illinois

Blackhawks Years of Service: 1990–99

Acquired: From Montreal with a second-round pick in 1991 for Denis Savard on June 29, 1990.

Career Highlights: Recorded twenty-one points in eighteen games to set a new club record for most points by a defenseman in one playoff year. His six-playoff goals also set a new club record for most goals in a playoff year by a defenseman. Led the team in scoring in 1995–96 with seventy-two points, becoming the first defenseman in team history to accomplish that feat.

The 2000–2001 hockey season will be a historic one for the storied Chicago Blackhawks franchise as it celebrates its seventy-fifth anniversary as a member of the National Hockey League. As part of that celebration, Blackhawks fans from around the world had an opportunity to select their all-time favorite Blackhawks team. The fan balloting began on January 14 and ran through April 30, 2000. The ballot consisted of ten players from each position: goaltenders, defensemen, centers, right wingers, and left wingers. The ballot also consisted of six coaches. Fans were asked to choose eighteen players, three players from each category, except for defensemen where they were asked to choose six. In the event that a player of their choice was not listed on the ballot, a space was provided for write-in votes. They were also asked to choose the three top coaches in Blackhawks history. Nearly a half-million ballots were cast by Blackhawks fans from around the world as their enthusiasm

proved once again why they are the greatest fans in all of sport.

Fan balloting was conducted online at www.chicagoblackhawks.com; at the United Center; the Edge Ice Arena, the Blackhawks practice facility in Bensenville; HawkQuarters at 333 North Michigan Avenue; in the *Chicago Sun-Times;* and in the *Red & White,* the official Blackhawks newsletter.

As usual, Blackhawks fans came through with flying colors in selecting an outstanding group of players who truly exemplify what playing for the Blackhawks is all about. The seventy-fifth anniversary team balloting has given fans an opportunity to debate who the all-time great Blackhawks players are. And while that debate will continue for years to come, we can certainly agree that this group of players is a dynamic lineup of extraordinarily talented individuals.

ANNIVERSARY ALL-STAR TEAM

ALWAYS AN ORIGINAL

1926

75TH ANNIVERSARY

RIGHT WINGS

HAROLD "MUSH" MARCH

Born: October 18, 1908, in Silton, Saskatchewan

Blackhawks Years of Service: 1928–45

Acquired: From the Regina Falcons (Jrs.) in 1928.

Career Highlights: Played his entire professional hockey career as a Blackhawk. Scored the first goal in the Maple Leaf Gardens on November 12, 1931. Scored the goal in sudden-death overtime that gave the Blackhawks their first Stanley Cup in 1934. Won his second Stanley Cup with the Blackhawks in 1938.

STEVE LARMER

Born: June 16, 1961, in Peterborough, Ontario

Blackhawks Years of Service: 1980–93

Acquired: Was the Blackhawks' sixth-round draft choice in the 1980 entry draft.

Career Highlights: His forty-three goals and ninety points during the 1982–83 season helped produce the highest scoring line in Blackhawks history with 297 points and the most goals by a line in a season with 132. Scored forty-four goals and added fifty-seven assists for 101 points in 1990–91. Holds the Blackhawks' "Iron Man" record having played in 884 consecutive games.

TONY AMONTE

Born: August 2, 1970, in Hingham, Massachusetts

Blackhawks Years of Service: 1994–present

Acquired: From the New York Rangers in 1994.

Career Highlights: Had been selected by *The Hockey News* as 1991–92 Rookie of the Year. Recorded the first hat trick in the United Center on January 22, 1996. Became the thirteenth Blackhawks player to score forty or more goals in a single season. Led the NHL in goal scoring over two seasons (1998–99 and 1999–2000) with eighty-seven.

COACHES

ROBERT J. PULFORD

Born: March 31, 1936, in Newton Robinson, Ontario

Blackhawks Years of Service: 1977–present

Career Highlights: Retired from play after 1972–73 season. Took on the responsibility as head coach of the Los Angeles Kings in 1972–73, and received the Jack Adams Award as "Coach of the Year" in 1975. Became the head coach and general manager of the Blackhawks in 1977. The Blackhawks made the playoffs in nineteen of the twenty seasons that Pulford was general manager and coach. Was elevated to the role of senior vice president in 1990.

Hockey Hall of Fame: Inducted in 1991.

WILLIAM "BILLY" REAY

Born: August 21, 1918, in Winnipeg, Manitoba

Blackhawks Years of Service: 1963–1977

Career Highlights: Began his hockey career as a forward for the Detroit Red Wings and later the Montreal Canadiens. Retired from active play following 1952–53 season. Joined the Blackhawks in 1963 as head coach and led the team through 1,012 games. Brought the team to six first-place finishes and three Stanley Cup finals. Received a Milestone Award from the NHL for coaching 542 victories in his NHL career. His 516 coaching wins as the coach of the Blackhawks is a team record.

MIKE KEENAN

Born: October 21, 1949, in Bowmanville, Ontario

Blackhawks Years of Service: 1988–92

Career Highlights: Took the Philadelphia Flyers to the Stanley Cup finals in 1985 and 1987, becoming the first coach in NHL history to win forty or more games in each of his first three seasons. Became the head coach of the Blackhawks and led them to the Presidents' Trophy in 1991 and the Stanley Cup finals in 1992.

During their last decade of the twentieth century, the Blackhawks iced some splendid teams, and were regarded throughout the NHL as a constant threat to seize another Stanley Cup. Unfortunately for the franchise and its fans, there were no Cups, but there were several close calls. The Blackhawks didn't beat the champions, but they badly bruised them.

In fact, the Blackhawks had a habit of producing some of their best hockey at the same time that other teams were just a shade better. In the 1989 Clarence Campbell Conference finals, for instance, the Blackhawks were eliminated by the Calgary Flames, who went on to win the Cup. In 1990, the Edmonton Oilers seized their fifth Stanley Cup, but not before surviving a gritty conference final against the Blackhawks. That felt similar to the sting of the 1980s, when Wayne Gretzky and the Oilers earned four Cups, but only after emerging from a conference that included the Blackhawks.

In the 1991 playoffs, the Blackhawks entered as favorites, having garnered the Presidents' Trophy for the best regular-season record in the entire league. The Blackhawks were upset by the Minnesota North Stars, who, in turn, advanced to the Stanley Cup finals. But in 1992, the Blackhawks showed their resilience with a brilliant playoff run that included eleven consecutive victories. Alas, once again, the Blackhawks encountered another dynasty. The Pittsburgh Penguins and star Mario Lemieux inherited the mantle as league powerhouse, and the Penguins won their second straight Cup by whipping the Blackhawks, who were left stranded at the altar once more.

During the mid-1990s, two other giants came to the fore—the Detroit Red Wings and Colorado Avalanche. Both were in the Blackhawks' conference, and both had to go through Chicago en route to bigger things. In 1995, the Red Wings won a taut conference final against the Blackhawks—three games went into overtime—to reach the Stanley Cup finals for the first time in three decades.

REBOUNDING CONFIDENCE

NATIONAL HOCKEY LEAGUE PRESIDENTS' TROPHY

Left: The Presidents' Trophy for the team finishing first place overall. Far left: Chris Chelios in classic form protecting the blue line on December 10, 1992, against his off-ice buddy and ex-Blackhawk Steve Thomas. Neither Chelios nor Thomas has his stick anywhere near the ice in a display of old-time hockey where open ice hits were delivered at the blue line by rugged defensemen like Blackhawks great Johnny Mariucci.

The next year, it was Colorado's turn to claim its first Stanley Cup, after a memorable conference playoff against the Blackhawks, who won two games in overtime and lost two in overtime. So, in a matter of a few short seasons, the Blackhawks missed out on the Stanley Cup, but they incurred defeat with honor against Edmonton, Calgary, Pittsburgh, Detroit, and Colorado. In fact, after Detroit managed to shake off the Blackhawks in 1995, only to be swept in the Cup final, the Red Wings cited their difficult and physical series against the Blackhawks as a reason for losing to New Jersey. The Blackhawks were fun to watch, but not fun to play.

Of course, the Blackhawks did a lot more than prepare opponents for Stanley Cup celebrations during the 1990s. The Blackhawks developed an entirely new cast of stars without missing a beat. Replenishing rosters on the fly is no simple task, but the Blackhawks were able to replace Denis Savard and Steve Larmer with the likes of Jeremy Roenick, a fearless forward who was discovered at Thayer Academy in New England, and Tony Amonte, a schoolboy pal of Roenick's in Massachusetts. Amonte was acquired from the New York Rangers and caught fire in Chicago. The Blackhawks also filled in when necessary with veterans such as Michel Goulet, one of the best natural scorers in NHL history. Goulet collected his landmark 500th goal with the Blackhawks on his way to the Hockey Hall of Fame.

The Blackhawks bowed to progress, too, with their emotional move from the Chicago Stadium after sixty-five years to the palatial United Center across the street. The relocation was placed on hold by a labor-management impasse that affected the league, but when the season began, the Blackhawks debuted against Edmonton in January 1995. Joe Murphy—another pretty fair sniper—scored the first goal at the United Center before a standing-room-only throng. The quaint and creaky Stadium would not be forgotten, but the Blackhawks' spectacular new arena quickly earned rave reviews for its conveniences and sightlines. All other hockey or basketball franchises pondering the construction of a new facility have regarded the United Center as a must-see. It has become one of the most popular, and most copied, buildings in North America.

As the 1999–2000 NHL season ended, the Blackhawks had reason to be optimistic about their immediate future. Although the Blackhawks missed the playoffs for a third consecutive year, they closed their regular schedule with a rush. In the last month or so of the season, no team wanted to meet up with the Blackhawks, who had knocked

Above: The puck used in the 1992 Stanley Cup games. Below: Tony Amonte, one of the fastest skaters in the game, was a genius for piercing the smallest opening in the net. Far right: Doug Gilmour, fully airborne, still scored the goal.

off in back-to-back games during the final weekend the defending Stanley Cup champion Dallas Stars, the talent-laden Detroit Red Wings, and the St. Louis Blues—the same Blues who earned the best record in the NHL throughout the eighty-two-game regular schedule.

"We will make the playoffs next season," promised Senior Vice President and Hall of Fame member Bob Pulford, who temporarily left his office in December to join head coach Lorne Molleken on the bench after the

Blackhawks endured a slow start. Molleken benefited greatly by learning from Pulford, and obviously the players did, too, as the team evolved into a unit with stability, consistency, and—last but not least—confidence.

In mid-season, the Blackhawks also took a major step to fortify their executive branch when they hired Mike Smith to become Manager of Hockey Operations. Smith has a keen eye for talent, and is credited with much of the success of the Toronto Maple Leafs, for whom he worked before coming to Chicago, and of the Phoenix Coyotes, who were the Winnipeg Jets when Smith helped build them into a league force.

Tony Amonte, one of the most prolific scorers in the league, broke the forty-goal mark for the second consecutive season and third in his last four. But the Blackhawks were blessed by a balanced offense that included five other players who tallied twenty goals or more each—Doug Gilmour, Steve Sullivan, Alex Zhamnov, Michael Nylander, and Eric Daze. Few other teams boasted such an array of top guns. Sullivan was acquired during the season from the Toronto Maple Leafs, as was Nylander

from the Tampa Bay Lightning, and by year's end, each was a valuable part of the team chemistry. Also, Boris Mironov, a gifted defenseman who started the season late, finished with a flourish. The Blackhawks also settled down with their tandem of goalkeepers, Jocelyn Thibault and Steve Passmore.

By fielding a contending team that qualified for the playoffs from 1970 through 1997, a remarkable string of successes, the Blackhawks invariably paid a price for their good fortune. Like any other franchise in professional sports, the Blackhawks would prefer it if their best players never grew old. But that's obviously not feasible, and so it is the chore of all teams to restock talent pools through the draft of college or junior players. However, there are caveats to that process. The lower a team finishes in the overall standings, the higher it may draft young players each off-season. By employing this inverse order, the league strives for balance. All franchises fall victim at one time or another to the downside of posting winning records season after season.

In 1999–2000, for the first time in history, only two of the Original Six teams—Detroit and Toronto—made the playoffs. Conversely, when the Blackhawks were challenging for the Stanley Cup during the 1980s and early 1990s, the Red Wings and the Maple Leafs were down and out and in a rebuilding mode. The Colorado Avalanche won the Stanley Cup in 1996, but during the 1989–90 season while operating as the Quebec Nordiques, they won just twelve of eighty games! The Penguins, who ruled the early 1990s, missed the playoffs for six of the previous seven seasons before achieving greatness.

There is no easy way around it. While the Blackhawks were winning all those games during those wildly entertaining winters, they faced the flip side of the equation every spring by drafting low and late, after the best young prospects had been snagged by teams that achieved less and required more help. Only once during the 1990s did the Blackhawks select from among the top ten. In 1987, when they selected eighth, they grabbed Roenick.

However, what goes up comes down, and the corollary is also true. If you've read these pages, you know that history has not always been kind to the Blackhawks, but the Blackhawks have rebounded from much more ominous circumstances. In the early 1950s, the Blackhawks lacked a fan base, financial wherewithal, and a plan. There is no such scenario now. Given the continuity and commitment of their ownership and the loyalty of their fans, the Chicago Blackhawks have reason to be optimistic about the 2000–2001 season. And the team has shown every sign of upward mobility heading into the new century.

Far left: Alex Zhamnov, a former Moscow Dynamo and a Canada Cup and Olympic star, who joined the Blackhawks in 1996–97. The alternate captain portrays perfect form: crouched low, rear knee fully bent, skate blades digging into the ice, and eyes firmly on target. Left: Chicago's beloved Eddie Olczyk, who was the Blackhawks' first-round pick in the 1984 draft and who has the distinction of having played his first and his thousandth NHL game as a Blackhawk.

106 POINTS IN 1991

The 1990–91 Blackhawks accomplished a feat no other team in franchise history has: winning the Presidents' Trophy, which since 1986 has been awarded for the best regular-season record in the NHL. Under Coach Mike Keenan, there was a steady progression from sixty-six points in 1988–89 to eighty-eight points in 1989–90, and 106 in 1990–91, gleaned from a franchise-high forty-nine victories, only twenty-three defeats, and eight ties. Only two teams in Blackhawk annals, 1970–71 and 1971–72, amassed more points (107).

However, the 1990–91 Blackhawks by no means cruised to first place in the Norris Division. They were pushed to the end by the St. Louis Blues, who finished second with 105 points, the league's second-best mark.

The 1990–91 team was deep and well balanced. Steve Larmer, a superlative two-way winger, led the offense with forty-four goals and fifty-seven assists for 101 points. Jeremy Roenick added forty-one goals and fifty-three assists. Michel Goulet (twenty-seven goals), Dirk Graham (twenty-four), and Adam Creighton (twenty-two) contributed to the attack. The Blackhawks

were also the stingiest team in the league, yielding just 211 goals, thirty-nine fewer than St. Louis. Ed Belfour, the workhorse goalie, played seventy-four games and posted a sparkling 2.47 goals against average. He was in the net for all five Chicago wins against St. Louis (against two losses and one tie) in pivotal head-to-head meetings with the Blues.

The defense was anchored by Chicago-born Chris Chelios, who was playing his first season with the Blackhawks after being acquired from Montreal. Doug Wilson, one of the best defensemen in Blackhawks history, again was a valuable asset, despite missing twenty-five games with an ankle injury. Dave Manson and Bob McGill provided toughness on the blue line, and Steve Konroyd was reliable in a stay-at-home role. Also, the roster was liberally sprinkled with quality veterans such as Troy Murray, Greg Gilbert, Wayne Presley, and Steve Thomas.

After a grueling regular schedule, however, the Blackhawks took some ill-advised penalties in their first playoff series against the Minnesota North Stars, who eliminated Chicago, four games to two. The success of

the North Stars, who finished fourth in the Norris Division, was no fluke. They upset St. Louis in the second round and the Edmonton Oilers in the Clarence Campbell Conference finals, losing only three games along the way before being whipped in the Stanley Cup finals by the Pittsburgh Penguins.

It's a merry day after Christmas as the Blackhawks battle the Penguins at the United Center on December 26, 1999. Darius Kasparaitis, the Penguins' in-your-face resident bad boy, gets a dose of his own medicine from Blackhawks heavyweight champ Bob Probert, whose fistful of glove sends him sprawling to the ice.

RIVALRIES

Below: Action-packed drama plays out as emotions run high during a game between the Leafs and Blackhawks. Far right: Chris Chelios takes a bite out of a body-slamming Bruin in an altercation along the boards.

Mirror, mirror on the wall, who's the Blackhawks' fiercest rival of them all? That's a tough call. It depends on the eyes and ears of the beholder. One could certainly make a case for any of the other five teams from the Original Six. The Blackhawks have met the Montreal Canadiens in seventeen different playoff series since 1930, and the Canadiens have won all but five. A few of those Montreal triumphs really hurt, too. But expansion and realignment have altered the frequency with which establishment franchises meet. The Blackhawks, for instance, didn't visit New York's Madison Square Garden once last season. Based on geography, the most visceral games the Blackhawks play might be those against the Detroit Red Wings.

The Blackhawks didn't qualify for the playoffs in 1999–2000, but they still won the regular-season series from Detroit.

Some of the Blackhawks' angriest games during the 1980s were against the Minnesota North Stars, who have since moved to Dallas. The St. Louis Blues always seem to get up for the Blackhawks, and vice versa. The Blackhawks and the Colorado Avalanche staged two terrific playoff series during the mid-1990s: twelve games total, five in overtime. Some of the best Blackhawks teams a few years ago seemed to run up against the Edmonton Oilers every spring, and the Oilers have five Stanley Cups. When the Oilers finally cooled off, the Blackhawks had to deal with the Pittsburgh Penguins, who claimed successive Stanley Cups, one after sweeping Chicago in the finals.

So, it's a dealer's choice. But if you want to elicit a little extra feeling from the Blackhawks and their fans, you probably can't go wrong by inviting the Detroit Red Wings and their fans to the United Center. Regardless of whether the teams are up or down, you can bet they'll try to knock each other sideways.

WEARING IT PROUDLY

The Blackhawks uniform is without equal in the world of hockey. No team in the NHL even comes close to it. The red and white stripes at the elbows and around the waist, the tomahawk patch on the arm, and the Indian-head logo across the chest: the Blackhawks' jersey is one of the most colorful and distinctive jerseys in professional sports.

The original uniforms designed by Major McLaughlin were funeral black. For the 1935–36 season, McLaughlin's then wife, Irene Castle, a famous dancer from the 1920s, hired a Hollywood stylist to enliven the uniform in art-deco style. This style quickly yielded to the more familiar barber-pole uniform.

While the uniform has changed considerably over the years, the team's logo has not. The exact origin of the Indian head itself is murky. Some believe Irene Castle contributed to its design, while others believe it was created from a sketch by McLaughlin, but there is simply no evidence to know either way. Whatever its origins, the Indian head has remained a central icon on the Blackhawks' uniform and in its spirit.

The biggest change in the logo came in the 1954–55 season. Previously, the Indian head appeared as a crest circumscribed by the words "Black Hawks Chicago."

(The name was written as two words until the 1986–87 season when William Wirtz had it changed to one word after he noticed it was written that way in the original 1926 charter.) The crest and the words were dropped, leaving only the Indian head (remade much larger), and the arm patches with the crossed tomahawks were added. This redesign was made by Dorothy Ivan, the wife of Tommy Ivan. Tiny modifications to the Indian head itself have been made from year to year, such as changing the colors of the feathers or slightly altering the facial expression, but for the most part, the icon has remained the same as it was in the beginning.

The Indian head is, of course, emblematic of Black Hawk (Indian name, Ma-ka-tai-me-she-kia-kiak), the Sauk Indian leader, who lived from 1767 to 1838 and who valiantly defended Sauk and Fox lands along the Rock River in Illinois, siding with the British in the War of 1812. While the team name is twice removed from its original source (Major McLaughlin named the team after his World War I army division), the logo has come to represent perseverance, tenacity, and courage—all characteristics of the hockey team that shares the famous Sauk chief's name.

No other team wears its uniform and logo with more pride than the Chicago Blackhawks. The Indian-head logo inspires great loyalty in its players, and has earned its reputation as what Keith Magnuson has called, with classic Blackhawks pride, "the greatest trademark in the world."

Far right: For a Chicago hockey player or a Chicago hockey fan, the ultimate compliment is, "He's got the Indian head tattooed on his heart." There is a certain mystique about Chief Black Hawk. This sweater was worn in 1942–43 by the "Dipsy-Doodle-Dandy" Max Bentley, one of the best stick-handlers ever to skate in the NHL. Below: An arm patch depicting the logo worn by the Black Hawk Battalion.

BLACKHAWKS JERSEYS

DOUG BENTLEY'S JERSEY, 1947—48

EARL SEIBERT'S JERSEY, 1935—36

ROY CONACHER'S JERSEY, 1953—54

THE STAT BOX

CHICAGO BLACKHAWKS ALL-STARS

Since 1930—31, the Professional Hockey Writers Association has named an all-star team at the end of each National Hockey League season. The following Blackhawks were named to these all-star teams.

FIRST TEAM

GOALTENDER

CHARLIE GARDINER	1931, 1932, 1934
LORNE CHABOT	1935
GLENN HALL	1958, 1960, 1963, 1964, 1966
TONY ESPOSITO	1970, 1972, 1980
ED BELFOUR	1991, 1993

DEFENSEMAN

LIONEL CONACHER	1934
EARL SEIBERT	1942, 1943, 1944
PIERRE PILOTE	1963, 1964, 1965, 1966, 1967
DOUG WILSON	1982
CHRIS CHELIOS	1993, 1995, 1996

CENTER

MAX BENTLEY	1946
STAN MIKITA	1962, 1963, 1964
	1966, 1967, 1968

LEFT WING

PAUL THOMPSON	1938
DOUG BENTLEY	1943, 1944, 1947
ROY CONACHER	1949
BOBBY HULL	1960, 1962, 1964, 1965, 1966,
	1967, 1968, 1969, 1970, 1972

RIGHT WING

KEN WHARRAM	1964, 1967

COACH

PAUL THOMPSON	1940

SECOND TEAM

GOALTENDER

CHARLIE GARDINER	1933
MIKE KARAKAS	1945
GLENN HALL	1961, 1962, 1967
TONY ESPOSITO	1973, 1974
ED BELFOUR	1995

DEFENSEMAN

ART COULTER	1935
EARL SEIBERT	1936, 1937, 1938, 1939, 1940, 1941
BILL GADSBY	1953, 1954
PIERRE PILOTE	1960, 1961, 1962
ELMER VASKO	1963—64
PAT STAPLETON	1966, 1971, 1972
BILL WHITE	1972, 1973, 1974
DOUG WILSON	1985, 1990
CHRIS CHELIOS	1991, 1997

CENTER

MAX BENTLEY	1947
DOUG BENTLEY	1949
ED LITZENBERGER	1957
STAN MIKITA	1965, 1970
DENIS SAVARD	1983

LEFT WING

PAUL THOMPSON	1936
JOHN GOTTSELIG	1939
GAYE STEWART	1948
BOBBY HULL	1963, 1971
DENNIS HULL	1973

RIGHT WING

BILL MOSIENKO	1945, 1946
BUD POILE	1948

COACH

DICK IRVIN	1931
JOHN GOTTSELIG	1946

BLACKHAWKS MEMBERS IN THE HOCKEY HALL OF FAME

PLAYER	SEASON	YEAR INDUCTED
SID ABEL	1952—53	1969
DOUG BENTLEY	1939—52	1964
MAX BENTLEY	1940—48	1966
GEORGE BOUCHER	1931—32	1960
FRANK BRIMSEK	1949—50	1966
WILLIAM BURCH	1932—33	1974
ART COULTER	1931—36	1974
CECIL "BABE" DYE	1926—27	1970
ANTHONY ESPOSITO	1969—84	1988
PHIL ESPOSITO	1963—67	1984
BILL GADSBY	1946—54	1970
CHARLES GARDINER	1927—34	1945
MICHEL GOULET	1990—94	1998
GLENN HALL	1957—67	1975
GEORGE HAY	1926—27	1958
BOBBY HULL	1957—72	1983
DICK IRVIN	1926—29	1958
GORDON "DUKE" KEATS	1928—29	1958
HUGH LEHMAN	1926—28	1958
TED LINDSAY	1957—60	1966
HARRY LUMLEY	1951—52	1980
DUNCAN MACKAY	1926—28	1952
STAN MIKITA	1958—80	1983
HOWIE MORENZ	1934—36	1945
BILL MOSIENKO	1941—55	1965
BERT OLMSTEAD	1948—51	1985
BOBBY ORR	1976—78	1979
PIERRE PILOTE	1955—68	1975
EARL SEIBERT	1936—44	1963
ALLAN STANLEY	1954—56	1981
JOHN STEWART	1950—52	1964

VETERAN	SEASON	YEAR INDUCTED
LIONEL CONACHER	1933—34	1994
ROY CONACHER	1947—52	1998
CLINT SMITH	1943—46	1991
HARRY WATSON	1954—57	1994

BUILDER		YEAR INDUCTED
AL ARBOUR		1996
THOMAS N. IVAN		1974
JOHN MARIUCCI		1985
FREDERIC MCLAUGHLIN		1963
JAMES D. NORRIS		1962
JAMES NORRIS		1958
RUDY PILOUS		1985
BUD POILE		1990
ARTHUR WIRTZ		1971
WILLIAM WIRTZ		1976

BLACKHAWKS MEMBERS IN THE U.S. HOCKEY HALL OF FAME

PLAYER	SEASON	YEAR INDUCTED
CLARENCE ABEL	1929—34	1973
FRANK BRIMSEK	1949—50	1973
CARL DAHLSTROM	1937—45	1973
VICTOR DESJARDINS	1930—31	1974
VICTOR HEYLIGER	1937—43	1974
VIRGIL JOHNSON	1937—45	1974
MICHAEL KARAKAS	1935—46	1973
SAM LOPRESTI	1940—42	1973
JOHN MARIUCCI	1940—48	1973
FIDO PURPUR	1941—45	1974
DOC ROMNES	1930—38	1973

COACH	SEASON	YEAR INDUCTED
WILLIAM J. STEWART	1937—39	1982

ADMINISTRATOR		YEAR INDUCTED
WILLIAM W. WIRTZ		1984

BLACKHAWKS ALL-TIME COACHING RECORDS

	REGULAR SEASON						CUP		
COACH	GAMES	WON	LOST	TIED	RT*	PCT.	WINS	SEA.	YEARS
BILL REAY	1012	516	335	161	—	.589	0	14	1963—77
BOB PULFORD	433	185	180	68	—	.506	0	7	1977—00
RUDY PILOUS	387	162	151	74	—	.514	1	6	1957—63
MIKE KEENAN	320	153	126	41	—	.542	0	4	1988—92
DARRYL SUTTER	216	110	80	26	—	.569	0	3	1992—95
CRAIG HARTSBURG	246	104	102	40	—	.504	0	3	1995—98
PAUL THOMPSON	272	104	127	41	—	.458	0	7	1938—45
ORVAL TESSIER	213	99	93	21	—	.514	0	3	1982—85
JOHN GOTTSELIG	187	62	105	20	—	.388	0	4	1944—48
CLEM LOUGHLIN	144	61	63	20	—	.493	0	3	1934—37
CHARLES CONACHER	162	56	84	22	—	.414	0	3	1948—50
KEITH MAGNUSON	132	49	57	26	—	.470	0	2	1980—82
DICK IRVIN	119	46	57	16	—	.454	0	2	1930—32
SID ABEL	140	39	79	22	—	.357	0	2	1952—54
EDDIE JOHNSTON	80	34	27	19	—	.544	0	1	1979—80
BOB MURDOCH	80	30	41	9	—	.413	0	1	1987—88
EBBIE GOODFELLOW	140	30	91	19	—	.282	0	2	1950—52
TOM GORMAN	73	28	28	17	—	.500	1	1	1933—34
BILL TOBIN	66	26	28	12	—	.485	0	3	1929—32
TOMMY IVAN	103	26	56	21	—	.354	0	2	1956—58
BILL STEWART	69	22	35	12	—	.406	1	2	1937—39
PETER MULDOON	44	19	22	3	—	.466	0	1	1926—27
LORNE MOLLEKEN	47	18	21	8	2	.489	0	2	1998—00
BILL WHITE	46	16	24	6	—	.413	0	1	1976—77
DIRK GRAHAM	59	16	35	8	—	.339	0	1	1998—99
FRANK EDDOLLS	70	13	40	17	—	.307	0	1	1954—55
TOM SHAUGHNESSY	21	10	8	3	—	.548	0	1	1929—30
EMIL IVERSON	21	8	7	6	—	.523	0	1	1932—33
HERB GARDINER	44	7	29	8	—	.250	0	1	1928—29
BARNEY STANLEY	23	4	17	2	—	.217	0	1	1927—28
HUGH LEHMAN	21	3	17	1	—	.167	0	1	1927—28
GODFREY MATHESON	2	0	2	0	—	.000	0	1	1932—33
TOTALS	4992	2056	2167	769	2	.489	3	74	

*Regulation Ties (RTs) were introduced by the NHL for the 1999—2000 season. Teams receive one point in the standings for each overtime loss.

REGULAR-SEASON TEAM MILESTONES

GAMES PLAYED	4,992	GOALS FOR	15,022
WINS	2,056	GOALS AGAINST	15,196
LOSSES	2,167	SHUTOUTS FOR	347
TIES	769	SHUTOUTS AGAINST	345
REGULATION TIES	2		

MILESTONE	DATE	OPPONENT	SCORE
1ST WIN	NOVEMBER 17, 1926	VS. TORONTO	4-1
100TH WIN	DECEMBER 8, 1932	VS. DETROIT	3-1
250TH WIN	JANUARY 7, 1941	AT NY RANGERS	3-2
500TH WIN	DECEMBER 20, 1953	VS. TORONTO	4-1
750TH WIN	JANUARY 23, 1964	AT BOSTON	3-1
1,000TH WIN	DECEMBER 2, 1970	VS. BOSTON	4-3
1,250TH WIN	JANUARY 30, 1977	VS. CLEVELAND	9-3
1,500TH WIN	NOVEMBER 17, 1984	AT HARTFORD	7-0
1,750TH WIN	OCTOBER 31, 1991	VS. NY ISLANDERS	4-3
2,000TH WIN	NOVEMBER 29, 1998	AT EDMONTON	3-2

BLACKHAWKS GOALTENDERS YEAR BY YEAR

YEAR	PLAYER	GP	W	L	T	MINS	GA	SO	AVG
1926–27	HUGH LEHMAN	44	19	22	3	2,797	116	5	2.49
1927–28	CHARLES GARDINER	40	6	32	2	2,420	114	3	2.83
	HUGH LEHMAN	4	1	2	1	250	20	1	4.80
1928–29	CHARLES GARDINER	44	7	29	8	2,758	85	5	1.85
1929–30	CHARLES GARDINER	44	21	18	5	2,750	111	3	2.42
1930–31	CHARLES GARDINER	44	24	17	3	2,710	78	12	1.72
1931–32	CHARLES GARDINER	48	18	18	11	2,989	92	4	1.85
	WILF CUDE	1	0	1	0	41	9	0	13.17
1932–33	CHARLES GARDINER	48	16	20	12	3,010	101	5	2.01
1933–34	CHARLES GARDINER	48	20	17	11	3,050	83	10	1.63
1934–35	LORNE CHABOT	48	26	17	5	2,940	88	8	1.80
1935–36	MIKE KARAKAS	48	21	19	8	2,990	92	9	1.85
1936–37	MIKE KARAKAS	48	14	27	7	2,978	131	5	2.64
1937–38	MIKE KARAKAS	48	14	25	9	2,980	139	1	2.80
1938–39	MIKE KARAKAS	48	12	28	8	2,998	132	5	2.65
1939–40	PAUL GOODMAN	31	16	10	5	1,920	62	4	1.94
	MIKE KARAKAS	17	7	9	1	1,050	58	0	3.31
1940–41	PAUL GOODMAN	21	7	10	4	1,320	55	2	2.50
	SAM LOPRESTI	27	9	15	3	1,670	84	1	3.02
1941–42	BILL DICKIE	1	1	0	0	60	3	0	3.00
	SAM LOPRESTI	47	21	23	3	2,860	152	3	3.19
1942–43	BERT GARDINER	50	17	18	15	3,020	180	1	3.58
1943–44	MIKE KARAKAS	26	12	9	5	1,560	79	3	3.04
	HEC HIGHTON	24	10	14	0	1,440	108	0	4.50
1944–45	MIKE KARAKAS	48	12	29	7	2,880	187	4	3.90
	DOUG STEVENSON	2	1	1	0	120	7	0	3.50
1945–46	MIKE KARAKAS	48	22	19	7	2,880	166	1	3.46
	DOUG STEVENSON	2	1	1	0	120	12	0	6.00
1946–47	PAUL BIBEAULT	41	13	25	3	2,460	170	1	4.15
	EMILE FRANCIS	19	6	12	1	1,140	104	0	5.47
1947–48	EMILE FRANCIS	54	18	31	5	3,240	183	1	3.39
	DOUG JACKSON	6	2	3	1	360	42	0	7.00
1948–49	JIM HENRY	60	21	31	8	3,600	211	0	3.52
1949–50	FRANK BRIMSEK	70	22	38	10	4,200	244	5	3.49
1950–51	HARRY LUMLEY	64	12	41	10	3,785	246	3	3.90
	MARCEL PELLETIER	6	1	5	0	355	29	0	4.90
	RALPH ALMAS	1	0	1	0	60	5	0	5.00
1951–52	HARRY LUMLEY	70	17	44	9	4,180	241	2	3.46
	MOE ROBERTS	1	0	0	0	20	0	0	0.00
1952–53	AL ROLLINS	70	27	28	15	4,200	175	6	2.50
1953–54	AL ROLLINS	66	12	47	7	3,960	213	5	3.23
	JEAN MAROIS	2	0	2	0	120	11	0	5.50
	JOHN GELINEAU	2	0	2	0	120	18	0	9.00
1954–55	AL ROLLINS	44	9	27	8	2,640	150	0	3.41
	HANK BASSEN	21	4	9	8	1,260	63	0	3.00
	RAY FREDERICK	5	0	4	1	300	22	0	4.40
1955–56	AL ROLLINS	58	17	30	11	3,480	174	3	3.00
	HANK BASSEN	12	2	9	1	720	42	1	3.50
1956–57	AL ROLLINS	70	16	39	15	4,200	225	3	3.21
1957–58	GLENN HALL	70	24	39	7	4,200	202	7	2.89
1958–59	GLENN HALL	70	28	29	13	4,200	208	1	2.97
1959–60	GLENN HALL	70	28	29	13	4,200	180	6	2.57
1960–61	GLENN HALL	70	29	24	17	4,200	180	6	2.57
1961–62	GLENN HALL	70	31	26	13	4,200	186	9	2.66
1962–63	GLENN HALL	66	30	20	15	3,910	166	5	2.55
	DENIS DEJORDY	5	2	1	2	290	12	0	2.48
1963–64	GLENN HALL	65	34	19	11	3,860	148	7	2.30
	DENIS DEJORDY	6	2	3	1	340	19	0	3.35
1964–65	GLENN HALL	41	18	17	5	2,440	99	4	2.57
	DENIS DEJORDY	30	16	11	3	1,760	74	3	2.52
1965–66	GLENN HALL	63	34	21	7	3,747	164	4	2.61
	DAVE DRYDEN	11	3	4	1	453	23	0	3.10
1966–67	DENIS DEJORDY	44	22	12	7	2,536	104	4	2.71
	GLENN HALL	32	19	5	5	1,664	66	2	2.38
1967–68	DENIS DEJORDY	50	23	15	11	2,981	128	4	3.14
	DAVE DRYDEN	27	7	8	5	1,268	69	1	3.26
	JACK NORRIS	7	2	3	0	334	22	1	3.95
1968–69	DENIS DEJORDY	53	22	22	7	2,981	156	2	3.14
	DAVE DRYDEN	30	11	11	2	1,479	79	3	3.32
	JACK NORRIS	3	1	0	0	100	10	0	6.00
1969–70	TONY ESPOSITO	63	38	17	8	3,763	136	15	2.17
	GERRY DESJARDINS	4	4	0	0	240	8	0	2.00
	DENIS DEJORDY	10	3	5	1	557	25	0	2.69
1970–71	TONY ESPOSITO	57	35	14	7	3,325	126	6	2.27
	GERRY DESJARDINS	22	12	6	2	1,217	49	0	2.42
	GILLES MELOCHE	2	2	0	0	120	6	0	3.00
	KEN BROWN	1	0	0	0	18	1	0	3.33
1971–72	TONY ESPOSITO	48	31	10	6	2,780	82	9	1.77
	GARY SMITH	28	14	5	6	1,540	62	5	2.42
	GERRY DESJARDINS	6	1	2	3	360	21	0	3.53
1972–73	TONY ESPOSITO	56	32	17	7	3,340	140	4	2.51
	GARY SMITH	23	10	10	2	1,340	79	0	3.54

YEAR	PLAYER	GP	W	L	T	MINS	GA	SO	AVG
1973–74	TONY ESPOSITO	70	34	14	21	4,143	141	10	2.04
	MIKE VEISOR	10	7	0	2	537	20	1	2.23
1974–75	TONY ESPOSITO	71	34	30	7	4,219	193	6	2.74
	MICHEL DUMAS	3	2	0	0	121	7	0	3.47
	MIKE VEISOR	9	1	5	1	460	36	0	4.70
1975–76	TONY ESPOSITO	68	30	23	13	4,003	198	4	2.97
	GILLES VILLEMURE	15	2	7	5	797	57	0	4.29
1976–77	TONY ESPOSITO	69	25	36	8	4,067	234	2	3.45
	MICHEL DUMAS	5	0	1	2	241	17	0	4.23
	MIKE VEISOR	3	1	2	0	180	13	0	4.33
	GILLES VILLEMURE	6	0	4	1	312	28	0	5.38
1977–78	MIKE VEISOR	12	3	4	5	720	31	2	2.58
	TONY ESPOSITO	64	28	22	14	3,840	168	5	2.63
	ED JOHNSTON	4	1	3	0	240	17	0	4.25
1978–79	TONY ESPOSITO	63	24	28	11	3,780	206	4	3.27
	MIKE VEISOR	17	5	8	4	1,020	60	0	3.53
1979–80	TONY ESPOSITO	69	31	22	16	4,140	205	6	2.97
	MIKE VEISOR	11	3	5	3	660	37	0	3.36
1980–81	TONY ESPOSITO	66	29	23	14	3,935	246	0	3.75
	MURRAY BANNERMAN	15	2	10	2	865	62	0	4.30
1981–82	TONY ESPOSITO	52	19	25	8	3,069	231	1	4.52
	MURRAY BANNERMAN	29	11	12	4	1,671	116	1	4.17
	WARREN SKORODENSKI	1	0	1	0	60	5	0	5.00
1982–83	TONY ESPOSITO	39	23	11	5	2,340	135	1	3.46
	MURRAY BANNERMAN	41	24	12	5	2,460	127	4	3.10
1983–84	MURRAY BANNERMAN	56	23	29	4	3,335	188	2	3.38
	TONY ESPOSITO	18	5	10	3	1,095	88	1	4.82
1984–85	MURRAY BANNERMAN	60	27	25	4	3,371	215	0	3.83
	WARREN SKORODENSKI	27	11	9	3	1,396	75	2	3.22
	DARREN PANG	1	0	1	0	60	4	0	4.00
	CHRIS CLIFFORD	1	0	0	0	20	0	0	0.00
1985–86	MURRAY BANNERMAN	48	20	19	6	2,689	201	1	4.48
	BOB SAUVE	38	19	13	2	2,099	138	0	3.94
	WARREN SKORODENSKI	1	0	1	0	60	6	0	6.00
1986–87	BOB SAUVE	46	19	19	5	2,660	159	1	3.59
	MURRAY BANNERMAN	39	9	18	8	2,059	142	0	4.14
	WARREN SKORODENSKI	3	1	0	1	155	7	0	2.71
1987–88	DARREN PANG	45	17	23	1	2,548	163	0	3.84
	BOB MASON	41	13	18	8	2,312	160	0	4.15
1988–89	ALAIN CHEVRIER	27	13	11	2	1,573	92	0	3.51
	DARREN PANG	35	10	11	6	1,644	120	0	4.38
	ED BELFOUR	23	4	12	3	1,148	74	0	3.87
	JIM WAITE	11	0	7	1	494	43	0	5.22
	CHRIS CLIFFORD	1	0	0	0	4	0	0	0.00
1989–90	JACQUES CLOUTIER	43	18	15	2	2,178	112	2	3.09
	GREG MILLEN	10	5	4	1	575	32	0	3.34
	ALAIN CHEVRIER	39	16	14	3	1,894	132	0	4.18
	JIM WAITE	4	2	0	0	183	14	0	4.59
1990–91	ED BELFOUR	74	43	19	7	4,127	170	4	2.47
	JACQUES CLOUTIER	10	2	3	0	403	24	0	3.57
	JIM WAITE	1	0	0	0	60	2	0	2.00
	DOMINIK HASEK	5	3	0	1	195	8	0	2.46
	GREG MILLEN	3	0	1	0	58	4	0	4.14
1991–92	ED BELFOUR	52	21	18	10	2,928	132	5	2.70
	DOMINIK HASEK	20	10	4	1	1,014	44	1	2.60
	JIMMY WAITE	17	4	7	4	877	54	0	3.69
	RAY LEBLANC	1	1	0	0	60	1	0	1.00
1992–93	ED BELFOUR	71	41	18	11	4,106	177	7	2.59
	JIMMY WAITE	20	6	7	1	996	49	2	2.95
1993–94	ED BELFOUR	70	37	24	6	3,998	178	7	2.67
	JEFF HACKETT	22	2	12	3	1,084	62	0	3.43
	CHRISTIAN SOUCY	1	0	0	0	3	0	0	0.00
1994–95	ED BELFOUR	42	22	15	3	2,450	93	5	2.28
	JEFF HACKETT	7	1	3	2	328	13	0	2.38
	JIMMY WAITE	2	1	1	0	119	5	0	2.52
1995–96	ED BELFOUR	50	22	17	10	2,956	135	1	2.74
	JEFF HACKETT	35	18	11	4	2,000	80	4	2.40
	JIMMY WAITE	1	0	0	0	31	0	0	0.00
1996–97	ED BELFOUR	33	11	15	6	1,966	88	1	2.69
	JEFF HACKETT	41	19	18	4	2,473	89	2	2.16
	CHRIS TERRERI	7	4	1	2	429	19	0	2.66
	JIMMY WAITE	2	0	1	1	105	7	0	4.00
1997–98	JEFF HACKETT	58	21	25	11	3,441	126	8	2.20
	CHRIS TERRERI	21	8	10	2	1,222	49	2	2.41
	ANDREI TREFILOV	6	1	4	0	299	17	0	3.41
1998–99	JEFF HACKETT	10	2	6	1	524	33	0	3.78
	JOCELYN THIBAULT	52	21	26	5	3,014	136	4	2.71
	MARK FITZPATRICK	27	6	8	6	1,403	64	0	2.74
	ANDREI TREFILOV	1	0	1	0	20	4	0	9.60
1999–2000	STEVE PASSMORE	24	7	12	3	1,388	63	1	2.72
	JOCELYN THIBAULT	60	25	26	7	3,438	158	3	2.76
	MARC LAMOTHE	2	1	1	0	116	10	0	5.17

Chicago Blackhawks Year-by-Year Player Statistics 1926–27 Through 1999–2000

1926–27	GP	G	A	PTS	PIM
IRVIN, DICK	43	18	18	36	34
DYE, CECIL	41	25	5	30	14
MACKAY, MICKEY	34	14	8	22	23
HAY, GEORGE	35	14	8	22	12
FRASER, GORDON	44	14	6	20	89
MCVEIGH, CHARLES	43	12	4	16	23
WILSON, CULLY	39	8	4	12	40
TRAPP, BOB	44	4	2	6	92
RODDEN, EDDIE	19	3	3	6	0
DUTKOWSKI, DUKE	34	3	2	5	22
TRAUB, PERCY	37	0	2	2	93
RILEY, JACK	15	0	2	2	14
TOWNSEND, ART	4	0	0	0	0
MCFARLANE, GORDON	1	0	0	0	0
DORATY, KEN	20	0	0	0	0
LEHMAN, HUGH	44	0	0	0	0

1927–28	GP	G	A	PTS	PIM
KEATS, DUKE	32	14	8	22	55
MACKAY, MICKEY	36	17	4	21	23
MCVEIGH, CHARLES	39	6	7	13	10
ARBOUR, ERNEST	32	5	5	10	32
WENTWORTH, MARVIN	43	5	5	10	31
IRVIN, DICK	12	5	4	9	14
DENNENY, CORBETT	18	5	0	5	12
BROWNE, CECIL	12	2	0	2	4
MCCALMON, EDDIE	21	2	0	2	8
MILLER, EARL	21	1	1	2	32
TAYLOR, RALPH	22	1	1	2	39
MORAN, AMBY	21	1	1	2	14
FRASER, GORDON	11	1	1	2	10
TRAPP, BOB	34	0	2	2	37
RODDEN, ED	9	0	2	2	6
GRAHAM, TEDDY	19	1	0	1	8
WASNIE, NICK	15	1	0	1	22
LAFRANCE, LEO	14	1	0	1	4
HOFFINGER, VIC	15	0	1	1	18
STANLEY, BARNEY	2	0	0	0	0
DYE, CECIL	10	0	0	0	0
GARDINER, CHARLES	40	0	0	0	0
LEHMAN, HUGH	4	0	0	0	0

1928–29	GP	G	A	PTS	PIM
RIPLEY, VIC	39	11	2	13	31
GOTTSELIG, JOHN	44	5	3	8	26
IRVIN, DICK	39	6	1	7	30
ARBOUR, ERNEST	44	3	4	7	32
MARCH, HAROLD	35	3	3	6	6
COUTURE, ROSARIO	43	1	3	4	22
WENTWORTH, MARVIN	44	2	1	3	44
MCKINNON, ALEX	44	1	1	2	56
MILLER, EARL	17	1	1	2	24
LOUGHLIN, CLEM	24	0	1	1	16
KEATS, GORDON	3	0	1	1	0
TAYLOR, RALPH	38	0	0	0	56
BURNS, ROBERT	6	0	0	0	6
HOFFINGER, VIC	10	0	0	0	12
LESIEUR, ARTHUR	2	0	0	0	0
GARDINER, HERB	5	0	0	0	0
GARDINER, CHARLES	44	0	0	0	2

1929–30	GP	G	A	PTS	PIM
COOK, TOM	41	14	16	30	16
GOTTSELIG, JOHN	39	21	4	25	28
SOMERS, ART	44	11	13	24	74
ARBOUR, ERNEST	42	10	8	18	26
DUTKOWSKI, DUKE	44	7	10	17	42
MILLER, EARL	28	11	5	16	50
RIPLEY, VIC	38	8	8	16	33
COUTURE, ROSARIO	43	8	8	16	63
INGRAM, FRANK	35	6	10	16	28
MARCH, HAROLD	43	8	7	15	48
ADAMS, STEWART	26	4	6	10	16
WENTWORTH, MARVIN	37	3	4	7	28
ABEL, CLARENCE	38	3	3	6	42
GRAHAM, TED	26	1	2	3	23
TAYLOR, RALPH	17	1	0	1	42
BURNS, ROBERT	11	1	0	1	2
BOSTRUM, HELGE	21	0	1	1	8
GARDINER, CHARLES	44	0	0	0	0

1930–31	GP	G	A	PTS	PIM
GOTTSELIG, JOHN	42	20	12	32	14
COOK, TOM	44	15	14	29	34
INGRAM, FRANK	44	17	4	21	37
COUTURE, ROSARIO	44	8	11	19	30
ADAMS, STEWART	36	5	13	18	18
MARCH, HAROLD	44	11	6	17	36
DESJARDINS, VICTOR	38	3	12	15	11
RIPLEY, VIC	39	8	4	12	9
ROMNES, ELWYN	30	5	7	12	8
SOMERS, ART	33	3	6	9	33
WENTWORTH, MARVIN	44	4	4	8	12
MILLER, EARL	19	3	4	7	8
GRAHAM, TED	44	0	7	7	38
ARBOUR, ERNEST	41	3	3	6	12
BOSTRUM, HELGE	38	2	2	4	32
DUTKOWSKI, DUKE	25	1	3	4	28
ABEL, CLARENCE	43	0	1	1	45
JENKINS, ROGER	10	0	1	1	2
VOKES, ED	5	0	0	0	0
GARDINER, CHARLES	44	0	0	0	0

1931–32	GP	G	A	PTS	PIM
GOTTSELIG, JOHN	44	13	15	28	28
COOK, TOM	48	12	13	25	36
MARCH, HAROLD	48	12	10	22	59
THOMPSON, PAUL	48	8	14	22	34
RIPLEY, VIC	46	12	6	18	47
COUTURE, ROSARIO	48	9	9	18	8
WENTWORTH, CY	48	3	10	13	30
LOWREY, GERRY	48	8	3	11	32
ABEL, CLARENCE	48	3	3	6	34
HOLMES, LOUIS	41	2	4	6	6
BOUCHER, GEORGE	43	1	5	6	50
ADAMS, STEWART	26	0	5	5	26
INGRAM, FRANK	19	1	2	3	4
GRAHAM, TED	48	0	3	3	40
ROMNES, ELWYN	18	1	0	1	6
SHEA, PAT	10	1	0	1	0
COULTER, ART	14	0	1	1	23
BOSTRUM, HELGE	13	0	0	0	4
MILLER, EARL	9	0	0	0	0
GARDINER, CHARLES	48	0	0	0	0
CUDE, WILF	1	0	0	0	0

1932–33	GP	G	A	PTS	PIM
THOMPSON, PAUL	48	13	20	33	27
COOK, TOM	48	12	14	26	30
GOTTSELIG, JOHN	41	11	11	22	6
ROMNES, ELWYN	47	10	12	22	2
MARCH, HAROLD	48	9	11	20	38
COUTURE, ROSARIO	46	10	7	17	26
MCFAYDEN, DON	47	5	9	14	20
JENKINS, ROGER	46	3	10	13	42
GRAHAM, TED	48	3	8	11	57
MACKENZIE, BILL	36	4	4	8	13
RIPLEY, VIC	15	2	4	6	6
COULTER, ART	46	3	2	5	53
ABEL, CLARENCE	47	0	4	4	63
BURCH, BILL	24	2	0	2	2
BOSTRUM, HELGE	18	1	0	1	14
HOLMES, LOUIS	15	0	0	0	2
WEIBE, ART	4	0	0	0	0
GARDINER, CHARLES	48	0	0	0	0

1933–34	GP	G	A	PTS	PIM
THOMPSON, PAUL	48	20	16	36	17
GOTTSELIG, JOHN	48	16	14	30	4
ROMNES, ELWYN	47	8	21	29	6
CONACHER, LIONEL	48	10	13	23	87
MARCH, HAROLD	48	4	13	17	26
COOK, TOM	37	5	9	14	15
COUTURE, ROSARIO	48	5	8	13	21
LESWICK, JACK	37	1	7	8	16
COULTER, ART	41	5	2	7	39
SHEPPARD, JOHN	38	3	4	7	4
GOLDSWORTHY, LEROY	27	3	3	6	0
JENKINS, ROGER	48	2	2	4	37
TRUDEL, LOUIS	34	1	3	4	13
MCFAYDEN, DON	34	1	3	4	20
KENDALL, BILL	21	3	0	3	0
ABEL, CLARENCE	46	2	1	3	28
STARKE, JOE	2	0	0	0	0
DUTKOWSKI, DUKE	5	0	0	0	2
GARDINER, CHARLES	48	0	0	0	0

1934–35	GP	G	A	PTS	PIM
THOMPSON, PAUL	48	16	23	39	20
GOTTSELIG, JOHN	48	19	18	37	16
MORENZ, HOWIE	48	8	26	34	21
COOK, TOM	48	13	18	31	33
MARCH, HAROLD	48	13	17	30	48
ROMNES, ELWYN	35	10	14	24	8
TRUDEL, LOUIS	47	11	11	22	28
COUTURE, ROSARIO	47	7	9	16	14
COULTER, ART	48	4	8	12	68
KENDALL, BILL	47	6	4	10	16
LEVINSKY, ALEX	23	3	4	7	16
LOCKING, NORMAN	38	2	5	7	19
MCFAYDEN, DON	36	2	5	7	4
BURKE, MARTY	48	2	2	4	29
WIEBE, ART	42	2	1	3	27
KENNY, ERNEST	4	0	0	0	18
GOLDSWORTHY, LEROY	7	0	0	0	2
CHABOT, LORNE	48	0	0	0	0

1935–36	GP	G	A	PTS	PIM
THOMPSON, PAUL	45	17	23	40	19
ROMNES, ELWYN	48	13	25	38	6
MARCH, HAROLD	48	16	19	35	42
GOTTSELIG, JOHN	41	14	15	29	4
MCFAYDEN, DON	47	4	16	20	33
MORENZ, HOWIE	23	4	10	14	20
COOK, TOM	47	4	8	12	20
BRYDSON, GLENN	22	6	4	10	30
LEVINSKY, ALEX	48	1	7	8	69
TRUDEL, LOUIS	46	3	4	7	27
SEIBERT, EARL	15	3	3	6	6
OUELLETTE, EDDIE	43	3	2	5	11
LAROCHELLE, WILDOR	27	2	1	3	8
KENDALL, BILL	22	2	1	3	0
BURKE, MARTY	48	0	3	3	49
COULTER, ART	25	0	2	2	18
WIEBE, ART	46	1	0	1	25
LOCKING, NORMAN	14	0	1	1	7
KARAKAS, MIKE	48	0	0	0	0

1936–37	GP	G	A	PTS	PIM
THOMPSON, PAUL	47	17	18	35	28
GOTTSELIG, JOHN	47	9	21	30	10
LAROCHELLE, WILDOR	43	9	10	19	6
TRUDEL, LOUIS	42	6	12	18	11
ROMNES, ELWYN	28	4	14	18	2
KELLY, REGIS	29	13	4	17	0
MARCH, HAROLD	36	11	6	17	31
PALANGIO, PETE	30	8	9	17	16
SEIBERT, EARL	43	9	6	15	46
BRYDSON, GLENN	30	7	7	14	20
LEVINSKY, ALEX	48	0	8	8	32
BURKE, MARTY	42	1	3	4	28
JACKSON, HAROLD	38	1	3	4	6
KENDALL, BILL	17	3	0	3	6
KLINGBEIL, ERNEST	5	1	2	3	2
BLAIR, ANDY	43	0	3	3	33
COOK, TOM	15	0	2	2	0
WIEBE, ART	43	0	2	2	6
LAPRAIRIE, BUN	6	0	0	0	0
SUOMI, AL	5	0	0	0	0
SCHAEFFER, PAUL	5	0	0	0	6
BRINK, MILTON	5	0	0	0	0
KARAKAS, MIKE	48	0	0	0	2

1937–38	GP	G	A	PTS	PIM
THOMPSON, PAUL	48	22	22	44	14
GOTTSELIG, JOHN	48	13	19	32	22
ROMNES, ELWYN	44	10	22	32	4
MARCH, HAROLD	42	11	17	28	16
TRUDEL, LOUIS	42	6	16	22	15
SEIBERT, EARL	48	8	13	21	38
DAHLSTROM, CARL	48	10	9	19	11
VOSS, CARL	34	3	8	11	0
JENKINS, ROGER	37	1	8	9	26
SHILL, JACK	23	4	3	7	8
LEVINSKY, ALEX	48	3	2	5	18
BRYDSON, GLENN	19	1	3	4	6
PALANGIO, PETE	19	2	1	3	4
MACKENZIE, BILL	35	1	2	3	20
CONNOLLY, BERT	16	1	2	3	4
WIEBE, ART	43	0	3	3	24
JOHNSON, VIRGIL	25	0	2	2	2
NICHOLSON, IVAN	2	1	0	1	0
KENDALL, BILL	9	0	1	1	2
BURKE, MARTY	12	0	0	0	8
HANSON, OSCAR	8	0	0	0	0
HEYLIGER, VIC	7	0	0	0	0
JACKSON, HAROLD	3	0	0	0	0
KARAKAS, MIKE	48	0	0	0	0

1938–39	GP	G	A	PTS	PIM
GOTTSELIG, JOHN	48	16	23	39	15
DESILETS, JOFFRE	48	11	13	24	28
MARCH, HAROLD	47	10	11	21	29
DAHLSTROM, CARL	48	6	14	20	2
THOMS, BILL	36	6	11	17	16
THOMPSON, PAUL	33	5	10	15	33
SEIBERT, EARL	48	4	11	15	57
BLINCO, RUSSELL	47	3	12	15	2
ROBINSON, EARL	47	9	6	15	13
NORTHCOTT, LAWRENCE	46	5	7	12	9
GRACIE, BOB	31	4	6	10	27
SHILL, JACK	28	2	4	6	4
COOPER, JOE	17	3	3	6	10
LEVINSKY, ALEX	30	1	3	4	36
BESLER, PHIL	17	1	3	4	16
MASON, CHARLIE	13	1	3	4	0
ROMNES, ELWYN	12	0	4	4	0
WIEBE, ART	47	1	2	3	24
JENKINS, ROGER	14	1	1	2	2
MACKENZIE, BILL	47	1	0	1	36
DE MARCO, ALBERT	2	1	0	1	0
KARAKAS, MIKE	48	0	0	0	2

1939–40	GP	G	A	PTS	PIM
DAHLSTROM, CARL	45	11	19	30	15
MARCH, HAROLD	47	9	14	23	49
CARSE, BILL	48	10	13	23	10
GOTTSELIG, JOHN	39	8	15	23	7
THOMS, BILL	47	9	13	22	4
ALLEN, GEORGE	47	10	12	22	26
HERGESHEIMER, PHIL	42	9	11	20	6
BENTLEY, DOUG	39	12	7	19	12
CUNNINGHAM, LES	37	6	11	17	2
DESILETS, JOFFRE	26	6	7	13	6
COOPER, JOE	44	4	7	11	59
CHAD, JOHN	22	8	3	11	11
SEIBERT, EARL	37	3	7	10	35
CARSE, BOB	22	3	5	8	11
PORTLAND, JACK	16	1	4	5	20
SMITH, DES	24	1	4	5	27
DE MARCO, ALBERT	18	0	5	5	17
WIEBE, ART	47	2	2	4	20
MACKENZIE, BILL	19	0	1	1	14
ALLUM, BILL	1	0	0	0	0
GOODMAN, PAUL	31	0	0	0	0
KARAKAS, MIKE	17	0	0	0	0

1940–41	GP	G	A	PTS	PIM
THOMS, BILL	47	13	19	32	8
ALLEN, GEORGE	44	14	17	31	22
BENTLEY, DOUG	46	8	20	28	12
DAHLSTROM, CARL	40	11	14	25	6
CHAD, JOHN	44	7	18	25	16
HERGESHEIMER, PHIL	47	8	16	24	9
CARSE, BILL	30	5	15	20	12
SEIBERT, EARL	44	3	17	20	52
CARSE, BOB	42	9	9	18	9
MARCH, HAROLD	43	8	9	17	16
BENTLEY, MAX	36	7	10	17	6
COOPER, JOE	40	5	5	10	66
KELLY, REGIS	21	5	3	8	7
WIEBE, ART	45	3	2	5	28
GOTTSELIG, JOHN	5	1	4	5	5
MARIUCCI, JOHN	24	0	5	5	33
PAPIKE, JOE	9	2	2	4	2
MACKAY, DAVE	27	3	0	3	26
PORTLAND, JACK	5	0	0	0	4
GOODMAN, PAUL	21	0	0	0	0
LOPRESTI, SAM	27	0	0	0	0

1941–42	GP	G	A	PTS	PIM
THOMS, BILL	47	15	30	45	8
MARCH, HAROLD	46	6	26	32	22
BENTLEY, MAX	38	13	17	30	2
KALETA, ALEX	47	7	21	28	24
HAMILL, ROBERT	34	18	9	27	21
DAHLSTROM, CARL	33	13	14	27	6
CARSE, BILL	43	13	14	27	16
BENTLEY, DOUG	38	12	14	26	11
CARSE, BOB	32	7	16	23	10
SEIBERT, EARL	45	7	14	21	52
ALLEN, GEORGE	42	7	13	20	21
COOPER, JOE	46	6	14	20	58
MOSIENKO, BILL	11	6	8	14	4
HERGESHEIMER, PHIL	23	3	11	14	2
MARIUCCI, JOHN	46	5	8	13	44
WIEBE, ART	43	2	4	6	20
JOHNSTON, GEORGE	2	2	0	2	0

	GP	G	A	PTS	PIM
TUTEN, AUDLEY	5	1	1	2	10
STEWART, KEN	6	1	1	2	0
PAPIKE, JOE	9	1	0	1	0
MITCHELL, BILL	1	0	0	0	4
PURPUR, CLIFFORD	8	0	0	0	0
DICKIE, BILL	1	0	0	0	0
LOPRESTI, SAM	47	0	0	0	0

1942–43	GP	G	A	PTS	PIM
BENTLEY, DOUG	50	33	40	73	18
BENTLEY, MAX	47	26	44	70	2
HAMILL, ROBERT	50	28	16	44	44
THOMS, BILL	47	15	28	43	11
MARCH, HAROLD	50	7	29	36	46
CARSE, BOB	47	10	22	32	6
SEIBERT, EARL	44	5	27	32	48
PURPUR, CLIFFORD	50	13	16	29	14
DAHLSTROM, CARL	38	11	13	24	10
ALLEN, GEORGE	47	10	14	24	26
JOHNSTON, GEORGE	30	10	7	17	0
TUTEN, AUDLEY	34	3	7	10	38
GOTTSELIG, JOHN	10	2	6	8	2
WIEBE, ART	33	1	7	8	25
HERGESHEIMER, PHIL	9	1	3	4	0
BENTLEY, REGINALD	11	1	2	3	2
MOSIENKO, BILL	2	2	0	2	0
MITCHELL, BILL	42	1	1	2	47
MATTE, JOE	12	0	2	2	8
CARBOL, LEO	6	0	1	1	4
GARDINER, BERT	50	0	0	0	0

1943–44	GP	G	A	PTS	PIM
BENTLEY, DOUG	50	38	39	77	22
SMITH, CLINT	50	23	49	72	4
MOSIENKO, BILL	50	32	38	70	10
DAHLSTROM, CARL	50	20	22	42	8
ALLEN, GEORGE	45	17	24	41	36
MARCH, HAROLD	48	10	27	37	16
SEIBERT, EARL	50	8	25	33	40
GOTTSELIG, JOHN	45	8	15	23	6
PURPUR, CILFFORD	40	9	10	19	13
JOHNSON, VIRGIL	48	1	8	9	23
THOMS, BILL	7	3	5	8	2
WIEBE, ART	21	2	4	6	2
HEYLIGER, VIC	26	2	3	5	2
CAMPBELL, DONALD	17	1	3	4	8
TOUPIN, JACK	8	1	2	3	0
GRIGOR, GEORGE	2	1	0	1	0
COOPER, JOE	13	1	0	1	17
DYTE, JACK	27	1	0	1	21
BUTTREY, GORDON	10	0	0	0	0
FARRANT, WHITEY	1	0	0	0	0
HARMS, JOHN	1	0	0	0	0
THOMPSON, PAUL	1	0	0	0	0
KARAKAS, MIKE	26	0	0	0	0
HIGHTON, HEC	24	0	0	0	0

1944–45	GP	G	A	PTS	PIM
MOSIENKO, BILL	50	28	26	54	0
SMITH, CLINT	50	23	31	54	0
HORECK, PETE	50	20	16	36	44
COOPER, JOE	50	4	17	21	50
DAHLSTROM, CARL	40	6	13	19	0
MCDONALD, BYRON	26	6	13	19	0
GROSSO, DON	21	9	6	15	4
SEIBERT, EARL	22	7	8	15	13
BRAYSHAW, RUSSELL	43	5	9	14	14
MARCH, HAROLD	38	5	5	10	12
HARMS, JOHN	43	5	5	10	21
FRASER, HARVEY	21	5	4	9	0
PURPUR, CLIFFORD	21	2	7	9	11
CHECK, LUDE	26	6	2	8	4
THOMS, BILL	21	2	6	8	8
FIELD, WILFRED	39	3	4	7	22
MITCHELL, BILL	40	3	4	7	16
RAMSEY, LES	11	2	2	4	2
SIMON, JOHN	29	0	1	1	9
KARAKAS, MIKE	48	0	1	1	0
JOHNSON, VIRGIL	2	0	1	1	2
PAPIKE, JOE	2	0	1	1	2
GOTTSELIG, JOHN	1	0	0	0	0
ZABROSKI, MARTIN	1	0	0	0	2
BRETTO, JOE	3	0	0	0	4
STEVENSON, DOUG	2	0	0	0	0

1945–46	GP	G	A	PTS	PIM
BENTLEY, MAX	47	31	30	61	6
SMITH, CLINT	50	26	24	50	2
MOSIENKO, BILL	40	18	30	48	12
KALETA, ALEX	49	19	27	46	17
HORECK, PETE	50	20	21	41	34
BENTLEY, DOUG	36	19	21	40	16
HAMILL, ROBERT	38	20	17	37	23
GEE, GEORGE	35	14	15	29	12
ALLEN, GEORGE	44	11	15	26	16
GROSSO, DON	47	7	10	17	17
WARES, EDDIE	45	4	11	15	34
MARIUCCI, JOHN	50	3	8	11	58
JOHNSTON, GEORGE	16	5	4	9	2
COOPER, JOE	50	2	7	9	46
HAMILTON, REG	48	1	7	8	31
CHAD, JOHN	13	0	1	1	2
REISE, LEO, JR.	6	0	0	0	6
KARAKAS, MIKE	48	0	0	0	5
STEVENSON, DOUG	2	0	0	0	0

1946–47	GP	G	A	PTS	PIM
BENTLEY, MAX	60	29	43	72	12
BENTLEY, DOUG	52	21	34	55	18
MOSIENKO, BILL	59	25	27	52	2
KALETA, ALEX	57	24	20	44	37
HAMILL, ROBERT	60	21	19	40	12
GEE, GEORGE	60	20	20	40	26
BROWN, ADAM	42	11	25	36	59
SMITH, CLINT	52	9	17	26	6
GADSBY, BILL	48	8	10	18	31
WARES, EDDIE	60	4	7	11	21
MARIUCCI, JOHN	52	2	9	11	110
HORECK, PETE	18	4	6	10	12
ASHWORTH, FRANK	18	5	4	9	2
NATTRASS, RALPH	35	4	5	9	34
JACKSON, JACK	48	2	5	7	38
JOHNSTON, GEORGE	10	3	1	4	0
BLADE, HENRY	18	1	3	4	2
HAMILTON, REG	10	0	3	3	2
DICK, HARRY	12	0	1	1	12
FOWLER, TOM	24	0	1	1	18
REISE, LEO, JR.	17	0	0	0	18
BIBEAULT, PAUL	41	0	0	0	2
FRANCIS, EMILE	19	0	0	0	0

1947–48	GP	G	A	PTS	PIM
BENTLEY, DOUG	60	20	37	57	16
STEWART, GAYE	54	26	29	55	74
POILE, NORMAN	54	23	29	52	14
CONACHER, ROY	52	22	27	49	4
GEE, GEORGE	60	14	25	39	18
BODNAR, GUS	46	13	22	35	23
KALETA, ALEX	52	10	16	26	40
MOSIENKO, BILL	40	16	9	25	0
HAMILL, ROBERT	60	11	13	24	18
DICKENS, ERNIE	54	5	15	20	30
PRYSTAI, METRO	54	7	11	18	25
BROWN, ADAM	32	7	10	17	41
NATTRASS, RALPH	60	5	12	17	79
GADSBY, BILL	60	6	10	16	66
GOLDHAM, BOB	38	2	9	11	38
BENTLEY, MAX	6	3	3	6	0
MARIUCCI, JOHN	51	1	4	5	63
BUTLER, DICK	7	2	0	2	0
BLADE, HENRY	6	1	0	1	0
THOMAS, CY	6	1	0	1	8
MICHALUK, ART	5	0	0	0	0
BALDWIN, DOUG	5	0	0	0	2
FRANCIS, EMILE	54	0	0	0	6
JACKSON, DOUG	6	0	0	0	0

1948–49	GP	G	A	PTS	PIM
CONACHER, ROY	60	26	42	68	8
BENTLEY, DOUG	58	23	43	66	38
CONACHER, JIM	55	25	23	48	41
BODNAR, GUS	59	19	26	45	14
MOSIENKO, BILL	60	17	25	42	6
STEWART, GAYE	54	20	18	38	57
GUIDOLIN, BEP	56	4	17	21	116
BROWN, ADAM	58	8	12	20	69
PRYSTAI, METRO	59	12	7	19	19
NATTRASS, RALPH	60	4	10	14	99
GADSBY, BILL	50	3	10	13	85
HAMILL, ROBERT	57	8	4	12	16
GOLDHAM, BOB	60	1	10	11	43
DICKENS, ERNIE	59	2	3	5	14
MCCAIG, DOUGLAS	55	1	3	4	60
OLMSTEAD, BERT	9	0	2	2	4
GEE, GEORGE	4	0	2	2	4
POILE, BUD	4	0	0	0	2
HENRY, JIM	60	0	0	0	0

1949–50	GP	G	A	PTS	PIM
CONACHER, ROY	70	25	31	56	16
BENTLEY, DOUG	64	20	33	53	28
PRYSTAI, METRO	65	29	22	51	31
GUIDOLIN, BEP	70	17	34	51	42
OLMSTEAD, BERT	70	20	29	49	40
MOSIENKO, BILL	69	18	28	46	10
STEWART, GAYE	70	24	19	43	43
BODNAR, GUS	70	11	28	39	6
GADSBY, BILL	70	10	24	34	138
CONACHER, JIM	66	13	20	33	14
NATTRASS, RALPH	68	5	11	16	96
DICKENS, ERNIE	70	0	13	13	22
GOLDHAM, BOB	67	2	10	12	57
HAMILL, ROBERT	59	6	2	8	6
BROWN, ADAM	25	2	2	4	16
MCCAIG, DOUGLAS	63	0	4	4	49
STASIUK, VIC	17	1	1	2	2
LEIER, ED	5	0	1	1	0
BEDARD, JIM	5	0	0	0	2
MILLER, JACK	6	0	0	0	0
BRIMSEK, FRANK	70	0	0	0	2

1950–51	GP	G	A	PTS	PIM
CONACHER, ROY	70	26	24	50	16
BABANDO, PETE	70	18	19	37	36
CONACHER, JIM	52	10	27	37	16
MOSIENKO, BILL	65	21	15	36	18
GUIDOLIN, BEP	69	12	22	34	56
BENTLEY, DOUG	44	9	23	32	20
BROWN, ADAM	53	10	12	22	61
POWELL, RAY	31	7	15	22	2
MORRISON, DON	59	8	12	20	6
BODNAR, GUS	44	8	12	20	8
DEWSBURY, AL	67	5	14	19	79
LUNDY, PAT	61	9	9	18	9
FOGOLIN, LEE	35	3	10	13	63
BLACK, STEVE	39	4	6	10	22
GADSBY, BILL	25	3	7	10	32
DICKENS, ERNIE	70	2	8	10	20
STASIUK, VIC	20	5	3	8	6
MCCAIG, DOUGLAS	53	2	5	7	29
FASHOWAY, GORDON	13	3	2	5	14
OLMSTEAD, BERT	15	2	1	3	0
COFLIN, HUGH	31	0	3	3	33
LEIER, ED	11	2	0	2	2
BEDARD, JIM	17	1	1	2	6
STEWART, JACK	26	0	2	2	49
HUCUL, FRED	3	1	0	1	2
MILLER, JACK	11	0	0	0	4
SMITH, GLEN	2	0	0	0	0
HAMILL, ROBERT	2	0	0	0	0
MICHALUK, JOHN	1	0	0	0	0
FIELDER, GUYLE	3	0	0	0	0
LUMLEY, HARRY	64	0	0	0	4
PELLETIER, MARCEL	6	0	0	0	2
ALMAS, RALPH	1	0	0	0	0

1951–52	GP	G	A	PTS	PIM
MOSIENKO, BILL	70	31	22	53	10
GEE, GEORGE	70	18	31	49	39
BODNAR, GUS	69	14	26	40	26
PETERS, JIM	70	15	21	36	16
MCFADDEN, JIM	70	10	24	34	14
GUIDOLIN, BEP	67	13	18	31	78
BABANDO, PETE	49	11	14	25	29
DEWSBURY, AL	69	7	17	24	99
GADSBY, BILL	59	7	15	22	87
HORECK, PETER	60	9	11	20	22
FINNEY, SID	35	6	5	11	0
WITIUK, STEVE	33	3	8	11	14
HUCUL, FRED	34	3	7	10	37
FOGOLIN, LEE	69	0	9	9	96
BENTLEY, DOUG	8	2	3	5	4
RAGLAN, CLARE	35	0	5	5	28
CONACHER, ROY	12	3	1	4	0
STEWART, JACK	37	1	3	4	12
HRYMNAK, STEVE	18	2	1	3	4
MARTIN, CLARE	31	1	2	3	8
TAYLOR, HARRY	15	1	1	2	0
CONACHER, PETE	2	0	1	1	0
CONACHER, JIM	5	0	1	1	0
QUACKENBUSH, MAX	14	0	1	1	4
WHARRAM, KEN	1	0	0	0	0
BUCHANAN, MIKE	1	0	0	0	0
PRICE, JOHN	1	0	0	0	0
POETA, TONY	1	0	0	0	0
LUMLEY, HARRY	70	0	0	0	2
ROBERTS, MOE	1	0	0	0	0

1952–53	GP	G	A	PTS	PIM
MCFADDEN, JIM	70	23	21	44	29
PETERS, JIM	69	22	19	41	16
GEE, GEORGE	67	18	21	39	99
COUTURE, GERRY	70	19	18	37	22
MOSIENKO, BILL	65	17	20	37	8
GARDNER, CAL	70	11	24	35	60
BODNAR, GUS	66	16	13	29	26
MORTSON, GUS	68	5	18	23	88
GADSBY, BILL	68	2	20	22	84
DEWSBURY, AL	69	5	16	21	97
HUCUL, FRED	57	5	7	12	25
CONACHER, PETE	41	5	6	11	7
FOGOLIN, LEE	70	2	8	10	79
LYNN, VIC	29	0	10	10	23
ABEL, SID	39	5	4	9	6
BABANDO, PETE	28	5	4	9	10
FINNEY, SID	18	4	2	6	4
GLOVER, FRED	31	4	2	6	37
RAGLAN, CLARE	32	1	3	4	10
SCLISIZZI, ENIO	14	0	2	2	0
MCBURNEY, JIM	1	0	1	1	0
PRICE, JACK	10	0	0	0	2
KRYZANOWSKI, ED	5	0	0	0	0
ROLLINS, AL	70	0	0	0	0

1953–54	GP	G	A	PTS	PIM
WILSON, LARRY	66	9	33	42	22
GADSBY, BILL	70	12	29	41	108
MOSIENKO, BILL	65	15	19	34	17
CONACHER, PETE	70	19	9	28	23
JANKOWSKI, LOU	68	15	13	28	7
GEE, GEORGE	69	10	16	26	59
BODNAR, GUS	44	6	15	21	20
DEWSBURY, AL	69	6	15	21	44
MORTSON, GUS	68	5	8	13	132
PETERS, JIM	46	6	4	10	21
MCINTYRE, JACK	23	8	3	11	4
COUTURE, GERRY	40	6	5	11	14
PRICE, JACK	46	4	6	10	22
TOPPAZZINI, JERRY	14	5	3	8	18
WHARRAM, KEN	29	1	7	8	8
ZEIDEL, LARRY	64	1	6	7	102
MCFADDEN, JIM	19	3	3	6	6
COSTELLO, MURRAY	40	3	2	5	6
HILDEBRAND, IKE	7	1	4	5	4
HUCUL, FRED	27	0	3	3	19
LYNN, VIC	11	1	0	1	2
FOGOLIN, LEE	68	0	1	1	95
ROLLINS, AL	66	0	0	0	20
MAROIS, JEAN	2	0	0	0	0
GELINEAU, JACK	2	0	0	0	0
MENARD, HILLARY	1	0	0	0	0
WILSON, BOB	1	0	0	0	0
LALANDE, HEC	2	0	0	0	2
SLEAVER, JOHN	1	0	0	0	2
ABEL, SID	3	0	0	0	4
FINNEY, SID	3	0	0	0	0
SASAKAMOOSE, FRED	11	0	0	0	6

1954–55	GP	G	A	PTS	PIM
SULLIVAN, GEORGE	69	19	42	61	51
LITZENBERGER, ED	44	16	24	40	28
WATSON, HARRY	43	14	16	30	4
MICKOSKI, NICK	52	10	19	29	42
MCINTYRE, JACK	65	16	13	29	40
MOSIENKO, BILL	64	12	15	27	24
TOPPAZZINI, JERRY	70	9	18	27	59
STANLEY, ALLAN	52	10	15	25	22
PRYSTAI, METRO	57	11	13	24	28
WILSON, LARRY	63	12	11	23	39
CREIGHTON, DAVE	49	7	7	14	6
MORTSON, GUS	65	2	11	13	133
MCCORMACK, JOHN	63	5	7	12	8
MARTIN, FRANK	66	4	8	12	35
HOLLINGWORTH, GORD	70	3	9	12	135
GADSBY, BILL	18	3	5	8	17
CONACHER, PETE	18	2	4	6	2
JANKOWSKI, LOU	39	3	2	5	8
GAMBLE, DICK	14	2	0	2	6
TIMGREN, RAY	14	1	1	2	2
MASNICK, PAUL	11	1	0	1	8
FOGOLIN, LEE	9	0	1	1	16
DEWSBURY, AL	12	0	1	1	10
SULLIVAN, FRANK	1	0	0	0	0
HILDEBRAND, IKE	3	0	0	0	0
HASSARD, BOB	17	0	0	0	4
ROLLINS, AL	44	0	0	0	0
BASSEN, HENRY	21	0	0	0	0
FREDERICK, RAY	5	0	0	0	0
DAVIS, LORNE	8	0	0	0	4

1955–56	GP	G	A	PTS	PIM
SULLIVAN, GEORGE	63	14	26	40	58
MICKOSKI, NICK	70	19	20	39	52
LITZENBERGER, ED	70	10	29	39	36
WILSON, JOHN	70	24	9	33	12
CIESLA, HANK	70	8	23	31	22
SKOV, GLEN	70	7	20	27	26
LALANDE, HEC	65	8	18	26	70
WATSON, HARRY	55	11	14	25	6
LESWICK, TONY	70	11	11	22	71
SANDFORD, ED	57	12	9	21	56
STANLEY, ALLAN	59	4	14	18	70
MCINTYRE, JACK	46	10	5	15	14
MORTSON, GUS	52	5	10	15	87
DEWSBURY, AL	37	3	12	15	22
MARTIN, FRANK	61	3	11	14	21
WOIT, BEN	63	1	8	9	46
PILOTE, PIERRE	20	3	5	8	34
FOGOLIN, LEE	51	0	8	8	88
CORCORAN, NORMAN	23	1	3	4	19
PRYSTAI, METRO	8	1	3	4	8
WHARRAM, KEN	3	0	0	0	0
WILSON, LARRY	2	0	0	0	2
SULLIVAN, FRANK	1	0	0	0	0
ROLLINS, AL	58	0	0	0	10
BASSEN, HENRY	12	0	0	0	2

1956–57	GP	G	A	PTS	PIM
LITZENBERGER, ED	70	32	32	64	48
WILSON, JOHN	70	18	30	48	24
SKOV, GLEN	67	14	28	42	69
MICKOSKI, NICK	70	16	20	36	24
MCINTYRE, JACK	70	18	14	32	32
WATSON, HARRY	70	11	19	30	9
LALANDE, HEC	50	11	17	28	38
NESTERENKO, ERIC	24	8	15	23	32
MORTSON, GUS	70	5	18	23	147
KENNEDY, FORBES	69	8	13	21	102
CIESLA, HANK	70	10	8	18	28
PILOTE, PIERRE	70	3	14	17	117
VASKO, ELMER	64	3	12	15	31
KACHUR, ED	34	5	7	12	21
HERGESHEIMER, WALLY	41	2	8	10	12
MARTIN, FRANK	70	1	8	9	12
INGRAM, RON	45	1	6	7	21
MOSDELL, KEN	25	2	4	6	10
SLEAVER, JOHN	12	1	0	1	4
MAZUR, ED	15	0	1	1	4
ROLLINS, AL	70	0	1	1	9
WOIT, BEN	9	0	0	0	2
TOPPAZZINI, ZELLIO	7	0	0	0	0
CUSHENAN, IAN	11	0	0	0	13

1957–58	GP	G	A	PTS	PIM
LITZENBERGER, ED	70	32	30	62	63
HULL, BOB	70	13	34	47	62
LINDSAY, TED	68	15	24	39	110
NESTERENKO, ERIC	70	20	18	38	104
SKOV, GLEN	70	17	18	35	35
PILOTE, PIERRE	70	6	24	30	91
MURPHY, RON	69	11	17	28	32
VASKO, ELMER	59	6	20	26	51
REIBEL, EARL	40	4	12	16	6
FERGUSON, LORNE	38	6	9	15	24
DEA, BILL	34	5	8	13	4
DINEEN, BILL	41	4	9	13	10
MORTSON, GUS	67	3	10	13	62
KACHUR, ED	62	5	7	12	14
MICKOSKI, NICK	28	5	6	11	20
THOMSON, JIM	70	4	7	11	75
CUSHENAN, IAN	61	2	8	10	67
BAILEY, BOB	28	3	6	9	38
LALANDE, HEC	22	2	2	4	10
MCINTYRE, JACK	27	0	4	4	10
BARKLEY, DOUG	3	0	0	0	0
WARD, DON	3	0	0	0	0
MARTIN, FRANK	3	0	0	0	10
HALL, GLENN	70	0	0	0	10

1958–59	GP	G	A	PTS	PIM
LITZENBERGER, ED	70	33	44	77	37
SLOAN, TOD	59	27	35	62	79
LINDSAY, TED	70	22	36	58	184
HULL, BOB	70	18	32	50	50
MURPHY, RON	59	17	30	47	52
PILOTE, PIERRE	70	7	30	37	79
NESTERENKO, ERIC	70	16	18	34	81
LEWICKI, DAN	58	8	14	22	4
WHARRAM, KEN	66	10	9	19	14
BALFOUR, EARL	70	10	8	18	10
FERGUSON, LORNE	67	7	10	17	44
VASKO, ELMER	63	6	10	16	52
ST. LAURENT, DOLLARD	70	4	8	12	28
ARBOUR, AL	70	2	10	12	86
EVANS, JACK	70	1	8	9	75
SKOV, GLEN	70	3	5	8	4
MCKENZIE, JOHN	32	3	4	7	22
MALONEY, PHIL	24	2	2	4	6
JOHNSON, NORM	7	1	0	1	8
MIKITA, STAN	3	0	1	1	4
GLOVER, HOWARD	13	0	1	1	2
HALL, GLENN	70	0	0	0	0

1959–60	GP	G	A	PTS	PIM
HULL, BOB	70	39	42	81	68
HAY, BILL	70	18	37	55	31
PILOTE, PIERRE	70	7	38	45	100
SLOAN, TOD	70	20	20	40	54
MURPHY, RON	63	15	21	36	18
NESTERENKO, ERIC	61	13	23	36	71
BALFOUR, MURRAY	61	18	12	30	55
VASKO, ELMER	69	3	27	30	110
LITZENBERGER, ED	52	12	18	30	15
MIKITA, STAN	67	8	18	26	119
LINDSAY, TED	68	7	19	26	91
WHARRAM, KEN	59	14	11	25	16
ST. LAURENT, DOLLARD	68	4	13	17	60
MALONEY, PHIL	21	6	4	10	0
BALFOUR, EARL	70	3	5	8	16
SKOV, GLEN	69	3	4	7	16
ARBOUR, AL	57	1	5	6	66
EVANS, JACK	68	0	4	4	60
HALL, GLENN	70	0	1	1	2
BARKLEY, DOUG	3	0	0	0	2

1960–61	GP	G	A	PTS	PIM
HAY, BILL	69	11	48	59	45
HULL, BOB	67	31	25	56	43
MIKITA, STAN	66	19	34	53	100
BALFOUR, MURRAY	70	21	27	48	123
WHARRAM, KEN	64	16	29	45	12
MURPHY, RON	70	21	19	40	30
NESTERENKO, ERIC	68	19	19	38	125
PILOTE, PIERRE	70	6	29	35	165
SLOAN, TOD	67	11	23	34	48
MCDONALD, AB	61	17	16	33	22
LITZENBERGER, ED	62	10	22	32	14
VASKO, ELMER	63	4	18	22	40
ST. LAURENT, DOLLARD	67	2	17	19	58
FLEMING, REG	66	4	4	8	145
EVANS, JACK	69	0	8	8	58
BALFOUR, EARL	68	3	3	6	4
ARBOUR, AL	53	3	2	5	40
HALL, GLENN	70	0	1	1	0
HICKS, WAYNE	1	0	0	0	0

1961–62	GP	G	A	PTS	PIM
HULL, BOB	70	50	34	84	35
MIKITA, STAN	70	25	52	77	97
HAY, BILL	60	11	52	63	34
HORVATH, BRONCO	68	17	29	46	21
PILOTE, PIERRE	59	7	35	42	97
MCDONALD, AB	65	22	18	40	8
WHARRAM, KEN	62	14	23	37	24
BALFOUR, MURRAY	49	15	15	30	72
NESTERENKO, ERIC	68	15	14	29	97
MURPHY, RON	60	12	16	28	41
VASKO, ELMER	64	2	22	24	87
MELNYK, JERRY	63	5	16	21	6
EVANS, JACK	70	3	14	17	80
FLEMING, REG	70	7	9	16	71
ST. LAURENT, DOLLARD	64	0	13	13	44
TURNER, BOB	69	8	2	10	52
MAKI, CHICO	16	4	6	10	2
HILLMAN, WAYNE	19	0	2	2	14
HALL, MURRAY	2	0	0	0	0
HALL, GLENN	70	0	0	0	12

1962–63	GP	G	A	PTS	PIM
MIKITA, STAN	65	31	45	76	69
HULL, BOB	65	31	31	62	27
MCDONALD, AB	69	20	41	61	12
HAY, BILL	64	12	33	45	36
WHARRAM, KEN	55	20	18	38	17
MURPHY, RON	68	18	16	34	28
BALFOUR, MURRAY	65	10	23	33	75
LUNDE, LEN	60	6	22	28	30
NESTERENKO, ERIC	67	12	15	27	103
PILOTE, PIERRE	59	8	18	26	57
MAKI, CHICO	65	7	17	24	35
MACNEIL, AL	70	2	19	21	100
FLEMING, REG	64	7	7	14	99
VASKO, ELMER	64	4	9	13	70
HILLMAN, WAYNE	67	3	5	8	74
EVANS, JACK	68	0	8	8	46
TURNER, BOB	70	3	3	6	20
ERICKSON, AUTRY	3	0	0	0	8
HALL, GLENN	66	0	0	0	0
DEJORDY, DENIS	5	0	0	0	0

1963–64	GP	G	A	PTS	PIM
MIKITA, STAN	70	39	50	89	146
HULL, BOB	70	43	44	87	50
WHARRAM, KEN	70	39	32	71	18
HAY, BILL	70	23	33	56	30
PILOTE, PIERRE	70	7	46	53	84
MCDONALD, AB	70	14	32	46	19
NESTERENKO, ERIC	70	7	19	26	93
MACNEIL, AL	70	5	19	24	91
MAKI, CHICO	68	8	14	22	70
VASKO, ELMER	70	2	18	20	65
MURPHY, RON	70	11	8	19	32
MCKENZIE, JOHN	45	9	9	18	50
BALFOUR, MURRAY	41	2	10	12	36
FLEMING, REG	61	3	6	9	140
YOUNG, HOWARD	39	0	7	7	99
ESPOSITO, PHIL	27	3	2	5	2
HILLMAN, WAYNE	59	1	4	5	51
HALL, MURRAY	23	2	0	2	4
HALL, GLENN	65	0	2	2	2
ERICKSON, AUTRY	31	0	1	1	34
DEJORDY, DENIS	6	0	0	0	0

1964–65	GP	G	A	PTS	PIM
MIKITA, STAN	70	28	59	87	154
HULL, BOB	61	39	32	71	32
PILOTE, PIERRE	68	14	45	59	162
ESPOSITO, PHIL	70	23	32	55	44
WHARRAM, KEN	68	24	20	44	27
MAKI, CHICO	65	16	24	40	58
HAY, BILL	69	11	26	37	36
MOHNS, DOUG	49	13	20	33	84
NESTERENKO, ERIC	56	14	16	30	63
RAVLICH, MATT	61	3	16	19	80
MCKENZIE, JOHN	51	8	10	18	46
STANFIELD, FRED	58	7	10	17	14
JARRETT, DOUG	46	2	15	17	34
HULL, DENNIS	55	10	4	14	18
ROBINSON, DOUG	40	2	9	11	8
VASKO, ELMER	69	1	10	11	56
MACNEIL, AL	69	3	7	10	119
HENRY, CAMILLE	22	5	3	8	2
BRENNEMAN, JOHN	17	1	0	1	2
HILLMAN, WAYNE	19	0	1	1	8
DEJORDY, DENIS	30	0	1	1	0
HODGE, KEN	1	0	0	0	2
MICKEY, LARRY	1	0	0	0	0
HALL, GLENN	41	0	0	0	2

1965–66	GP	G	A	PTS	PIM
HULL, BOB	65	54	43	97	70
MIKITA, STAN	68	30	48	78	58
ESPOSITO, PHIL	69	27	26	53	49
HAY, BILL	68	20	31	51	20
MOHNS, DOUG	70	22	27	49	63
MAKI, CHICO	68	17	31	48	41
WHARRAM, KEN	69	26	17	43	28
NESTERENKO, ERIC	67	15	25	40	58
PILOTE, PIERRE	51	2	34	36	60
STAPLETON, PAT	55	4	30	34	52
HODGE, KEN	63	6	17	23	47
JARRETT, DOUG	66	4	12	16	71
RAVLICH, MATT	62	0	16	16	78
ANGOTTI, LOU	30	4	10	14	12
LUNDE, LEN	24	4	7	11	4
VASKO, ELMER	56	1	7	8	44
HULL, DENNIS	25	1	5	6	6
STANFIELD, FRED	39	2	2	4	2
MISZUK, JOHN	2	1	1	2	2
HALL, GLENN	63	0	2	2	14
DRYDEN, DAVE	11	0	1	1	0
MACNEIL, AL	51	0	1	1	34
STRATTON, ART	2	0	0	0	0
RICHARDSON, DAVE	3	0	0	0	2

1966–67	GP	G	A	PTS	PIM
MIKITA, STAN	70	35	62	97	12
HULL, BOB	66	52	28	80	52
WHARRAM, KEN	70	31	34	65	21
ESPOSITO, PHIL	69	21	40	61	40
MOHNS, DOUG	61	25	35	60	58
PILOTE, PIERRE	70	6	46	52	90
HULL, DENNIS	70	25	17	42	33
MAKI, CHICO	56	9	29	38	14
NESTERENKO, ERIC	68	14	23	37	38
HODGE, KEN	69	10	25	35	59
STAPLETON, PAT	70	3	31	34	54
JARRETT, DOUG	70	5	21	26	76
HAY, BILL	36	7	13	20	12
VAN IMPE, ED	61	8	11	19	111
ANGOTTI, LOU	63	6	12	18	21
BOYER, WALLY	42	5	6	11	15
RAVLICH, MATT	62	0	3	3	39
SMITH, WAYNE	2	1	1	2	2
STANFIELD, FRED	10	1	0	1	0
MISZUK, JOHN	3	0	0	0	0
DEJORDY, DENIS	44	0	0	0	0
HALL, GLENN	28	0	0	0	10

1967–68	GP	G	A	PTS	PIM
MIKITA, STAN	72	40	47	87	14
HULL, BOB	71	44	31	75	39
WHARRAM, KEN	74	27	42	69	18
MOHNS, DOUG	65	24	29	53	53
STAPLETON, PAT	67	4	34	38	34
PILOTE, PIERRE	74	1	36	37	69
NESTERENKO, ERIC	71	11	25	36	37
MARTIN, PIT	63	16	19	35	36
HULL, DENNIS	74	18	15	33	34
MAKI, CHICO	60	8	16	24	4
JARRETT, DOUG	74	4	19	23	48
MAROTTE, GILLES	73	0	21	21	122
MAKI, WAYNE	49	5	5	10	32
TERBENCHE, PAUL	68	3	7	10	8
SCHMAUTZ, BOB	13	3	2	5	6
ORBAN, BILL	39	3	2	5	17
REID, TOM	56	0	4	4	25
GOYER, GERRY	40	1	2	3	4
SHELTON, DOUG	5	0	1	1	2
POWIS, GEOFFREY	2	0	0	0	0
DEJORDY, DENIS	50	0	0	0	0
DRYDEN, DAVE	27	0	0	0	0
NORRIS, JACK	7	0	0	0	0

1968–69	GP	G	A	PTS	PIM
HULL, BOB	74	58	49	107	48
MIKITA, STAN	74	30	67	97	52
PAPPIN, JIM	75	30	40	70	49
WHARRAM, KEN	76	30	39	69	19
HULL, DENNIS	72	30	34	64	25
MARTIN, PIT	76	23	38	61	73
STAPLETON, PAT	75	6	50	56	44
MOHNS, DOUG	65	22	19	41	47
MAROTTE, GILLES	68	5	29	34	120
NESTERENKO, ERIC	72	15	17	32	29
MAKI, CHICO	66	7	21	28	30
SCHMAUTZ, BOB	63	9	7	16	37
BOUDRIAS, ANDRE	20	4	10	14	4
RAVLICH, MATT	60	2	12	14	57
JARRETT, DOUG	69	0	13	13	58
ORBAN, BILL	45	4	6	10	33
YOUNG, HOWARD	57	3	7	10	67
MCMAHON, MIKE	20	0	8	8	6
LEBLANC, J.P.	6	1	2	3	0
REID, TOM	30	0	3	3	12
SHMYR, PAUL	3	1	0	1	8
MCKAY, RAY	9	0	1	1	12
DEJORDY, DENIS	53	0	1	1	2
DRYDEN, DAVE	30	0	1	1	0
MAKI, WAYNE	1	0	0	0	0
WISTE, JIM	3	0	0	0	0
NORRIS, JACK	3	0	0	0	0

1969–70	GP	G	A	PTS	PIM
MIKITA, STAN	76	39	47	86	50
HULL, BOB	61	38	29	67	8
MARTIN, PIT	73	30	33	63	61
PAPPIN, JIM	66	28	25	53	68
HULL, DENNIS	76	17	35	52	31
STAPLETON, PAT	49	4	38	42	28
PINDER, GERRY	75	19	20	39	41
ANGOTTI, LOU	70	12	26	38	25
KOROLL, CLIFF	73	18	19	37	44
NESTERENKO, ERIC	67	16	18	34	26
MAKI, CHICO	75	10	24	34	27
MOHNS, DOUG	66	6	27	33	46
JARRETT, DOUG	72	4	20	24	78
MAGNUSON, KEITH	76	0	24	24	213
MAROTTE, GILLES	51	5	13	18	52
WISTE, JIM	26	0	8	8	8

	GP	G	A	PTS	PIM
MENARD, HOWIE	19	2	3	5	8
WHITE, BILL	21	0	5	5	18
SHMYR, PAUL	24	0	4	4	26
UBRIACO, GENE	21	1	1	2	2
CAMPBELL, BRYAN	14	1	1	2	2
ESPOSITO, TONY	63	0	2	2	2
DESJARDINS, GERRY	4	0	1	1	0
CAFFERY, TERRY	6	0	0	0	0
DEJORDY, DENIS	10	0	0	0	0
MCKAY, RAY	17	0	0	0	23

1970–71	GP	G	A	PTS	PIM
HULL, BOB	78	44	52	96	32
MIKITA, STAN	74	24	48	72	85
HULL, DENNIS	78	40	26	66	16
MARTIN, PIT	62	22	33	55	40
CAMPBELL, BRYAN	78	17	37	54	26
STAPLETON, PAT	76	7	44	51	30
KOROLL, CLIFF	72	16	34	50	85
MAKI, CHICO	72	22	26	48	18
PAPPIN, JIM	58	22	23	45	40
PINDER, GERRY	74	13	18	31	35
MALONEY, DAN	74	12	14	26	174
ANGOTTI, LOU	65	9	16	25	19
WHITE, BILL	67	4	21	25	64
NESTERENKO, ERIC	76	8	15	23	28
MAGNUSON, KEITH	76	3	20	23	291
KORAB, JERRY	46	4	14	18	152
JARRETT, DOUG	51	1	12	13	46
SHMYR, PAUL	57	1	12	13	41
O'SHEA, DANNY	18	4	7	11	10
MOHNS, DOUG	39	4	6	10	16
ROMANCHYCH, LARRY	10	0	2	2	2
FOLEY, RICK	2	0	1	1	8
ESPOSITO, TONY	57	0	1	1	4
MCKAY, RAY	2	0	0	0	0
DESJARDINS, GERRY	22	0	0	0	6
MELOCHE, GILLES	2	0	0	0	0
BROWN, KEN	1	0	0	0	0

1971–72	GP	G	A	PTS	PIM
HULL, BOB	78	50	43	93	24
MARTIN, PIT	78	24	51	75	56
HULL, DENNIS	78	30	39	69	10
MIKITA, STAN	74	26	39	65	46
PAPPIN, JIM	64	27	21	48	38
MAKI, CHICO	62	13	34	47	22
KOROLL, CLIFF	76	22	23	45	51
STAPLETON, PAT	78	3	38	41	47
WHITE, BILL	76	7	22	29	58
JARRETT, DOUG	78	6	23	29	68
MAGNUSON, KEITH	74	2	19	21	201
CAMPBELL, BRYAN	75	5	13	18	22
ANGOTTI, LOU	65	5	10	15	23
O'SHEA, DANNY	48	6	9	15	28
BORDELEAU, CHRISTIAN	25	6	8	14	6
KORAB, JERRY	73	9	5	14	95
NESTERENKO, ERIC	38	4	8	12	27
MAGGS, DARRYL	59	7	4	11	4
LACROIX, ANDRE	51	4	7	11	6
BORDELEAU, J.P.	3	0	2	2	2
ESPOSITO, TONY	48	0	1	1	2
SMITH, GARY	28	0	0	0	0
DESJARDINS, GERRY	6	0	0	0	0

1972–73	GP	G	A	PTS	PIM
PAPPIN, JIM	76	41	51	92	82
HULL, DENNIS	78	39	51	90	27
MARTIN, PIT	78	29	61	90	30
MIKITA, STAN	57	27	56	83	32
KOROLL, CLIFF	77	33	24	57	38
WHITE, BILL	72	9	38	47	80
ANGOTTI, LOU	77	15	22	37	26
MAKI, CHICO	77	13	19	32	10
STAPLETON, PAT	75	10	21	31	14
BORDELEAU, J.P.	73	15	15	30	6
MALONEY, DAN	57	13	17	30	63
REDMOND, DICK	52	9	19	28	4
KORAB, JERRY	77	12	15	27	94
RUSSELL, PHIL	76	6	19	25	156
MAGNUSON, KEITH	77	0	19	19	140
MARKS, JOHN	55	3	10	13	21
JARRETT, DOUG	49	2	11	13	18
BACKSTROM, RALPH	16	6	3	9	2
OGILVIE, BRIAN	12	1	2	3	4
ESPOSITO, TONY	56	0	2	2	0
KRYSKOW, DAVE	11	1	0	1	0
L'ABBE, MAURICE	5	0	1	1	0
LEDINGHAM, WALT	9	0	1	1	4
MAGGS, DARRYL	17	0	0	0	4
SMITH, GARY	23	0	0	0	5

1973–74	GP	G	A	PTS	PIM
MIKITA, STAN	76	30	50	80	46
MARTIN, PIT	78	30	47	77	43
PAPPIN, JIM	78	32	41	73	76
HULL, DENNIS	74	29	39	68	15
REDMOND, DICK	76	17	42	59	69
KOROLL, CLIFF	78	21	25	46	32
WHITE, BILL	69	5	31	36	52
RUSSELL, PHIL	75	10	25	35	184
MAKI, CHICO	69	9	26	35	12
TALLON, DALE	65	15	19	34	36
ROTA, DARCY	74	21	12	33	58
MARKS, JOHN	76	13	18	31	22
POWIS, LYNN	57	8	13	21	6
BORDELEAU, J.P.	64	11	9	20	11
KRYSKOW, DAVE	72	7	12	19	22
GAGNON, GERMAINE	14	3	14	17	4
JARRETT, DOUG	67	5	11	16	45
FRIG, LEN	66	4	10	14	35
MAGNUSON, KEITH	57	2	11	13	105
ESPOSITO, TONY	70	0	1	1	0
VEISOR, MIKE	10	0	1	1	0
DONALDSON, GARY	1	0	0	0	0
PALMER, ROB	1	0	0	0	0

1974–75	GP	G	A	PTS	PIM
MIKITA, STAN	79	36	50	86	48
BOLDIREV, IVAN	80	24	43	67	54
PAPPIN, JIM	71	36	27	63	94
KOROLL, CLIFF	80	27	32	59	27
REDMOND, DICK	80	14	43	57	90
GAGNON, GERMAINE	80	16	35	51	21
MARKS, JOHN	80	17	30	47	56
MARTIN, PIT	70	19	26	45	34
ROTA, DARCY	78	22	22	44	93
HULL, DENNIS	69	16	21	37	10
RUSSELL, PHIL	80	5	24	29	260
WHITE, BILL	51	4	23	27	20
JARRETT, DOUG	79	5	21	26	66
BORDELEAU, J.P.	59	7	8	15	4
TALLON, DALE	35	5	10	15	28
MAGNUSON, KEITH	48	2	12	14	117
MULVEY, GRANT	74	7	4	11	36
DAIGLE, ALAIN	52	5	4	9	6
WYLIE, DUANE	6	1	3	4	2
WILSON, ROGER	7	0	2	2	6
PALMER, ROB	13	0	2	2	2
HOLT, RANDY	12	0	1	1	13
ESPOSITO, TONY	71	0	1	1	11
VEISOR, MIKE	9	0	0	0	0
DUMAS, MICHEL	3	0	0	0	0

1975–76	GP	G	A	PTS	PIM
MARTIN, PIT	80	32	39	71	44
HULL, DENNIS	80	27	39	66	28
BOLDIREV, IVAN	78	28	34	62	33
TALLON, DALE	80	15	47	62	101
KOROLL, CLIFF	80	25	33	58	29
MIKITA, STAN	48	16	41	57	37
MARKS, JOHN	80	21	23	44	43
RUSSELL, PHIL	74	9	29	38	194
ROTA, DARCY	79	20	17	37	73
REDMOND, DICK	53	9	27	36	25
SHEEHAN, BOBBY	78	11	20	31	18
BORDELEAU, J.P.	76	12	18	30	6
MULVEY, GRANT	64	11	17	28	72
DAIGLE, ALAIN	71	15	9	24	15
WHITE, BILL	59	1	9	10	44
MAGNUSON, KEITH	48	1	6	7	99
MAKI, CHICO	22	0	6	6	2
JOHNSTON, JOEY	32	0	5	5	6
MURRAY, BOB	64	1	2	3	44
PALMER, ROB	2	0	1	1	0
ESPOSITO, TONY	68	0	1	1	2
LOGAN, DAVE	2	0	0	0	0
HOLT, RANDY	12	0	0	0	13
GAGNON, GERMAINE	5	0	0	0	2
VILLEMURE, GILLES	15	0	0	0	0

1976–77	GP	G	A	PTS	PIM
BOLDIREV, IVAN	80	24	38	62	40
MARTIN, PIT	75	17	36	53	22
MIKITA, STAN	57	19	30	49	20
REDMOND, DICK	80	22	25	47	30
ROTA, DARCY	76	24	22	46	82
RUSSELL, PHIL	76	9	36	45	233
HARRISON, JIM	60	18	23	41	97
KOROLL, CLIFF	80	15	26	41	8
HULL, DENNIS	75	16	17	33	2
BORDELEAU, J.P.	60	15	14	29	20
MULVEY, GRANT	80	10	14	24	111
BOWMAN, KIRK	55	10	13	23	6
ORR, BOBBY	20	4	19	23	25
MARKS, JOHN	80	7	15	22	41
MURRAY, BOB	77	10	11	21	71
TALLON, DALE	70	5	16	21	65
DAIGLE, ALAIN	73	12	8	20	11
MAGNUSON, KEITH	37	1	6	7	86
HOLT, RANDY	12	0	3	3	14
WYLIE, DUANE	8	2	0	2	0
LOGAN, DAVE	34	0	2	2	61
ESPOSITO, TONY	69	0	2	2	6
DUMAS, MICHEL	5	0	1	1	0
MCDILL, JEFF	1	0	0	0	0
BULLEY, TED	2	0	0	0	0
ARCHAMBAULT, MICHEL	3	0	0	0	0
MCKEGNEY, IAN	3	0	0	0	2
VAYDIK, GREG	5	0	0	0	0
HINTON, DAN	14	0	0	0	16
VILLEMURE, GILLES	6	0	0	0	0
VEISOR, MIKE	3	0	0	0	0

1977–78	GP	G	A	PTS	PIM
BOLDIREV, IVAN	80	35	45	80	34
MIKITA, STAN	76	18	41	59	35
BULLEY, TED	79	23	28	51	141
BORDELEAU, J.P.	76	15	25	40	32
MULVEY, GRANT	78	14	24	38	135
ROTA, DARCY	78	17	20	37	67
MARKS, JOHN	80	15	22	37	26
WILSON, DOUG	77	14	20	34	72
KOROLL, CLIFF	73	16	15	31	19
MURRAY, BOB	70	14	17	31	41
PLANTE, PIERRE	77	10	18	28	59
RUSSELL, PHIL	57	6	20	26	139
TALLON, DALE	75	4	20	24	66
SAVARD, JEAN	31	7	11	18	20
KELLY, BOB	75	7	11	18	95
DAIGLE, ALAIN	53	6	6	12	13
HARRISON, JIM	26	2	8	10	31
HICKS, DOUG	13	1	7	8	2
MAGNUSON, KEITH	67	2	4	6	145
LOGAN, DAVE	54	1	5	6	77
BOWMAN, KIRK	33	1	4	5	13
ESPOSITO, TONY	64	0	4	4	0
O'CONNELL, MIKE	6	1	1	2	2
MARTIN, PIT	7	1	1	2	0
KERR, REG	2	0	2	2	0
HOFFMEYER, BOB	5	0	1	1	12
VEISOR, MIKE	12	0	0	0	0
JOHNSTON, ED	4	0	0	0	0
HOLT, RANDY	6	0	0	0	20

1978–79	GP	G	A	PTS	PIM
BOLDIREV, IVAN	66	29	35	64	25
MIKITA, STAN	65	19	36	55	34
MURRAY, BOB	79	19	32	51	38
BULLEY, TED	75	27	23	50	153
MARKS, JOHN	80	21	24	45	35
KERR, REG	73	16	24	40	50
BORDELEAU, J.P.	63	15	21	36	34
MULVEY, GRANT	80	19	15	34	99
KOROLL, CLIFF	78	12	19	31	20
RUSSELL, PHIL	66	8	23	31	122
ROTA, DARCY	63	13	17	30	77
WILSON, DOUG	56	5	21	26	37
O'CONNELL, MIKE	48	4	22	26	20
DAIGLE, ALAIN	74	11	14	25	55
HIGGINS, TIM	36	7	16	23	30
LOGAN, DAVE	76	1	14	15	176
LYSIAK, TOM	14	0	10	10	14
WALTON, MIKE	26	6	3	9	4
HARRISON, JIM	21	4	5	9	22
HICKS, DOUG	44	1	8	9	15
KELLY, BOB	63	2	5	7	85
MAGNUSON, KEITH	26	1	4	5	41
FOX, GREG	14	0	5	5	16
ORR, BOBBY	6	2	2	4	4
RIBBLE, PAT	12	1	3	4	8
PHILLIPOFF, HAROLD	14	0	4	4	6
HOFFMEYER, BOB	6	0	2	2	5
LECUYER, DOUG	2	1	0	1	0
SAVARD, JEAN	11	0	1	1	9
VEISOR, MIKE	17	0	1	1	0
ESPOSITO, TONY	63	0	1	1	2
ZAHARKO, MILES	1	0	0	0	0

1979–80	GP	G	A	PTS	PIM
RUSKOWSKI, TERRY	74	15	55	70	252
LYSIAK, TOM	77	26	43	69	31
MULVEY, GRANT	80	39	26	65	122
PRESTON, RICH	80	31	30	61	70
WILSON, DOUG	73	12	49	61	70
MURRAY, BOB	74	16	34	50	60
BULLEY, TED	66	14	17	31	136
O'CONNELL, MIKE	78	8	22	30	52
HIGGINS, TIM	74	13	12	25	50
SEDLBAUER, RON	45	13	10	23	14
BORDELEAU, J.P.	45	7	14	21	28
MARKS, JOHN	74	6	15	21	51
BROWN, KEITH	76	2	18	20	27
KERR, REG	49	9	8	17	17
DAIGLE, ALAIN	66	7	9	16	22
TRIMPER, TIM	30	6	10	16	10
FOX, GREG	71	4	11	15	73
LECUYER, DOUG	53	3	10	13	59
KOROLL, CLIFF	47	3	4	7	6
MIKITA, STAN	17	2	5	7	12
LOGAN, DAVE	12	2	3	5	34
HUTCHISON, DAVE	38	0	5	5	73
RIBBLE, PAT	23	1	2	3	14
SUTTER, DARRYL	8	2	0	2	2
PATERSON, RICK	11	0	2	2	0
ESPOSITO, TONY	69	0	1	1	2
MAGNUSON, KEITH	3	0	0	0	4
PHILLIPOFF, HAROLD	9	0	0	0	20
VEISOR, MIKE	11	0	0	0	0

1980–81	GP	G	A	PTS	PIM
LYSIAK, TOM	72	21	55	76	20
SAVARD, DENIS	76	28	47	75	47
SUTTER, DARRYL	76	40	22	62	86
KERR, REG	70	30	30	60	56
MURRAY, BOB	77	13	47	60	93
HIGGINS, TIM	78	24	35	59	86
RUSKOWSKI, TERRY	72	8	51	59	225
WILSON, DOUG	76	12	39	51	80
BROWN, KEITH	80	9	34	43	80
BULLEY, TED	68	18	16	34	95
MULVEY, GRANT	42	18	14	32	81
SHARPLEY, GLEN	35	10	16	26	12
SECORD, AL	41	13	9	22	145
PRESTON, RICH	47	7	14	21	24
O'CONNELL, MIKE	34	5	16	21	32
FOX, GREG	75	3	16	19	112
SEDLBAUER, RON	39	12	3	15	12
MARKS, JOHN	39	8	6	14	28
ZAHARKO, MILES	42	3	11	14	40
HUTCHISON, DAVE	59	2	9	11	124
PATERSON, RICK	49	8	2	10	18
MARSH, PETER	29	4	6	10	10
ROBIDOUX, FLORENT	39	6	2	8	75
ESPOSITO, TONY	66	0	3	3	0
SOLHEIM, KEN	5	2	0	2	0
YOUNG, BRIAN	8	0	2	2	6
CROSSMAN, DOUG	9	0	2	2	2
LARMER, STEVE	4	0	1	1	0
GARDNER, BILL	1	0	0	0	0
LECUYER, DOUG	14	0	0	0	41
BANNERMAN, MURRAY	15	0	0	0	0

1981–82	GP	G	A	PTS	PIM
SAVARD, DENIS	80	32	87	119	82
WILSON, DOUG	76	39	46	85	54
LYSIAK, TOM	71	32	50	82	84
SECORD, AL	80	44	31	75	303
HIGGINS, TIM	74	20	30	50	85
MULVEY, GRANT	73	30	19	49	141
PRESTON, RICH	75	15	28	43	30
CROSSMAN, DOUG	70	12	28	40	24
KERR, REG	59	11	28	39	39
RUSKOWSKI, TERRY	60	7	30	37	120
SUTTER, DARRYL	40	23	12	35	31
BULLEY, TED	59	12	18	30	120
MURRAY, BOB	45	8	22	30	48
MARSH, PETER	57	10	18	28	47
BROWN, KEITH	33	4	20	24	26
GARDNER, BILL	69	8	15	23	20
HUTCHISON, DAVE	66	5	18	23	246
FOX, GREG	79	2	19	21	137
SHARPLEY, GLEN	36	9	7	16	11
PATERSON, RICK	48	4	7	11	8
DUPONT, JEROME	34	0	4	4	51
LUDZIK, STEVE	8	2	1	3	2
ROBIDOUX, FLORENT	4	1	2	3	0
ZAHARKO, MILES	15	1	2	3	18

FEAMSTER, DAVE	29	0	2	2	29
ESPOSITO, TONY	52	0	2	2	0
MARKS, JOHN	13	1	0	1	7
BANNERMAN, MURRAY	29	0	1	1	0
MURRAY, TROY	1	0	0	0	0
TANTI, TONY	2	0	0	0	0
LARMER, STEVE	3	0	0	0	0
SKORODENSKI, WARREN	1	0	0	0	0

1982–83	GP	G	A	PTS	PIM
SAVARD, DENIS	78	35	86	121	99
LARMER, STEVE	80	43	47	90	28
SECORD, AL	80	54	32	86	180
WILSON, DOUG	74	18	51	69	58
SUTTER, DARRYL	80	31	30	61	53
LYSIAK, TOM	61	23	38	61	27
PRESTON, RICH	79	25	28	53	64
CROSSMAN, DOUG	80	13	40	53	46
GARDNER, BILL	77	15	25	40	12
MURRAY, BOB	79	7	32	39	73
BROWN, KEITH	50	4	27	31	20
LUDZIK, STEVE	66	6	19	25	63
HIGGINS, TIM	64	14	9	23	63
PATERSON, RICK	79	14	9	23	14
MARSH, PETER	68	6	14	20	55
FRASER, CURT	38	6	13	19	77
FEAMSTER, DAVE	78	6	12	18	69
MURRAY, TROY	54	8	8	16	27
CYR, DENIS	41	7	8	15	2
FOX, GREG	76	0	12	12	81
O'CALLAHAN, JACK	39	0	11	11	46
FIDLER, MIKE	4	2	1	3	4
RUSKOWSKI, TERRY	5	0	2	2	12
TANTI, TONY	1	1	0	1	0
BANNERMAN, MURRAY	41	0	1	1	2
ESPOSITO, TONY	39	0	0	0	0
DUPONT, JEROME	1	0	0	0	0
MULVEY, GRANT	3	0	0	0	0

1983–84	GP	G	A	PTS	PIM
SAVARD, DENIS	75	37	57	94	71
LARMER, STEVE	80	35	40	75	34
WILSON, DOUG	66	13	45	58	64
GARDNER, BILL	79	27	21	48	12
MURRAY, BOB	78	11	37	48	78
LYSIAK, TOM	54	17	30	47	35
SUTTER, DARRYL	59	20	20	40	44
BROWN, KEITH	74	10	25	35	94
WILSON, BEHN	59	10	22	32	143
MURRAY, TROY	61	15	15	30	45
LUDZIK, STEVE	80	9	20	29	73
PRESTON, RICH	75	10	18	28	50
CYR, DENIS	46	12	13	25	19
LARMER, JEFF	36	9	13	22	20
FRASER, CURT	29	5	12	17	26
O'CALLAHAN, JACK	70	4	13	17	67
PATERSON, RICK	72	7	6	13	41
FEAMSTER, DAVE	46	6	7	13	42
YAREMCHUK, KEN	47	6	7	13	19
MARSH, PETER	43	4	6	10	44
SECORD, AL	14	4	4	8	77
HIGGINS, TIM	32	1	4	5	21
FOX, GREG	24	0	5	5	31
DIETRICH, DON	17	0	5	5	0
BOYD, RANDY	23	0	4	4	16
MCMURCHY, TOM	27	3	1	4	42
DUPONT, JEROME	36	2	2	4	116
BANNERMAN, MURRAY	56	0	4	4	17
ESPOSITO, TONY	18	0	3	3	0
ANHOLT, DARRELL	1	0	0	0	0
CAMAZZOLA, JIM	1	0	0	0	0
CASSIDY, BRUCE	1	0	0	0	0
FRAWLEY, DAN	3	0	0	0	0
PELENSKY, PERRY	4	0	0	0	5
JANECYK, BOB	8	0	0	0	2
ROBIDOUX, FLORENT	9	0	0	0	0

1984–85	GP	G	A	PTS	PIM
SAVARD, DENIS	79	38	67	105	56
LARMER, STEVE	80	46	40	86	16
WILSON, DOUG	78	22	54	76	44
MURRAY, TROY	80	26	40	66	82
GARDNER, BILL	74	17	34	51	12
FRASER, CURT	73	25	25	50	109
OLCZYK, ED	70	20	30	50	67
LYSIAK, TOM	74	16	30	46	13
MURRAY, BOB	80	5	38	43	56
SUTTER, DARRYL	49	20	18	38	12
WILSON, BEHN	76	10	23	33	185
LUDZIK, STEVE	79	11	20	31	86
SECORD, AL	51	15	11	26	193
YAREMCHUK, KEN	63	10	16	26	16
BROWN, KEITH	56	1	22	23	55
PATERSON, RICK	79	7	12	19	25
O'CALLAHAN, JACK	66	6	8	14	105
DUPONT, JEROME	55	3	10	13	105
MACMILLAN, BOB	36	5	7	12	12
FRAWLEY, DAN	30	4	3	7	64
BERGEVIN, MARC	60	0	6	6	54
FEAMSTER, DAVE	16	1	3	4	14
MCMURCHY, TOM	15	1	2	3	13
PRESLEY, WAYNE	3	0	1	1	0
BANNERMAN, MURRAY	60	0	1	1	8
BOYD, RANDY	3	0	0	0	6
LARMER, JEFF	7	0	0	0	0
SKORODENSKI, WARREN	27	0	0	0	2
PANG, DARREN	1	0	0	0	0
CLIFFORD, CHRIS	1	0	0	0	0

1985–86	GP	G	A	PTS	PIM
SAVARD, DENIS	80	47	69	116	111
MURRAY, TROY	80	45	54	99	94
OLCZYK, ED	79	29	50	79	47
SECORD, AL	80	40	36	76	201
LARMER, STEVE	80	31	45	76	47
FRASER, CURT	61	29	39	68	84
WILSON, DOUG	79	17	47	64	82
WILSON, BEHN	69	13	38	51	113
BROWN, KEITH	70	11	29	40	87
MURRAY, BOB	80	9	29	38	75
YAREMCHUK, KEN	78	14	20	34	43
SUTTER, DARRYL	50	17	10	27	42
WATSON, BILL	52	8	16	24	2
O'CALLAHAN, JACK	80	4	19	23	116
LYSIAK, TOM	51	2	19	21	14
PRESLEY, WAYNE	38	7	8	15	38
DUPONT, JEROME	75	2	13	15	173
BERGEVIN, MARC	71	7	7	14	60
GARDNER, BILL	46	3	10	13	6
PATERSON, RICK	70	9	3	12	24
LUDZIK, STEVE	49	6	5	11	21
BANNERMAN, MURRAY	48	0	2	2	6
BOUDREAU, BRUCE	7	1	0	1	2
SAUVE, BOB	38	0	1	1	27
CASSIDY, BRUCE	1	0	0	0	0
LAVARRE, MARK	2	0	0	0	0
SKORODENSKI, WARREN	1	0	0	0	0
LARMER, JEFF	2	0	0	0	0
POSA, VICTOR	2	0	0	0	2
MCMURCHY, TOM	4	0	0	0	2

1986–87	GP	G	A	PTS	PIM
SAVARD, DENIS	70	40	50	90	108
LARMER, STEVE	80	28	56	84	22
MURRAY, TROY	77	28	43	71	59
PRESLEY, WAYNE	80	32	29	61	114
SECORD, AL	77	29	30	59	206
OLCZYK, ED	79	16	35	51	119
FRASER, CURT	75	25	25	50	182
WILSON, DOUG	69	16	32	48	36
MURRAY, BOB	79	6	38	44	80
WATSON, BILL	51	13	19	32	6
NYLUND, GARY	80	7	20	27	190
BROWN, KEITH	73	4	23	27	86
LA VARRE, MARK	58	8	15	23	33
DONNELLY, DAVE	71	6	12	18	81
PRESTON, RICH	73	8	9	17	19
LUDZIK, STEVE	52	5	12	17	34
SUTTER, DARRYL	44	8	6	14	16
BERGEVIN, MARC	66	4	10	14	66
O'CALLAHAN, JACK	48	1	13	14	59
STAPLETON, MIKE	39	3	6	9	6
MANSON, DAVE	63	1	8	9	146
SANIPASS, EVERETT	7	1	3	4	2
SAUVE, BOB	46	0	4	4	6
PATERSON, RICK	22	1	2	3	6
BANNERMAN, MURRAY	39	0	1	1	4
CASSIDY, BRUCE	2	0	0	0	0
CAMAZZOLA, JIM	2	0	0	0	0
SCEVIOUR, DARIN	1	0	0	0	0
SKORODENSKI, WARREN	3	0	0	0	0

1987–88	GP	G	A	PTS	PIM
SAVARD, DENIS	80	44	87	131	95
LARMER, STEVE	80	41	48	89	42
VAIVE, RICK	76	43	26	69	108
MURRAY, TROY	79	22	36	58	96
GRAHAM, DIRK	42	17	19	36	32
WILSON, DOUG	27	8	24	32	28
NOONAN, BRIAN	77	10	20	30	44
WILSON, BEHN	58	6	23	29	166
THOMAS, STEVE	30	13	14	27	40
MURRAY, BOB	62	6	20	26	44
PRESLEY, WAYNE	42	12	10	22	52
LUDZIK, STEVE	73	6	15	21	40
SANIPASS, EVERETT	57	8	12	20	126
NYLUND, GARY	76	4	15	19	212
VINCELETTE, DAN	69	6	11	17	107
SUTTER, DUANE	37	7	9	16	70
CASSIDY, BRUCE	21	3	10	13	6
MCGILL, BOB	67	4	7	11	133
STAPLETON, MIKE	53	2	9	11	59
FRASER, CURT	27	4	6	10	57
YAWNEY, TRENT	15	2	8	10	15
WILSON, RIK	14	4	5	9	6
BROWN, KEITH	24	3	6	9	45
COCHRANE, GLEN	72	1	8	9	204
BERGEVIN, MARC	58	1	6	7	83
MANSON, DAVE	54	1	6	7	185
PANG, DARREN	45	0	6	6	2
PLAYFAIR, JIM	12	1	3	4	21
MACKEY, DAVE	23	1	3	4	71
WATSON, BILL	9	2	0	2	2
LA VARRE, MARK	18	1	1	2	25
MASON, BOB	41	0	2	2	0
GARDNER, BILL	2	1	0	1	2
PAYNTER, KENT	2	0	0	0	2

1988–89	GP	G	A	PTS	PIM
LARMER, STEVE	80	43	44	87	54
SAVARD, DENIS	58	23	59	82	110
GRAHAM, DIRK	80	33	45	78	89
WILSON, DOUG	66	15	47	62	69
MANSON, DAVE	79	18	36	54	352
MURRAY, TROY	79	21	30	51	115
THOMAS, STEVE	45	21	19	40	69
PRESLEY, WAYNE	71	21	19	40	100
CREIGHTON, ADAM	43	15	14	29	92
VAIVE, RICK	30	12	13	25	60
YAWNEY, TRENT	69	5	19	24	116
HUDSON, MIKE	41	7	16	23	20
BASSEN, BOB	49	4	12	16	62
ROENICK, JEREMY	20	9	9	18	4
KONROYD, STEVE	57	5	7	12	40
BROWN, KEITH	74	2	16	18	84
SUTTER, DUANE	75	7	9	16	214
EAGLES, MIKE	47	5	11	16	44
NOONAN, BRIAN	45	4	12	16	28
VINCELETTE, DAN	66	11	4	15	119
SANIPASS, EVERETT	50	6	9	15	167
MURRAY, BOB	15	2	4	6	25
NYLUND, GARY	23	3	2	5	63
MCGILL, BOB	68	0	4	4	155
MACKEY, DAVE	23	1	2	3	78
PANG, DARREN	35	0	3	3	4
GARDNER, BILL	6	1	1	2	0
DOYON, MARIO	7	1	1	2	6
CASSIDY, BRUCE	9	0	2	2	4
TORKKI, JARI	4	1	0	1	0
LUDZIK, STEVE	6	1	0	1	8
WATSON, BILL	3	0	1	1	4
STAPLETON, MIKE	7	0	1	1	7
BELFOUR, ED	23	0	1	1	6
GILBERT, GREG	4	0	0	0	0
CHEVRIER, ALAIN	27	0	0	0	0
CLIFFORD, CHRIS	1	0	0	0	0
PAYNTER, KENT	1	0	0	0	2
RUCINSKI, MIKE	1	0	0	0	0
RYCHEL, WARREN	2	0	0	0	17
PLAYFAIR, JIM	7	0	0	0	28
VAN DORP, WAYNE	8	0	0	0	28
WAITE, JIM	11	0	0	0	0
BERGEVIN, MARC	11	0	0	0	18
COCHRANE, GLEN	6	0	0	0	13

1989–90	GP	G	A	PTS	PIM
LARMER, STEVE	80	31	59	90	40
SAVARD, DENIS	60	27	53	80	56
WILSON, DOUG	70	23	50	73	40
THOMAS, STEVE	76	40	30	70	91
CREIGHTON, ADAM	80	34	36	70	224
ROENICK, JEREMY	78	26	40	66	54
MURRAY, TROY	68	17	38	55	86
GRAHAM, DIRK	73	22	32	54	102
GILBERT, GREG	70	12	25	37	54
MANSON, DAVE	59	5	23	28	301
BROWN, KEITH	67	5	20	25	87
MURRAY, BOB	49	5	19	24	45
SECORD, AL	43	14	7	21	131
LEMIEUX, JOCELYN	39	10	11	21	47
HUDSON, MIKE	49	9	12	21	56
YAWNEY, TRENT	70	5	15	20	82
SUTTER, DUANE	72	4	14	18	156
KONROYD, STEVE	75	3	14	17	34
PRESLEY, WAYNE	49	6	7	13	69
MCGILL, BOB	69	2	10	12	204
VAN DORP, WAYNE	61	7	4	11	303
GOULET, MICHEL	8	4	1	5	9
SANIPASS, EVERETT	12	2	2	4	17
EAGLES, MIKE	23	1	2	3	34
CASSIDY, BRUCE	2	1	1	2	0
BASSEN, BOB	6	1	1	2	8
NOONAN, BRIAN	8	0	2	2	6
RUSSELL, CAM	19	0	1	1	27
MILLEN, GREG	10	0	1	1	0
CLOUTIER, JACQUES	43	0	0	0	8
WAITE, JIM	4	0	0	0	0
VINCELETTE, DAN	2	0	0	0	4
PELUSO, MIKE	2	0	0	0	15

1990–91	GP	G	A	PTS	PIM
LARMER, STEVE	80	44	57	101	79
ROENICK, JEREMY	79	41	53	94	80
GOULET, MICHEL	74	27	38	65	65
CHELIOS, CHRIS	77	12	52	64	192
THOMAS, STEVE	69	19	35	54	129
CREIGHTON, ADAM	72	22	29	51	135
GRAHAM, DIRK	80	24	21	45	88
WILSON, DOUG	51	11	29	40	32
MURRAY, TROY	75	14	23	37	74
PRESLEY, WAYNE	71	15	19	34	122
MANSON, DAVE	75	14	15	29	191
GILBERT, GREG	72	10	15	25	58
HUDSON, MIKE	55	7	9	16	62
YAWNEY, TRENT	61	3	13	16	77
KUCERA, FRANTISEK	40	2	12	14	32
LEMIEUX, JOCELYN	67	6	7	13	119
KONROYD, STEVE	70	0	12	12	40
BROWN, KEITH	45	1	10	11	55
MCGILL, BOB	77	4	5	9	151
PELUSO, MIKE	53	6	1	7	320
MCNEILL, MIKE	23	2	2	4	6
GILLIS, PAUL	13	0	5	5	53
NOONAN, BRIAN	7	0	4	4	2
BELFOUR, ED	74	0	3	3	34
GRIMSON, STU	35	0	1	1	183
STAPLETON, MIKE	7	0	1	1	2
MCKEGNEY, TONY	9	0	1	1	4
RUSSELL, CAM	3	0	0	0	5
MILLEN, GREG	3	0	0	0	0
WAITE, JIM	1	0	0	0	0
HASEK, DOMINIK	5	0	0	0	0
CLOUTIER, JACQUES	10	0	0	0	2

1991–92	GP	G	A	PTS	PIM
ROENICK, JEREMY	80	53	50	103	98
LARMER, STEVE	80	29	45	74	65
GOULET, MICHEL	75	22	41	63	69
CHELIOS, CHRIS	80	9	47	56	245
SUTTER, BRENT	61	18	32	50	30
GRAHAM, DIRK	80	17	30	47	89
NOONAN, BRIAN	65	19	12	31	81
SMITH, STEVE	76	9	21	30	304
HUDSON, MIKE	76	14	15	29	92
BROWN, KEITH	57	6	10	16	69
LEMIEUX, JOCELYN	78	6	10	16	80
BROWN, ROB	25	5	11	16	32
KONROYD, STEVE	49	2	14	16	65
MARCHMENT, BRYAN	58	5	10	15	168
MATTEAU, STEPHANE	20	5	8	13	45
KUCERA, FRANTISEK	61	3	10	13	36
GILBERT, GREG	50	7	5	12	35
CREIGHTON, ADAM	11	6	6	12	16
PELUSO, MIKE	63	6	3	9	408
KRAVCHUK, IGOR	18	1	8	9	4
STAPLETON, MIKE	19	4	4	8	8
VINCELETTE, DAN	29	3	5	8	56
THOMAS, STEVE	11	2	6	8	26
TONELLI, JOHN	33	1	7	8	37
HORACEK, TONY	12	1	4	5	21
GRIMSON, STU	54	2	2	4	234
DYKHUIS, KARL	6	1	3	4	4
BUSKAS, ROD	42	0	4	4	80
HRKAC, TONY	18	1	2	3	6
MCAMMOND, DEAN	5	0	2	2	0
BELFOUR, ED	52	0	2	2	40

	GP	G	A	PTS	PIM
MCGILL, RYAN	9	0	2	2	20
WAITE, JIMMY	17	0	1	1	0
LAUER, BRAD	6	0	0	0	4
BYRAM, SHAWN	1	0	0	0	0
JACKSON, JEFF	1	0	0	0	2
LANZ, RICK	1	0	0	0	2
WILLIAMS, SEAN	2	0	0	0	4
CONN, ROB	2	0	0	0	2
BENNETT, ADAM	5	0	0	0	12
RUSSELL, CAM	19	0	0	0	34
HASEK, DOMINIK	20	0	0	0	8
LEBLANC, RAY	1	0	0	0	0
GILLIS, PAUL	2	0	0	0	6

1992–93	GP	G	A	PTS	PIM
ROENICK, JEREMY	84	50	57	107	86
CHELIOS, CHRIS	84	15	58	73	282
LARMER, STEVE	84	35	35	70	48
SMITH, STEVE	78	10	47	57	214
SUTTER, BRENT	65	20	34	54	67
RUUTTU, CHRISTIAN	84	17	37	54	134
GOULET, MICHEL	63	23	21	44	43
GRAHAM, DIRK	84	20	17	34	139
MATTEAU, STEPHANE	79	15	18	33	98
GILBERT, GREG	77	13	19	32	57
LEMIEUX, JOCELYN	81	10	21	31	111
NOONAN, BRIAN	63	16	14	30	82
MARCHMENT, BRYAN	78	5	15	20	313
KUCERA, FRANTISEK	71	5	14	19	59
CHRISTIAN, DAVE	60	4	14	18	12
MURPHY, JOE	19	7	10	17	18
KRAVCHUK, IGOR	38	6	9	15	30
BROWN, KEITH	33	2	6	8	39
BROWN, ROB	15	1	6	7	33
HUDSON, MIKE	36	1	6	7	44
RUSSELL, CAM	67	2	4	6	151
DYKHUIS, KARL	12	0	5	5	0
MURRAY, TROY	22	1	3	4	25
BELFOUR, ED	71	0	3	3	28
GRIMSON, STU	78	1	1	2	193
BENNETT, ADAM	16	0	2	2	8
LAUER, BRAD	7	0	1	1	2
TICHY, MILAN	13	0	1	1	30
MUNI, CRAIG	9	0	0	0	8
WAITE, JIMMY	20	0	0	0	0
KRIVOKRASOV, SERGEI	4	0	0	0	2
ANDRIEVSKI, ALEXANDR	1	0	0	0	0
BANCROFT, STEVE	1	0	0	0	0
TEPPER, STEVE	1	0	0	0	0
BUSKAS, ROD	4	0	0	0	26

1993–94	GP	G	A	PTS	PIM
ROENICK, JEREMY	84	46	61	107	125
MURPHY, JOE	81	31	39	70	111
CHELIOS, CHRIS	76	16	44	60	212
SUTTER, BRENT	73	9	29	38	43
NOONAN, BRIAN	64	14	21	35	57
GRAHAM, DIRK	67	15	18	33	45
MATTEAU, STEPHANE	65	15	16	31	55
GOULET, MICHEL	56	16	14	30	26
RUUTTU, CHRISTIAN	54	9	20	29	68
SMITH, STEVE	57	5	22	27	174
SUTTER, RICH	83	12	14	26	108
WEINRICH, ERIC	54	3	23	26	31
POULIN, PATRICK	58	12	13	25	40
LEMIEUX, JOCELYN	66	12	8	20	63
KUCERA, FRANTISEK	60	4	13	17	34
SHANTZ, JEFF	52	3	13	16	30
WILKINSON, NEIL	72	3	9	12	116
TODD, KEVIN	35	5	6	11	16
YSEBAERT, PAUL	11	5	3	8	8
CARNEY, KEITH	30	3	5	8	35
DUBINSKY, STEVE	27	2	6	8	16
RUSSEL, CAM	67	1	7	8	200
CUNNEYWORTH, RANDY	16	4	3	7	13
KIMBLE, DARIN	65	4	2	6	133
SUTER, GARY	16	2	3	5	18
MARCHMENT, BRYAN	13	1	4	5	42
AMONTE, TONY	7	1	3	4	6
MUNI, CRAIG	9	0	4	4	4
BELFOUR, ED	70	0	4	4	61
CHRISTIAN, DAVE	9	0	3	3	0
KRIVOKRASOV, SERGEI	9	1	0	1	4
DROPPA, IVAN	12	0	1	1	12
HACKETT, JEFF	22	0	1	1	2
MURRAY, TROY	12	0	1	1	6
SOUCY, CHRISTIAN	1	0	0	0	0
HORACEK, TONY	7	0	0	0	53
DIRK, ROBERT	6	0	0	0	26
SMYTH, GREG	38	0	0	0	108

1994–95	GP	G	A	PTS	PIM
NICHOLLS, BERNIE	48	22	29	51	32
MURPHY, JOE	40	23	18	41	89
CHELIOS, CHRIS	48	5	33	38	72
SUTER, GARY	48	10	27	37	42
AMONTE, TONY	48	15	20	35	41
ROENICK, JEREMY	33	10	24	34	14
POULIN, PATRICK	45	15	15	30	53
KRIVOKRASOV, SERGEI	41	12	7	19	33
SHANTZ, JEFF	45	6	12	18	33
SUTTER, BRENT	47	7	8	15	51
GRAHAM, DIRK	40	4	9	13	42
WEINRICH, ERIC	48	3	10	13	33
SMITH, STEVE	48	1	12	13	128
YSEBAERT, PAUL	15	4	5	9	6
SAVARD, DENIS	12	4	4	8	8
CRAVEN, MURRAY	16	4	3	7	2
RUUTTU, CHRISTIAN	20	2	5	7	6
GRIEVE, BRENT	24	1	5	6	23
CUMMINS, JIM	27	3	1	4	117
DIDUCK, GERALD	13	1	0	1	48
RUSSELL, CAM	33	1	3	4	88
SMYTH, GREG	22	0	3	3	33
BELFOUR, ED	42	0	3	3	11
DAZE, ERIC	4	1	1	2	2
JOHANSSON, ROGER	11	1	0	1	6
CARNEY, KEITH	18	1	0	1	11
HORACEK, TONY	19	0	1	1	25
WAITE, JIM	2	0	0	0	0
GAUTHIER, DANIEL	5	0	0	0	0
HACKETT, JEFF	7	0	0	0	0
KIMBLE, DARIN	14	0	0	0	30
SUTTER, RICH	15	0	0	0	28
DUBINSKY, STEVE	16	0	0	0	8

1995–96	GP	G	A	PTS	PIM
CHELIOS, CHRIS	81	14	58	72	140
ROENICK, JEREMY	66	32	35	67	109
SUTER, GARY	82	20	47	67	80
AMONTE, TONY	81	31	32	63	62
NICHOLLS, BERNIE	59	19	41	60	60
DAZE, ERIC	80	30	23	53	18
MURPHY, JOE	70	22	29	51	86
SAVARD, DENIS	69	13	35	48	102
CRAVEN, MURRAY	66	18	29	47	36
PROBERT, BOB	78	19	21	40	237
SUTTER, BRENT	80	13	27	40	56
SHANTZ, JEFF	78	6	14	20	24
CARNEY, KEITH	82	5	14	19	94
KRIVOKRASOV, SERGEI	46	6	10	16	32
POULIN, PATRICK	38	7	8	15	16
WEINRICH, ERIC	77	5	10	15	65
ULANOV, IGOR	53	1	8	9	92
SMITH, STEVE	37	0	9	9	71
BLACK, JAMES	13	3	3	6	16
GRIEVE, BRENT	28	2	4	6	180
CUMMINS, JIM	52	2	4	6	180
DUBINSKY, STEVE	43	2	3	5	14
MILLER, KIP	10	1	4	5	2
RUSSELL, CAM	61	2	2	4	129
BELFOUR, ED	50	0	2	2	36
MOREAU, ETHAN	8	0	1	1	4
CICCONE, ENRICO	11	0	1	1	48
HACKETT, JEFF	35	0	1	1	8
WAITE, JIMMY	1	0	0	0	0
COLE, DANTON	2	0	0	0	0
DROPPA, IVAN	7	0	0	0	2
WERENKA, BRAD	9	0	0	0	8
PROKOPEC, MIKE	9	0	0	0	5

1996–97	GP	G	A	PTS	PIM
AMONTE, TONY	81	41	36	77	64
ZHAMNOV, ALEX	74	20	42	62	56
CHELIOS, CHRIS	72	10	38	48	112
DAZE, ERIC	71	22	19	41	16
CRAVEN, MURRAY	75	8	27	35	12
WEINRICH, ERIC	81	7	25	32	62
MOREAU, ETHAN	82	15	16	31	123
MILLER, KEVIN	69	14	17	31	41
SUTER, GARY	82	7	21	28	70
SAVARD, DENIS	69	9	18	27	60
KRIVOKRASOV, SERGEI	67	13	11	24	42
BLACK, JAMES	64	12	11	23	20
PROBERT, BOB	82	9	14	23	326
CARNEY, KEITH	81	3	15	18	62
SUTTER, BRENT	39	7	7	14	18
DAHLEN, ULF	30	6	8	14	10
CUMMINS, JIM	65	6	6	12	199
SYKORA, MICHAL	28	1	9	10	10
CICCONE, ENRICO	67	2	2	4	233
CREIGHTON, ADAM	19	1	2	3	13
RUSSELL, CAM	44	1	1	2	65
LEROUX, JEAN-YVES	1	0	1	1	5
LAFLAMME, CHRISTIAN	4	0	1	1	2
GRONMAN, TUOMAS	16	0	1	1	13
HACKETT, JEFF	41	0	1	1	6
KLIMOVICH, SERGEI	1	0	0	0	2
WAITE, JIMMY	2	0	0	0	0
DUBINSKY, STEVE	5	0	0	0	0
PROKOPEC, MIKE	6	0	0	0	6
TERRERI, CHRIS	7	0	0	0	0
CHYZOWSKI, DAVE	8	0	0	0	6
MCRAE, BASIL	8	0	0	0	12
SMITH, STEVE	21	0	0	0	29
BELFOUR, ED	33	0	0	0	26

1997–98	GP	G	A	PTS	PIM
AMONTE, TONY	82	31	42	73	66
ZHAMNOV, ALEX	70	21	28	49	61
DAZE, ERIC	80	31	11	42	22
SUTER, GARY	73	14	28	42	74
CHELIOS, CHRIS	81	3	39	42	151
JOHNSON, GREG	69	11	22	33	38
SHANTZ, JEFF	61	11	20	31	36
KRIVOKRASOV, SERGEI	58	10	13	23	33
WEINRICH, ERIC	82	2	21	23	106
MOREAU, ETHAN	54	9	9	18	73
DUBINSKY, STEVE	82	5	13	18	57
BLACK, JAMES	52	10	5	15	8
CARNEY, KEITH	60	2	13	15	73
LEROUX, JEAN-YVES	66	6	7	13	55
KILGER, CHAD	22	3	8	11	6
NABOKOV, DMITRI	25	7	4	11	10
MILLER, KEVIN	37	4	7	11	8
LAFLAMME, CHRISTIAN	72	0	11	11	59
SUTTER, BRENT	52	2	6	8	28
SIMPSON, REID	38	3	2	5	102
FELSNER, BRIAN	12	1	3	4	12
SYKORA, MICHAL	28	1	3	4	12
PROBERT, BOB	14	2	1	3	48
MILLS, CRAIG	20	0	3	3	34
RUSSELL, CAM	41	1	1	2	79
MORE, JAY	17	0	2	2	8
CUMMINS, JIM	55	0	2	2	178
WHITE, TODD	7	1	0	1	2
YAWNEY, TRENT	45	1	0	1	76
VANDENBUSSCHE, RYAN	4	0	1	1	5
SKALDE, JARROD	7	0	1	1	4
TERRERI, CHRIS	21	0	1	1	2
HUSKA, RYAN	1	0	0	0	0
VARIS, PETRI	1	0	0	0	0
GENDRON, MARTIN	2	0	0	0	0
TREFILOV, ANREI	6	0	0	0	0
CLEARY, DAN	6	0	0	0	0
HACKETT, JEFF	58	0	0	0	8

1998–99	GP	G	A	PTS	PIM
AMONTE, TONY	82	44	31	75	60
ZHAMNOV, ALEX	76	20	41	61	50
GILMOUR, DOUG	72	16	40	56	56
DAZE, ERIC	72	22	20	42	22
CHELIOS, CHRIS	65	8	26	34	89
KILGER, CHAD	64	14	11	25	30
OLCZYK, EDDIE	61	10	15	25	29
PROBERT, BOB	78	7	14	21	206
MANSON, DAVE	64	6	15	21	107
DUMONT, JEAN-PIERRE	25	9	6	15	10
MOREAU, ETHAN	66	9	6	15	84
EMERSON, NELSON	27	4	10	14	13
ZMOLEK, DOUG	62	0	14	14	102
WHITE, TODD	35	5	8	13	20
LAFLAMME, CHRISTIAN	62	2	11	13	70
SIMPSON, REID	53	5	4	9	145
CLEARY, DAN	35	4	5	9	24
MIRONOV, BORIS	12	0	9	9	27
LEROUX, JEAN-YVES	40	3	5	8	21
BROWN, BRAD	61	1	7	8	184
ERIKSSON, ANDERS	11	0	8	8	0
MANELUK, MIKE	28	4	3	7	8
MARHA, JOSEF	22	2	5	7	4
MCAMMOND, DEAN	12	1	4	5	2
MUIR, BRYAN	53	1	4	5	50
ALLISON, JAMIE	39	2	2	4	62
WEINRICH, ERIC	14	1	3	4	12
COFFEY, PAUL	10	0	4	4	0
SHANTZ, JEFF	7	1	0	1	4
JANSSENS, MARK	60	1	0	1	65
FITZPATRICK, MARK	27	0	1	1	8
THIBAULT, JOCELYN	52	0	1	1	2
DUBINSKY, STEVE	1	0	0	0	0
TREFILOV, ANDREI	1	0	0	0	0
VOPAT, ROMAN	3	0	0	0	4
MURRAY, CHRIS	4	0	0	0	14
VANDENBUSSCHE, RYAN	6	0	0	0	17
CLOUTIER, SYLVAIN	7	0	0	0	0
MILLS, CRAIG	7	0	0	0	2
BICANEK, RADIM	7	0	0	0	6
RUSSELL, CAM	7	0	0	0	10
NASREDDINE, ALAIN	7	0	0	0	19
JONES, TY	8	0	0	0	12
HACKETT, JEFF	10	0	0	0	6
BONVIE, DENNIS	11	0	0	0	44
ROYER, REMI	18	0	0	0	67
YAWNEY, TRENT	20	0	0	0	32

1999–2000	GP	G	A	PTS	PIM
AMONTE, TONY	82	43	41	84	48
SULLIVAN, STEVE	73	22	42	64	52
ZHAMNOV, ALEX	71	23	37	60	61
GILMOUR, DOUG	63	22	34	56	51
NYLANDER, MICHAEL	66	23	28	51	26
MIRONOV, BORIS	58	9	28	37	72
DAZE, ERIC	59	23	13	36	28
MCAMMOND, DEAN	76	14	18	32	72
ERIKSSON, ANDERS	73	3	25	28	20
MCCABE, BRYAN	79	6	19	25	139
COTE, SYLVAIN	45	6	18	24	14
MARHA, JOSEF	81	10	12	22	18
DUMONT, JEAN-PIERRE	47	10	8	18	18
PROBERT, BOB	69	4	11	15	114
ATCHEYNUM, BLAIR	47	5	7	12	6
DEAN, KEVIN	27	2	8	10	12
ZMOLEK, DOUG	43	2	7	9	60
BROWN, BRAD	57	0	9	9	134
LEROUX, JEAN-YVES	54	2	5	8	43
MANSON, DAVE	37	0	7	7	40
GROSEK, MICHAL	14	2	4	6	12
JANSSENS, MARK	36	0	6	6	73
MUIR, BRYAN	11	2	3	5	13
OLCZYK, EDDIE	33	2	2	4	12
ALLISON, JAMIE	59	1	3	4	102
BICANEK, RADIM	11	0	3	3	4
MCCARTHY, STEVE	5	1	1	2	4
CLARK, WENDEL	13	2	0	2	13
CALDER, KYLE	8	1	1	2	2
PLANTE, DEREK	17	1	1	2	2
VANDENBUSSCHE, RYAN	52	0	1	1	143
WHITE, TODD	1	0	0	0	0
LAMOTHE, MARC	2	0	0	0	0
HERPERGER, CHRIS	9	0	0	0	5
PASSMORE, STEVE	24	0	0	0	9
THIBAULT, JOCELYN	60	0	0	0	2

INDEX

PHOTOGRAPHY CREDITS

Harold Barkley Archives Collection
117b, 120a—b

Bruce Bennett/Bruce Bennett Studios
76a, 94, 95, 135

Bruce Bennett Studios
21a, 124, 125b, 128—29, 148a, 149a, 150a

Chicago Blackhawks
endsheet (music), 1, 2—3, 4—5, 10—11, 13,
19, 22, 24—25b, 28—29a, 29b, 32a, 36,
37b, 38a, 43c—d, 45a, 54—55, 57, 58—59,
61, 66a, 68a, 72b, 79b, 80, 84, 88, 89, 91,
103a, 107a—b, 109, 111, 117a, 118a, 119b,
122b, 126a, 127, 130—31b, 138, 141a, 143,
146a, 151a, 152c, 166, 169b

Collection of William J. Martin
27, 30, 33a, 46a, 167

M. Digiacomo/Bruce Bennett Studios
86—87

Ray Grabowski
endsheet (background image), 6—7, 8—9,
14, 15, 16a—b, 17b, 20, 48, 49, 62—63a,
64a, 65, 66b, 68b, 69, 70—71, 74—75, 81,
98, 102, 119a, 126b, 130a, 137a, 137c, 139,
140, 142b, 144, 146c, 147a, 147c, 148c,
149b, 150b, 151b—c, 152a, 153, 156a—b,
158, 159, 160, 164, 165

Ray Grabowski/Blackhawks #1 Fan Collection
108b

Ray Grabowski/Lou Varga Collection
122—23a

Rob Grabowski
38b, 43a—b, 44—45, 52, 60, 67, 72a, 73,
110, 132a—b, 141b, 142a, 154, 157, 162—63

Rob Grabowski/Lou Varga Collection
64b, 122—23a

Graphic Artists/Hockey Hall of Fame
18, 79a, 83b, 122b

John Halligan Collection
85, 106, 121

Hockey Hall of Fame
21b, 24a, 31a, 32b, 44, 50, 51, 56a—b,
92—93, 96a—b, 101, 113a, 116b, 119c, 146b

The Hockey Information Service Inc.
31b, 46b, 113b, 116a, 148b

Imperial Oil-Turofsky/Hockey Hall of Fame
34—35, 40—41, 42, 45b, 112

Mitch Jaspan/Bruce Bennett Studios
152b

London Life-Portnoy/Hockey Hall of Fame
82, 123c, 133

Doug MacLellan/Hockey Hall of Fame
17a, 104a—f, 105a—g, 136a—c, 137b

Dave Sandford/Hockey Hall of Fame
23, 25a, 26, 33b, 37a, 47, 53a—b, 63b,
67a—b, 78, 83a, 90, 97, 99, 100, 108a,
118b, 125a, 131a, 168a—c, 169a, 169c

Slapshot Photo Collection
39, 103b, 114, 147b, 149c, 150c

Letters indicate image placement, clockwise from upper left.

HERE COME THE HAWKS

Words and Music by
J. WAYNE SWAYZEE